Shattering the Myth:
Plays by Hispanic Women

Edited by Linda Feyder

ARTE
PúBLICO
PRESS

Acknowledgements

This volume is made possible through a grant from the National Endowment for the Arts, a federal agency, and the Ford Foundation.

Arte Publico Press
University of Houston
Houston, Texas 77204-2090

Cover design by Mark Piñón
Original painting by Yreina D. Cervántez:
"Homenaje a Frida Kahlo," Copyright © 1978

Shattering the myth: plays by hispanic women / edited by Linda Feyder.
    p.   cm.
    ISBN 1-55885-041-4
    1. American drama—Hispanic American authors. 2. Hispanic American women—Drama. 3. American drama—Women authors. 4. Hispanic Americans—Drama. I. Feyder, Linda.
    PS628.H57S5 1992
    812'.540809287–dc20   91-40997
                                     CIP

The paper used in this publication meets the requirements of the American National Standard for Permanence of Paper for Printed Library Materials Z39.48-1984. ∞

Contents

INTRODUCTION

The six plays in this anthology represent something quite recent to contemporary American theater: the Hispanic female voice. The plays, written between the years 1986 to 1991, have been performed or read in theaters across the United States. They reflect a new generation of Hispanic-American women whose parents still hold strong cultural ties to the countries from which they immigrated. Their position is a unique one. Not only do they stand with each foot resting in a different culture, but as Hispanic-American women, they are members of two marginalized groups in American society: one of women, the other of color. Questioned in the six plays are the traditions so deeply rooted in the familial culture of which they are still a part, and equally explored is their need to reinterpret the inherited customs for a new identity in their present bicultural existence.

On all fronts—Hispanic culture, life in the United States, social class, gender and race—these playwrights are battling the myths and stereotypes that continue to circumscribe the freedom of expression and life fulfillment for Hispanic women. Their plays, indeed, shatter myths and, in so doing, are creating a broader, freer space for women's identity and cultural development.

Central to the plays is the problematic relationship Hispanic women have to their inherited customs. To begin with, there is the family. The traditional role of women in the Hispanic family is to serve their male counterparts, whether father, husband or son, and to have children. For many, the opportunity to have an advanced education or career is remote. Their future roles are prescribed for them by familial and cultural pressures. The familial restrictions share close covenant with the Catholic faith which, as evinced by the plays, provides an ambivalent source of worship for Hispanic women. On the one hand, their deep spiritual need is realized through a longstanding faith in a religion that has passed through their families. But on the other hand, it is a faith that has placed taboos on female sexuality making the Hispanic woman ashamed of her own body and unable to openly discuss her sexual experience outside secret confines.

For many of the playwrights in this anthology, the questions are addressed by returning to the women in their families—their mothers, grandmothers and aunts. Reevaluating the female relationships within the family allows the playwrights to explore how the female legacy has both helped and hindered the growth of the new generation of Hispanic women. Their female predecessors,

5

naturally, have carried the myths and scripts to them by way of an oral tradition received by young female ears that listened during the hours of gathering in the kitchen or across a table. It is this gathering of women during the course of everyday life that becomes significant to the new female voice. It is here in the company and safety of women that they experience a sense of freedom in their speech, a sense of taboos being lifted and thrown away, and a sense of creativity and power. They are free to talk about their sex lives, their desires, their dreams.

It is this oral tradition that lends itself so beautifully to drama, the genre expressing itself verbally. Evident in the plays is the trained ear of playwrights attuned to the detailed nuances and flavors of their spoken language, a language revealing what is deepest and most authentically Hispanic. These women, through dialogue, affirm their commitment to their oral history and, in the process, unveil the long-hidden Hispanic feminine discourse. They discover that Hispanic women have always been critical and rebellious of their social lot, always creative and subversive.

Cherríe Moraga's play, *Shadow of a Man*, was produced by Brava! For Women in the Arts and the Eureka Theatre Company in San Francisco in November 1990. The title suggests the omniscient and weighty presence of men in the lives of the female characters, a presence felt not only from the primary position of the men in their families, but from the position of Father as deity and priest of their religion as well. The play is set in the Rodriguez home, a Mexican family living in Los Angeles. It opens with Lupe, the twelve-year-old daughter in Catholic schoolgirl uniform, confessing to the bathroom mirror that she is unable to tell her secrets to the priest. The circle of women in the play include Lupe's elder sister, Leticia, a rebellious daughter aggressively seeking change for Chicana women; Rosario, the unwed, non-traditional aunt who speaks her mind into the ears of her young nieces; and Hortensia, the mother locked into what has become an abusive marriage.

The men in the play are dislocated from the family, although their problems loom heavily over the activities of the women. The only son, Rigo, planning to marry a *gringuita*, is slowly distancing himself from the family. The father, Manuel, hurting from his son's separation and the guilt of a previous transgression, becomes a withdrawn, abusive husband. The inevitable outcome leads to what Rosario calls a "house full of women, no más," a place where the women find solace in each other.

In *Miriam's Flowers* by Migdalia Cruz, a 1984–88 INTAR Theatre Playwright Resident and McKnight Fellow, the death of

Miriam's young brother, Puli, maims an already fragile Puerto Rican family. Set in the South Bronx of 1975, Miriam, age sixteen, and Puli, seven, are raised by their struggling mother, Delfina. Puli is hit by a train while chasing a baseball. The women of the family are devastated by his death. Young Miriam connects her pain to the physical suffering of the crucified Christ and seeks her own form of self-inflicted torture to feel she's alive. Her mother is not able to help her. Their only communion comes from the ritualistic bathings Miriam gives her mother.

This highly original drama is an exploration of the suffering inherent in the Catholic faith. It also suggests the sacrificial element in the sexual act for Hispanic women, the close relationship between suffering and sex. The women in this play become desperate, mutilated, no longer able to console one another outside the shared suffering that will hold them together in the afterlife.

Caridad Svich, a 1987 LaJolla Playhouse Resident and a INTAR Playwright Resident from 1988–90, chronicles a female friendship between two mid-twenties Cuban-American women in her play, *Gleaning/Rebusca*. They are roommates living in Florida and each possesses a different personality: Sonia is the reticent, practical friend; Barbara, the outgoing and romantic one. While folding clothes or cooking, their conversations are intimate and easy. They share their misgivings and anticipations about the men in their lives. They express their fears about the inevitable change of their friendship. Their thoughts and superstitions reflect the inheritance of their mother's myths: a fallen eyelash is pressed to the chest for a wish, a fly in the house means they should expect a visitor. In their conversations is the yearning for a life with better choices, one with better choices of men, jobs and fulfillments for single women.

Playwright Josefina López wrote her first play, *Simply María*, at the age of seventeen. It was first produced in San Diego and later aired on PBS. *Simply María* is a surreal exploration of the development of a Mexican woman in the United States. Most of the action takes place in a dream young María falls into after failing to convince her parents that she should attend college. Three specter girls serve as the different, conflicting voices inside María's mind; they represent the cultural myths María is being forced to accept. The myths begin with the American Dream and ironically lead to her role as Mexican mother and wife.

The dream ends with María on trial, but unable to speak in her own defense for her rebellion against marital duties. The play pokes fun at Mexican pop-culture, such as television *novelas* which

reinforce the myth of "happily everafter" to generations of Hispanic women, and the commercialization of the Mexican culture
in the United States, where advertisements promote Ajax cleanser
as the ideal gift for the perfect Mexican-American wife.

Edit Villarreal's *My Visits with MGM (My Grandmother Marta)*
was presented in the 1989 Hispanic Playwrights Project at South
Coast Repertory Theatre. It is a stylistic exploration of Marta Feliz's relationship to the two women who raised her: Marta Grande,
her grandmother, and Florinda, her grandmother's sister. As an
adult, Marta Feliz returns to the burnt shell of the home she once
shared with her grandmother and great aunt. The memories she
recovers while searching through the rubble bring forth the elder
female voices of her youth.

We find that Marta Grande persuaded Florinda to leave with
her from Mexico to America during the Revolution of 1910. They
are two sides of the same coin, both wanting to preserve their culture, yet in strikingly different ways. Florinda remains the reluc-
tant partner, becoming increasingly suspicious of those around her.
Marta Grande is able to integrate her two lives into what, Marta
Feliz discovers later in life, is a surprisingly liberated identity.

Diana Saenz's *A Dream of Canaries* is a time-displaced tale
about the weak and oppressed in a militaristic society. Saenz, re-
ceiver of the Isobel Aguirre Grant from Teatro de La Esperanza in
1989, creates characters living on the fringe of society, yet questioning and concerning themselves with the silent crimes committed
by the government in power.

Nita Durme is a young call-girl who plans to save money to
escape her life. In the meantime, she is hired by soldiers in the
Secret Service and by the daughter of the once revered head of the
Secret Service. Jesus Utimo is a recent recruit to the Secret Service. An ex-gigolo to a powerful woman agent, he's found himself
in this "elite" corps due to the agent's calculated manipulations.
Jesus hires Nita and the two form a caustic business relationship
until their involvement and knowledge of citizen "disappearances"
cause them to rely on each other as a way out of the existence in
which they are subjugated.

In all, the process of "shattering myths," breaking images, is
ultimately constructive. It is the necessary process that our culture
must experience in order to create new, more realistic images, more
humane roles and relationships. These Hispanic playwrights are
in the vanguard of not only creating new images—perhaps new
"myths"—but they are engaged in forging a new culture through
art and the empowerment of women.

Shadow of a Man

Cherríe Moraga

CHARACTERS

LUPE: the daughter, twelve.
ROSARIO: the aunt, mid-fifties.
HORTENSIA: the mother, mid-forties.
LETICIA: the older daughter, seventeen.
MANUEL: the father, early fifties.
CONRADO: the compadre,* early fifties.

PLACE

The action takes place in the home of the Rodríguez family in the Los Angeles area.

The play opens on the interior of the house in the places chiefly inhabited by mothers and daughters. The kitchen is the central feature with the bathroom at stage right and the daughters' bedroom at stage left. Downstage is the porch surrounded by the family garden of chiles, nopales and roses. Props and set pieces have been kept to a minimum, only present are what is essential to the action. Rooms are divided by representative walls that rise about sixteen inches from the floor. Although literal walls between spaces are absent on stage, they should give the impression of providing some minimal privacy for secrets both shared and concealed. There is an exit upstage center.

The backdrop to the house is a Mexican painting of a Los Angeles sunset. As the light descends into the garden, the smoggy sky takes on a faint mixture of orange and lavender, a pastel rose contrasts with the stark silhouette of cactus and palm trees, multiple plant life abounds.

TIME

The play begins in the Spring of 1969 and takes place over a period of about a year.

---

*"Compadre" refers to the relation of a godfather to the parents of a child. In Mexican culture, it is a very special bond, akin to that of blood ties, sometimes stronger.

ACT ONE
Spring, 1969

.... SCENE ONE ....

At rise, spot on LUPE, *staring into the bathroom mirror. She wears a catholic school uniform. She holds a votive candle under her chin and a rosary crucifix in her hand. Her face is a circle of light in the darkness. The shadow of the crucifix looms over the back wall.*

LUPE: Sometimes I think I should tell somebody about myself. It's a sin to have secrets. A'least the priest is a'pose to find out everything that's insida you. I try. I really do try, but no matter how many times I make confession, no matter how many times I try to tell the priest what I hold insida me, I know I'm still lying. Sinning. Keeping secrets. (*She pauses before the reflection, then blows out the candle. Fade out.*)

.... SCENE TWO ....

ROSARIO *appears in the garden. She wears a bandana around her head, and an apron around her thick middle. She picks a few chiles, tastes them.* LUPE *enters.*

ROSARIO: (*Chewing on a chile.*) I still say que los chiles no saben buenos aquí. I think it's the smog. They don' taste like not'ing. Aquí en Los Angeles the sun has to fight its way down to the plantas ... and to the peepo, too. (*Takes another bite, to* LUPE.) No sabe a nada. Try one. (*Gives* LUPE *one.*)
LUPE: No, these things are like fire.
ROSARIO: Pruébalo, gallina. (LUPE *very gingerly takes a bite off the tip of the chile.*)
LUPE: Hmm. Not so bad. (*Swallows.*) ¡Ay, tía! You tricked me. (*Fanning her mouth.*)
ROSARIO: (*Laughing.*) ¡Eres gringuita!

LUPE: I swear I dunno how you can eat them like they were nut'ing.

ROSARIO: Vas a ver when your tía kicks the bucket and is gone, you'll be there in your big Hollywood mansion haciendo tortillas y el chile, no más to remember me. Or maybe you'll get la criada mexicana to do it.

LUPE: I won't have a maid. I don't believe in that.

ROSARIO: Es trabajo like any other work. There will always be ricos an' the rich peepo always need someone to clean up after them. ¿Sabes qué? En México, half the women got criadas. Allá you don' have to be rico to have one.

LUPE: That's why it's better here.

ROSARIO: ¿Por qué?

LUPE: People don't have to be maids.

ROSARIO: Bueno, pero la tierra no me da ni un chile verdadero. (ROSARIO *crosses to the rose bushes, stage right.*) M'ijita, me traes el agua. Tienen tanta sed estas rosas. I don' know why I let them go so long sin agua. (LUPE *gives her the watering can.*) Gracias, m'ija. Make sure you cut a few of these para la mesa. Mañana es sábado.

LUPE: Flowers won't make this Saturday any better.

ROSARIO: Adió. It's your brother's wedding.

LUPE: (*Digging at the earth with the toe of her oxford.*) I'm never leaving home like Rigo.

ROSARIO: I know, m'ija. I know you love tus padres very much. (*After a beat,* ROSARIO *continues watering the roses.*) Ya, ya. No 'stén enojaditas conmigo. You're thirsty, ¿no, mis rositas? Tomen el agua. Ya, ya.

LUPE: Why do you talk to them, tía?

ROSARIO: To who, las plantas?

LUPE: Yeah.

ROSARIO: Because they got souls, the same as you an' me.

LUPE: You believe that?

ROSARIO: It's true.

LUPE: The nuns don't say that.

ROSARIO: You think the nuns are always right?

LUPE: I guess so.

ROSARIO: God is always right, not the Church. The Church is made by men. Men make mistakes, I oughta know. (*To the roses.*) ¡Ay pobrecitas! ¡Qué mala madre soy, mis pobres rositas! Tomen, tomen el agua. Ya, mis hijitas ... mis rositas.

LUPE: (*After a beat.*) Tía, you know how they say that ... that
    when you get tha' chill tha' goes through your body ...
ROSARIO: Es el diablo que te toca.
LUPE: Yeah, the devil. He comes up and kinda brushes past you,
    touching you on the shoulder or somet'ing, right?
ROSARIO: Sí, pero es un dicho, no más.
LUPE: ¿Pero sabe qué, tía? A veces I do feel him. El diablo me
    entra a mí. He's like a shadow. I can barely tell he's there,
    jus' kinda get a glimpse of him outta the corner of my eye,
    like he's following me or somet'ing, but when I turn my
    head, he's gone. I jus' feel the brush of his tail as he goes
    by me.
ROSARIO: ¿Tiene cola?
LUPE: Sí.
ROSARIO: El diablo.
LUPE: I tole you and I get a chill all over.
ROSARIO: No hables así, hija. I don't know what those monjas
    teach you at that school sometimes.
LUPE: They never tole me this.
ROSARIO: Well, take it out of your head. It's not good for you.
LUPE: It's not like I'm making myself think about it, it jus' keeps
    popping up in my head. It's like the more I try NOT to
    think about something, the more it stays in my head. I
    mean your mind jus' thinks what it wants to, doesn't it?
ROSARIO: No. You gottu train your mind. If you don', it could
    make you a very unhappy girl.
LUPE: I try, but I can't. At night, I try to stay awake cuz when
    I fall asleep that's when he sneaks inside me. I wake up
    con tanto miedo. It's like my whole body's on fire and I
    can hardly breathe. I try to call Lettie pero la voz no me
    sale. Nothing comes out of my mouth.
ROSARIO: You gottu stop thinking like that. Tu mamá y yo,
    we had a cousin, Fina, a very good-looking girl, but she
    thought about el diablo y la religión y todo eso so much
    that she went crazy. Se volvió loca, hija.
LUPE: You think I'm going to go crazy, tía?
ROSARIO: No, m'ija. But you gottu stop thinking this way.
LUPE: Is it a sin to think like this, tía?
ROSARIO: No sé, m'ija. I don't think so. Not if you can't help it.
LUPE: Sometimes I jus' feel like my eyes are too open. It's like
    the more I see, the more I got to be afraid of.
ROSARIO: ¿Quieres saber la verdad, Lupita?
LUPE: What?

ROSARIO: Only los estúpidos don't know enough to be afraid. The rest of us, we learn to live con nuestros diablitos. Tanto que if those little devils weren't around, we wouldn' even know who we were. (LUPE *smiles.* ROSARIO *gives her a hug.*) Vente. Today we think about las rosas. Sundee, cuando we go to church, there's plenty a time to think about el diablo. (*Fade out.*)

.... SCENE THREE ....

Crossfade to the kitchen, where a novela, a Mexican soap opera, plays on the T.V. HORTENSIA, wearing a housedress and apron, is rolling out tortillas on a chopping block. Her manner and bearing are more refined than her sister's. There is a kind of grace to her movements as she alternately moves to the stove where she heats the tortillas on the comal, then back to the board again. LUPE and ROSARIO are seated next to each other at the kitchen table, engrossed in the novela. For a few moments all that is heard are the muted voices of the novela and the steady beat of the rolling pin.

HORTENSIA: She can go to hell as far as I'm concern.
ROSARIO: Who, Hortensia?
HORTENSIA: La gringa. They di'nt even get married yet, and she's already got my son where she wants him. Ni lo conozco. He's a stranger. (*She puts the tortilla on the comal, watches it rise.*) The other day, Rigo comes home from the college. Manuel sees him in the door, and a'course he jumps up from the chair para darle un abrazo. And you know what Rigo does? He pushes Manuel away.
ROSARIO: No.
HORTENSIA: And you know what he says?
ROSARIO: ¿Qué?
HORTENSIA: He says, "No, Dad. I'm a man, now. We shake hands."
ROSARIO: No me digas.
HORTENSIA: Te digo. Does that sound like my son to you? (*She sits.*)
ROSARIO: No.
HORTENSIA: And to see the look on Manuel's face ... (*Pause.*) Y la girl standing there with a smile en la cara.
ROSARIO: ¡Qué barbaridad!

HORTENSIA: It's eating Manuel up. (*She gestures that* MANUEL
     has been drinking.)
ROSARIO: That's not so good, Tencha.
HORTENSIA: (*Intimately.*) Claro que no. ¿Pero qué puedo hacer
     yo?
LUPE: Miren. María's telling Enrique she's pregnant.
ROSARIO: No! ¿De veras? (*They all stop and watch, mesmerized.
     Muffled voices from the T.V., then a commercial.*)
LUPE: ¡Ay! Wait 'til he finds out quién es el padre.
ROSARIO: ¡Híjole!
HORTENSIA: (*Resuming her work.*) But I tell you, one of these
     days I'm goin' to tell esa gringuita everyt'ing I think of
     her. She thinks she goin' to keep my son, hold him all
     to herself? What's it hurt for her husband to stay close
     to his familia? But, they're a different kin'a peepo, los
     gringos ... gente fría. I try to tell Rigo this before they
     were novios, que iba a tener problemas con ella, pero no
     me quiso escuchar. So, what could I do? They might fool
     you with their pecas y ojos azules, but the women are cold.
ROSARIO: I bet her thing down there is frozen up.
HORTENSIA: (*Laughing.*) ¡Ay, Rosario! No digas eso.
ROSARIO: I may be old ... but my thing is still good 'n hot. ¿Ver-
     dad, m'ija? Us mexicanas keep our things muy calientes
     ... as hot as that comal allí, no?
LUPE: I dunno, tía.
ROSARIO: ¿No sabes? ¿Tú no sabes, eh? (*Playfully, snatching
     at* LUPE *between the legs.*) Is your fuchi fachi hot down
     there, too?
LUPE: (*Jumping away.*) Stop, tía!
HORTENSIA: ¡Chayo!
ROSARIO: ¡Ay! ¡Tú eres pura gallina! (LUPE *comes up behind*
     HORTENSIA *and takes a warm tortilla from the stack.*
     HORTENSIA *slaps her hand lightly.*)
HORTENSIA: With you around, the stack never gets any bigger.
LUPE: But my panza does. (*She sticks out her stomach.*)
ROSARIO: Now you look like María on the novela. (LUPE *begins
     to enact "la desesperada" role, when* LETICIA *enters. She
     is wearing late sixties radical Chicana attire: tight jeans,
     large looped earrings, an army jacket with a UFW [United
     Farm Workers] insignia on it, etc.*)
HORTENSIA: Allí viene la política. (*To* LETICIA.) I told you I
     don' want you to wear esa chaqueta.
ROSARIO: Es el estilo, Tencha.

LETICIA: (*Stealing a warm tortilla from the stack.*) Yeah.
HORTENSIA: (*Referring to tortilla.*) ¡Tú también!
LETICIA: (*Rolling up the tortilla.*) How can you stand watching
    those things? Those novelas are so phony. I mean, c'mon.
    What do you think the percentage of blondes is in Mexico?
ROSARIO: No sé.
LETICIA: I mean in relation to the whole population?
ROSARIO: No sé.
LETICIA: (*Putting butter on the tortilla.*) One percent? But no, the
    novelas make it look like half the population is Swedish
    or something. Even the maids are güeras. But, of course,
    the son of the patrón falls madly in love with one and they
    live happily everafter in luxury. Give me a break!
HORTENSIA: Ni modo, I enjoy them.
ROSARIO: Es pura fantasía. Pero, m'ija, they got so many prob-
    lems, it gets your mind off your own.
LETICIA: I guess that's the idea. (*Offstage a man's heavy labored
    steps.*)
MANUEL: Hortensia! Hortensia!
HORTENSIA: ¡Ay! Tha' man's goin' to make me crazy. Lupita,
    go see wha' your papi wan's.
LUPE: Sí, mami.
HORTENSIA: Y si te pide cigarros, don' give him none.
LUPE: Okay. (*She exits.*)
ROSARIO: ¿Todavía 'stá fumando?
LETICIA: Like a chimney.
HORTENSIA: Sure! He wan's to kill himself. He's not a'pose to
    smoke. Es otro día que no trabaja. I don' know what
    we're goin' to do if he keep missing work.
ROSARIO: He di'nt see el doctor?
LETICIA: Are you kidding?
HORTENSIA: He's scared a death a them. He complain que he
    pull somet'ing in his arm on the job, que le duele mucho.
    But I don' believe it. I think it's his heart. The other night
    he woke up in the middle of the night and he could har'ly
    breathe. He was burning up. I had to get up to change all
    the sheets y sus piyamas ... they were completely soaked.
    Now he's gottu take the sleeping pills jus' to close his eyes
    for a few hours. (*Pause.*) Pero vas a ver, tonight he'll go
    out again.
LETICIA: (*Kissing HORTENSIA on the cheek.*) Pues, ay te watcho.
HORTENSIA: ¿Adónde vas?
LETICIA: To Irma's.

HORTENSIA: ¿Qué vas a hacer con ésa?
LETICIA: Oh, we're jus' gonna hang out for a while.
HORTENSIA: Well, not on the street, do you hear me?
LETICIA: Aw, mom!
HORTENSIA: Aw, mom!
ROSARIO: Déjala, Tencha.
HORTENSIA: Pero, no la conoces, es callejera.
LETICIA: Shoot, I'll be graduating in a month.
HORTENSIA: You think graduating makes you una mujer. Eres
    mujer cuando te cases. Then your husband can worry
    about you, not me.
LETICIA: Yeah, but Rigo can come and go as he pleases whether
    he's married or not.
HORTENSIA: Claro. Es hombre.
LETICIA: Es hombre. Es hombre. I'm sick of hearing that. It's
    not fair.
HORTENSIA: Well, you better get use to things not being fair.
    Whoever said the world was goin' to be fair?
LETICIA: Well, my world's going to be fair! (LETICIA *exits up-*
    stage. ROSARIO *and* HORTENSIA *stare at the air in*
    silence.)
HORTENSIA: Te digo, the girl scares me sometimes.
LUPE: (*Entering.*) Papi wants his cigarettes. (*They turn to her.*
    A beat. Then all three simultaneously turn their attention
    back to the novela. The lights fade to black while the novela
    continues playing in the darkness.)

.... SCENE FOUR ....

Late that night. Offstage, a car pulls up, then a door slams. The
sound of keys being tossed and a man's heavy, drunken steps are
heard. MANUEL *enters drunk. He wears a hat and a light jacket.*
From the point of his entrance, the action takes on a stylized surreal
quality. Blue light. The characters' actions seem to slow down into
almost ritualized movement. (This scene replays itself in the lives
of the Rodríguez family.)

MANUEL: Rigo, m'ijo. I don't put my hands out to you no more.
    I have to tie them down to keep them from reaching for
    you. It goes against my nature, not to touch the face of
    my son. (*He sits. Puts his hat on the table.*) You use to sit
    and converse with me. Your eyes were so black, I forgot

myself in there sometimes. I watched the little fold of
indio skin above your eyes, and felt those eyes hold me to
the ground. They saw. I know they saw that I am a weak
man, but they did not judge me. Why do you judge me
now, hijo? How does the eye turn like that so suddenly?
(HORTENSIA *enters.*)

HORTENSIA: ¿A quién 'stás hablando?

MANUEL: (*As if snapping out of a trance.*) He doesn' got a mind
no more.

HORTENSIA: Who?

MANUEL: Who do you think? (*He looks at her. There is a pause.*)
She's took his mind.

HORTENSIA: (*Taking off his coat.*)   And whose mind you got,
talking to yourself como un loco?

MANUEL: (*Getting up.*) What was my son given huevos for? Tell
me. For some spoiled gabachita to come along an' squeeze
the blood from them until they turn white?

HORTENSIA: No hables cochino. Siéntate. (*He sits.* HORTEN-
SIA *removes his shoes.*)

MANUEL: You know wha' they call men like tha' que let the
women do their thinking for 'em. Pussywhipped, tha's
wha' they call 'em.

HORTENSIA: No seas grosero. The girls, they goin' to hear you.

MANUEL: My son is a pussywhipped.

HORTENSIA: 'Stás borracho. I dunno how you goin' to get up for
the wedding tomorrow. (*She methodically unbuttons his
shirt.*)

MANUEL: Ni modo. I'm not going.

HORTENSIA: No empieces.

MANUEL: No voy.

HORTENSIA: Quítate la camisa. (*She helps him off with the shirt.*)

MANUEL: We're not good enough for them, that's what they think!
Y tú eres igual que Rigo. You just wan' to put on the face
in front a those gringos. (*Digging at her.*) They don' even
let your sister come. (*This shames her.*)

HORTENSIA: They said it was a small ceremony.

MANUEL: ¡A la chingada! A small ceremony. (*She unbuckles his
pants.*)

HORTENSIA: How you think Rigo's goin' to feel without his padre
allí?

MANUEL: He's going to feel nothing. Rigo's got no feelings no
more. (*Beat.*) Where's my baby?

HORTENSIA: You're not goin' to do this to me, ¿m'oyes? (*He rises, hoists up his pants.*)

MANUEL: Quiero verla.

HORTENSIA: You're not goin' to leave us solitas to go into the church tomorrow.

MANUEL: (*Calling out.*) ¡M'ija! ¡M'ijita!

HORTENSIA: Leave the girls alone.

MANUEL: (*Calling out.*) ¡M'ija! (MANUEL *tries to fasten his pants, fumbling.*) ¡Lup-i-i-ta!

HORTENSIA: Why do you think your son left this house?

MANUEL: Because he's a gabachero!

HORTENSIA: Because you make him ashame, coming home smelling de los bars.

MANUEL: (*Going to her.*) Coming home con el cheque en la mano to feed you.

HORTENSIA: (*After a beat, she says severely.*) Tiene ojos. He can see what you are.

MANUEL: ¡Soy hombre! (*He takes a feeble swing at her, misses.*)

HORTENSIA: ¡Pégame! Es lo único que sabes ... (*A shot of pain rushes through his arm. He bends over.*) Your heart, te molesta.

MANUEL: No.

HORTENSIA: Pero sigues tomando. (*She starts for the bathroom.*) I'm goin' to get your pills.

MANUEL: ¡No, no necesito nada!

HORTENSIA: (*Stops, with disdain.*) I shou' let you die. (LETICIA *appears at the doorway.*)

MANUEL: (*To* LETICIA.) ¿Y qué quieres tú?

LETICIA: What did you do to her?

MANUEL: (*To* LETICIA.) I di'nt touch her.

LETICIA: (*To* HORTENSIA.) Did he hit you?

MANUEL: What I say is not good enough for you, metiche?

HORTENSIA: Déjala.

MANUEL: You wanna defend your mother? You think 'cause your brother's gone, que you're the macho around this house now?

LETICIA: No.

MANUEL: I'm sick of this house full of viejas.

LETICIA: Why don't you leave then?

HORTENSIA: Leticia!

MANUEL: ¿Eres fría, sabes? You're cold as a piece of ice ... just like your mother.

HORTENSIA: (*Glaring at* MANUEL.) I wish I had a heart of stone. (HORTENSIA *goes out to the porch, takes out a cigarette and lights it.* MANUEL *crosses to the girls' bedroom.* *Lights rise on* LUPE *in bed, the covers pulled up tight around her.* *She clutches a rosary in one hand.* MANUEL *stands at the doorway, his shadow filling it.*)

MANUEL: (*Softly.*) I know la chiquita is waiting for me. She's got a big heart, mi niñita. She makes sure her papacito comes home safe.

HORTENSIA: If he doesn't give a damn about himself, why should I care?

MANUEL: (*Going to* LUPE.) Lupita! ¿'Stás durmiendo, hijita? (*He lays his huge man's head on* LUPE*'s small shoulder.*) You'll never leave me. ¿No, m'ijita?

LUPE: No, papi.

MANUEL: Eres mi preferida, ¿sabes?

LUPE: Sí, papi.

MANUEL: You're different from the rest. You got a heart that was made to love. Don't ever leave me, baby.

LUPE: No, papi. I won't. (*He begins to weep softly. Her thin arm mechanically caresses his broad back. A muted tension falls over the scene. A few moments later,* LETICIA *enters the bedroom.*)

LETICIA: (*Bringing him to his feet.*) C'mon, dad. Let's get you to bed now. (*He gets up without resistance.* LETICIA *and* MANUEL *start to exit. Fade out.*)

.... SCENE FIVE ....

The next morning. LETICIA *and* LUPE *are in the bathroom, in their bathrobes.* LETICIA *is standing in front of the mirror fixing her hair, while* LUPE *polishes a pair of white dress shoes.* MANUEL *sits on the porch, drinking a beer, a six pack next to him. It is cloudy. Lucha Villa's "Que me lleva el tren" is playing on the radio.*

LUPE: I liked Teresa better.

LETICIA: I liked Teresa, too, but Rigo thought he was too good for a Chicana, so he's gonna marry a gringa.

LUPE: Well, he mus' love Karen.

LETICIA: Right.

LUPE: Doesn't he?

LETICIA: (*Referring to her hair.*) C'mere, Lupe. Help me.

LUPE: Well, does he?

LETICIA: Does he what?

LUPE: Love her. Does he love Karen?

LETICIA: Who knows what he feels, man. Jus' forget it. Do you
    hear me? Don't think about him no more. He's gone. In a
    couple of hours he'll be married and that's it. We'll never
    see him again. (*Referring to her hairdo.*) Lupe, hand me
    the Dippity Do. (*LUPE gets up, gives her the styling gel.
    LETICIA begins applying it to her bangs. LUPE moves in
    front of LETICIA to face the mirror. She stretches open
    her eyelids with her fingers.*) Lupe, get out of the way.

LUPE: You can see yourself in there ... in the darkest part.

LETICIA: What? (*LUPE leans into the mirror for a closer look.*)

LUPE: Two little faces, one in each eye. It's like you got other
    people living inside you. Maybe you're not really you.
    Maybe they're the real you and the big you is just a dream
    you.

LETICIA: I swear you give me the creeps when you talk about this
    stuff. You're gonna make yourself nuts.

LUPE: But I'm not kidding. I mean, how d'you know? How do
    you really know what's regular life and what's a sueño?

LETICIA: You're talking to me, aren't you? That's no dream. How
    many fingers do you see?

LUPE: Five.

LETICIA: Right! (*Grabs her face.*) Five fingers around your fat
    little face. You feel this?

LUPE: Yeah. Yeah.

LETICIA: That's what's real, 'manita. What you can see, taste,
    and touch ... that's real.

LUPE: I still say, you can't know for sure.

LETICIA: Say something else. You're boring me. (*LUPE sits. Puts
    her shoes on.*)

LUPE: I went over to Cholo Park yesterday.

LETICIA: You better not tell Mom. Some chick jus' got her lonche
    down there the other day. They found her naked, man,
    all chopped up.

LUPE: Ooooh. Shaddup.

LETICIA: Well, it's true. What were you doing down there?

LUPE: Nut'ing. Jus' hanging out with Frances and her brother,
    Nacho.

LETICIA: God, I hate that huevón. Stupid cholo ... he jus' hangs
    out with you guys cuz nobody his own age will have any-

thing to do with him. (*Beat.*) So what were you guys up to?

LUPE: (*Humming.*) Nut'ing.

LETICIA: C'mon. Fess up! Out with it!

LUPE: Nut'ing. The boys were jus' throwing cats.

LETICIA: What?

LUPE: They was throwing cats off the hill.

LETICIA: What d'yuh mean?

LUPE: Well, they stand up there, grab the gatos by the colas and swing 'em above their heads and let 'em go. Ay, they let out such a grito! It's horrible! It sounds like a baby being killed!

LETICIA: And you watch that shit?

LUPE: They was the ones doing it ... Most of the time the gatos land on their feet. But this one time this one got caught on these telephone wires. It jus' hung there in shock with its lengua así. (*She sticks out her tongue dramatically.*)

LETICIA: Ay, stop it! I swear you're really sick. How can you stand to see 'em do that?

LUPE: It's hard to take your eyes off it.

LETICIA: Si-ick. (*Holding her hair in place.*) Here, Lupe. Stick the bobby pin in for me.

LUPE: (*Taking the pin from* LETICIA.) Where?

LETICIA: Back here. C'mon, my arm's getting tired. (*She does.*) Ouch! ¡Bruta! You want to draw blood or what? (HORTENSIA *walks through the kitchen toward the porch. Her hair and face are done. She wears dress shoes and a house robe. She carries* MANUEL's *suit coat and pants.*)

HORTENSIA: I hear too much talking in there!

LUPE: We'll be right out, Mami!

HORTENSIA: We're goin' to be late for the wedding!

LETICIA: Ask me if I care. (*Cross fade to* HORTENSIA *at the screendoor of the porch.*)

HORTENSIA: (*To* MANUEL.) I got your clothes ready. (*He ignores her, turns up the volume on the radio. After a few moments,* ROSARIO *enters from the garden.*)

ROSARIO: If you listen too much to that music, you start to believe there's something good about suffering.

MANUEL: ¿Qué dices?

ROSARIO: I don't believe in suffering ... for nobody.

MANUEL: Siéntate.

ROSARIO: You're goin' to be late for la boda, Manuel.

MANUEL: (*Cracking open a beer for her.*) Toma. (*Hands it to her. She sits.* HORTENSIA *turns away. They watch her exit.* MANUEL *lowers the volume on the radio.*) Salud. (*They toast, clinking bottles.*) One a these days, I'm gonna get in the car, buy me a couple six packs and hit the road and I'm not gonna stop until I reach the desert. They got the road paved now all the way to my pueblito. I'll stop off and see my compadre in Phoenix. He's got a real nice life there. He's getting rich, I bet, pouring cement into holes in the ground. He's making swimming pools. Everybody's got a swimming pool out there. (*The sky begins to cloud.*)

ROSARIO: It's goin' to rain.

MANUEL: (*After a pause.*) In Arizona, it rains when you leas' expect it. You got thunder and lightning and the whole sky lights up. You can see the storm coming from a long ways off. (*Lightning lights the stage. Thunder is heard. He takes a swig of beer.*) I remember when I was a little esquincle, riding in the back of my tío's troque. We was coming back from digging ditches or something, me and a buncha primos all piled up in back, just watching the sky get darker and darker. Suddenly the lightning flashed and the whole desert lit up and you could see the mountain with the camelback clear as noontime. Then, crack! The thunder came and it started raining cats and dogs. In minutes, the water soaked up all the dust of the road and it smelled so clean ... Then right there in the open back of the troque, we tore off our clothes and took our showers in the rain. (*Another swig.*) Sometimes you know you want to be a boy like that again. The rain was better then, it cleaned something. (HORTENSIA, LETICIA *and* LUPE *enter the porch, dressed for the wedding. They stare at* MANUEL.)

LUPE: Papi? (*They all freeze. The lights and music fade out.*)

.... SCENE SIX ....

A few weeks later. Afternoon. HORTENSIA *is sorting beans at the table while* LETICIA *and* LUPE *show* ROSARIO *pictures from Rodrigo's wedding.*)

LETICIA: Mira, tía. Look-it all the stiffs, lined up in a row.

ROSARIO: Ay, Leticia!

LETICIA: You didn't miss much, tía. All they gave you was a little drop of lousy champagne and this white cake that stuck to the roof of your mouth. (*Showing her a picture.*) Don't we look miserable?

ROSARIO: I haf' to admit, you look like a buncha sourpusses.

LUPE: What bothered me was the stupid dress I had to wear.

HORTENSIA: You look purty, m'ija.

ROSARIO: Wasn' tha' the dress you wore for Easter?

LUPE: Yeah.

LETICIA: (*Showing* ROSARIO *another photo.*) Look. Karen's mother is 'spose to be younger than my mom and she already looks like she's ready for the grave!

HORTENSIA: (*To* ROSARIO.) You know how güeras' skin get arrugas so young.

ROSARIO: It's true.

LETICIA: Well, I feel sorry for Rigo cuz his wife is gonna be a has-been in no time. It runs in their genes, you can tell.

ROSARIO: Don' you have anyt'ing nice to say about the wedding?

HORTENSIA: Rigo looked real handsome. He smelled good, too. I got to say it, I got a good-looking boy. He had on a beautiful white ... como lino ... suit and a kin'a grey tie with a tiny design in it, muy fino ... I think era de seda.

LETICIA: Probably la vieja bought it for him, so he'd look classy enough for them.

HORTENSIA: Tu hermano has more class than all those peepo put together.

LETICIA: You don't have to tell me that! Tell him. He's the one trying to get over.

ROSARIO: (*After a beat.*) Déjame ver otra, Lupita.

LETICIA: (*Sarcastic.*) Chayo, you could of died of starvation there. We din't eat before because I thought they'd feed us at the wedding. Pero, you know, the peepo that got the most are the tightest with their money.

ROSARIO: Tha's why they got it.

LETICIA: I dunno. The cacahuates they had in the little platitos really filled me up.

LUPE: (*Sing-songy.*) Ca-ca-huates. Ca-ca-huates. I like that word!

LETICIA: You just like the "caca" part.

LUPE: Shaddup. (HORTENSIA *shows* ROSARIO *another photo.* LUPE *and* LETICIA *start exploring another packet of photos.*) This is el marido. Not a bad-looking man, really. (*Almost proud.*) He's a doctor.

ROSARIO: ¿De veras?

HORTENSIA: I think for the babies.
LETICIA: A pediatrician.
ROSARIO: Uh huh. (*Beat.*) ¿Y qué pasó when they saw Manuel wasn' with you?
HORTENSIA: When we came in, the mother ...
LETICIA: She knew something was up.
HORTENSIA: I guess she could tell from our faces. I felt so ashame to come without my husband and I sure wasn' goin' to tell her que he refuse to come. But she di'nt give me a chance to say nut'ing. She jus' grab me by the arm and right away like she har'ly notice, says to me, "Oh, I'm so sorry, Mr. Rodríguez couldn' make it. I hope it's not'ing serious." Pero muy suave.
LETICIA: And then she took us into this big room, introducing us to all these stiffs, going ... (*Very WASP, upper class.*) "Isn't it a pity that Mr. Road-ree-gays had to be ill today ... of all days!" It got me ill!
ROSARIO: ¿Había mucha gente?
LETICIA: ¡Montones! (*Pause.*)
HORTENSIA: Sí. Mucha. It was a lie that there was no room for our family.
LETICIA: They were afraid that if too many Mexicans got together, we'd take over the joint. Bring out the mariachis, spill guacamole over everything ...
HORTENSIA: They just din't want us.
LUPE: You should've been there, tía.
ROSARIO: (*A bit martyred.*) No importa. (*Beat.*) Y Rigo di'nt say not'ing about his papi?
HORTENSIA: Ni una palabra.
ROSARIO: ¡Válgame Dios!
HORTENSIA: When he came into the church, me besó en la cara. "Hello, mother," he says to me, muy formal ... y nada más.
ROSARIO: ¡No me digas!
HORTENSIA: Te digo ... y la girl had not'ing to say to me tampoco. She hug me ...
LETICIA: Cold enough to freeze the dead.
LUPE: (*Taking out an old photo.*) Oooh! I like this picture of you, Lettie. What grade were you in? (MANUEL *enters upstage, unnoticed. He approaches them from behind.*)
LETICIA: What grade, Mamá?
HORTENSIA: ¿Cómo? (*Examining it.*) Kinnergarten.
LUPE: I like your little curly top. (*They pass it around, amused.*)

ROSARIO: Se parece a Shirley Temple, ¿no? (HORTENSIA *tosses*
LETICIA's *hair.*)
LUPE: (*Taking out another photo.*) Who's this, Mami? (*She passes
it on to* HORTENSIA.)
HORTENSIA: Este ... that's ... Conrado.
LUPE: Who's that?
ROSARIO: A friend of your papi's, m'ija.
HORTENSIA: His compadre.
LUPE: He's really handsome. Where's he at?
HORTENSIA: No sé. I don't know where he is. Don't talk about
him.
LUPE: Why? Is he dead or somet'ing?
HORTENSIA: No, he's not dead, but it makes tu papi nervioso.
(MANUEL *takes the photo from* HORTENSIA's *hand.*)
MANUEL: I've been looking for this. (*He looks at the photo.*)
HORTENSIA: (*Gathering up the photos, to the* GIRLS.) Mira.
You messed up all my pictures. Next time I wannu find
somet'ing, I won' be able to. Put them away now. I can'
pass the whole day here contando los chismes. Put all
these fotos away now! (*As the rest of the lights fade, there's
a spot on* MANUEL *staring at the picture, lost in the past.
A few beats of "Sombras" by Javier Solis play. Fade out.*)

.... SCENE SEVEN ....

Months later. A Saturday afternoon. HORTENSIA *is changing Rodrigo's baby on top of the kitchen table, making the usual
exclamations a grandmother does over her first grandchild.*

HORTENSIA: ¡Ay mi chulito! ¡Riguito! ¡Qué precioso!
LETICIA: (*Offstage.*) Mom, I got the car!
HORTENSIA: Is that you, hijas? (LETICIA *and* LUPE *enter ex-
citedly.*)
LUPE: It's so tough, Mami!
HORTENSIA: Miren lo que tengo aquí.
LETICIA: It's just an old jalopy, but I can fix it up.
LUPE: Hey! When'd Sean come?
HORTENSIA: Ay! Don' call him tha'! It sounds like a girl's name.
LETICIA: That's what they called him.
HORTENSIA: Well, I call him Riguito ... como su papá, not ...
Shawn!

LETICIA: Yeah, well just don't try calling him that in front of
    Karen. What's he doing here anyway?
HORTENSIA: She left me the baby to watch. ¿Qué milagro, eh?
LUPE: That's for sure.
HORTENSIA: Una 'mergency came up. She tole me would I mind
    watching the baby. I said a'course not, even though they
    only call me when they need me.
LETICIA: Where's Rigo?
HORTENSIA: He has the Army this weekend. Ay! You should of
    seen how handsome he look in that uniform! He remind
    me of your papá.
LETICIA: The entire Raza's on the streets protesting the war and
    my brother's got to be strutting around in a uniform.
HORTENSIA: Es mejor que he shoulda gone to Vietnam?
LETICIA: No, but he doesn't have to go around parading it. God,
    I hope nobody I know saw him.
HORTENSIA: No te entiendo.
LUPE: Lettie got the car, Mom.
HORTENSIA: I know, m'ija. (*To* LETICIA.) But don' think this
    means you are free to go wherever you please now. Es
    para ir al trabajo, no más.
LETICIA: I paid for it.
HORTENSIA: And who's paid for you for the las' eighteen years
    of your life? (*She doesn't respond, takes out her keys and
    dangles them in front of the baby.*)
LETICIA: (*With a thick "chola" accent.*) Hey, little guy. You
    wannu go cruising with me, ése? (HORTENSIA *takes out
    a diaper and powder, etc. from the diaper bag.*)
HORTENSIA: She brought enough things for a week. And she gave
    me a long list of 'structions. (*Pulls out the list.*) You think
    I di'nt already have three babies of my own. (*To baby,
    changing the diaper.*) ¡Fuchi! Apestas. (*The baby sprays
    her.*) ¡Ay Dios! Miren. He soaked me. (*Wiping herself.*)
    No m'ijito, you haf' to learn not to shoot tu pajarito in
    the air. I forgot since I had you girls. Riguito use to do
    the same thing. I'd get it right in the face sometimes.
LUPE: Ugh!
HORTENSIA: They don' know yet to control their little peepees.
LUPE: Let me have the keys, Lettie. (*She gives them to her.*)
LETICIA: He is a little cutie, but I don't know about that blonde
    hair.
LUPE: (*Dangling the keys.*) The rest of him is brown.

HORTENSIA: Mi güerito. He's as purty as they get to be. (*Changing him.*) Miren, su pajarito es igual al de Rigo when he was a baby.

LETICIA: Please, spare me.

LUPE: (*Giggling.*) Really?

HORTENSIA: Igualito. (*To the baby.*) You got your papi's thing, mi Riguito. (*To her daughters.*) Dicen que esta parte siempre es the true color del hombre, el color de su ... nature.

LETICIA: Does that make him a real Mexican then?

HORTENSIA: Mira, que lindo es ... like a little jewel. Mi machito. Tha's one thing, you know, the men can never take from us. The birth of a son. Somos las creadoras. Without us women, they be not'ing but a dream.

LETICIA: Well, I don't see you getting so much credit.

HORTENSIA: But the woman knows. Tú no entiendes. Wait until you have your own son.

LETICIA: Who knows? Maybe I won't have kids.

HORTENSIA: Adió. Then you should of been born a man. (HORTENSIA *finishes changing the baby.*)

LETICIA: I'm gonna go wash the car. You want to help, Lupe?

LUPE: (*Dangling the keys above the baby.*) I'll be there in a second.

LETICIA: Well, give me the keys, then. (*She does.* LETICIA *starts to exit.*)

HORTENSIA: When you're done, you can go pick up the panza from Pedro's Place. I want to make menudo for the morning.

LETICIA: All right. All right. (*She exits.*)

HORTENSIA: Ay! They grow up so fast, Lupita. In only minutes, los muchachitos are already standing at the toilet, their legs straight like a man's. I remember sometimes being in the kitchen and hearing little Riguito ... he must of been only three or so, going to the toilet by himself. The toilet seat flipped back. Bang! it would go. Then the stream from his baby's body. But the sound was like a man's, full ... y fuerte. It gives you a kind of comfort, that sound. And I knew the time would fly so fast. In minutes, he would be a man. (*To the baby.*) You, too. ¿No, m'ijito? You got your papi's thing. El color de la tierra. A sleeping mountain, with a little worm of life in it. Una joya. (HORTENSIA *strokes the infant.*) Ya ya, duérmete, mi chulito.

LUPE: Duérmete. (*Fade out.*)

.... SCENE EIGHT ....

    LETICIA *is practicing dance steps in the bedroom to the tune
of "Grapevine." She sings to herself.*)

LETICIA:

    "Oh I heard it through the grapevine ...
    And I'm just about to loo-oose my mind."

        (*Cross fade to* LUPE *standing in front of the bathroom
        mirror. She is inspecting the black holes of her eyes. She
        holds a votive candle with a crucifix under her chin. Her
        face is a circle of light in the darkness. The shadow of
        the crucifix looms over the back wall.*) I have X-ray eyes.
        Sister Genevieve is naked. I can see through her habit,
        her thick black belt with the rosary hanging from it, her
        scapular, her square cotton slip. She has a naked body
        under there. I try not to see Sister Genevieve this way, jus'
        kin'a stare out the classroom window, wishing I was jus'
        one of those pigeons hanging out there on the roof. (*Pause,
        inspecting the reflection more closely.*) I can see her now
        standing with her thing pressed up against Jessie Alarcón's
        desk. She put Jessie up there in front cuz he's bad in
        school. I wish she wouldn' stand that way ... and there
        goes Jessie's stupid finger. It's his pajarito finger. (*She
        sticks out her middle finger, sliding it along an imaginary
        desktop.*) He's sliding it very slowly along the top of his
        desk. It's coming closer ... closer ... closer ... (*To Sister
        Genevieve.*) Move 'ster! Will you move? Please move.
        Whew! She moved jus' in time. I don' think Jessie wooda
        done it though. He's too chicken. (LUPE *steps back from
        the mirror.*) I think there's something wrong with me. I
        look at other kids' faces. Their eyes are smart like Frances
        Pacheco or sleepy like Chela La Bembona, but they seem
        to be seeing things purty much like they are. (*Pause.*) I
        mean, not X-ray or nut'ing. (*After a beat, she blows out*

the candle. Fade out.)

.... SCENE NINE ....

HORTENSIA *and* ROSARIO *are just finishing folding clothes on the porch. It is a humid evening.* HORTENSIA *wears a light robe.*

HORTENSIA: For weeks now, I walk around the house and hold my breath. Conrado is the only name on Manuel's lips. He don' talk about not'ing else.

ROSARIO: ¿Qué dice, Hortensia?

HORTENSIA: Estupideces. Half the time, I can't understand him. I see him sitting on the toilet, crying. I go to him, ¿Manuel, qué tienes? Pero, no me responde. His heart is as closed as this. (*She makes a fist.*) I can't make him open up to me. No puedo. (*Pause.*) He miss work already two times this week. And the week before, another two days. El patrón call him this morning. He wouldn' go to the phone.

ROSARIO: You're going to make yourself sick, worrying so much about him.

HORTENSIA: How often does he have anyt'ing to do with me? Once in a blue moon. I touch his feet in bed and he freezes, Chayo. No soy tan vieja. I don' wannu give up.

ROSARIO: (*After a pause.*) Tencha, I know sometimes you look at me and think there's something wrong with me becuz I coont stay with a husband.

HORTENSIA: That's not true, hermana.

ROSARIO: But after you see the other side of a man, your heart changes. It's harder to love. I've seen that side too many times, m'ija. (*Pause.*) Ahora, tengo mi casita, mi jardín, my kids are grown. What more do I need?

HORTENSIA: I need more, Chayo. (*She gets up with the basket of clothes, goes back into the house.* ROSARIO *follows.*) I think about Conrado sometimes ... the way he walked into a room ... like a warrior, un gallo. His plumas bien planchadas. His shoes shined, the crease in his pantalones, sharp like swords ... y tan perfumado, you could smell him before you saw him. I remember how when Conrado touched me ... jus' to grab my hand no más, and los vellitos on my arm would stand straight up. (*Pause.*)

I've never felt that with Manuel.

ROSARIO: Conrado was not the kin'a man you marry, m'ija.

HORTENSIA: He never ask me.

ROSARIO: Yo sé.

HORTENSIA: I don't wannu give up, Chayo. If I give up, I might as well put on the black dress and say. I'm a dead man's wife. (ROSARIO *goes to her.*)

ROSARIO: Don't give up, sister. Make your husband see you. (*She takes* HORTENSIA*'s face and turns it to her.*) Grab his face and make him see you. It's not that men don't love us. They just don't stop to see us.

HORTENSIA: Why don't they?

ROSARIO: They don't have to. Us women do all the loving for them. If a man sighs for no reason, we already know the reason. We watch their faces y sabemos cuando se vuelven máscaras. What they hide from us, we smell on their clothes and touch in our sleep. We know better than them what they feel ... and that's enough to make us believe it's love. That's a marriage.

HORTENSIA: Pues para mí, ya no. It's not a marriage for me. (MANUEL *can be seen coming up the porch steps.*)

ROSARIO: Allí viene.

MANUEL: (MANUEL *carries a caged canary. He sets it on the porch, removes his jacket. He wears a sleeveless undershirt. He sits and stares at the canary.*) Lupita's lying to me. I know it. She puts her little hand on my back and pats me real softly. "It's okay, Papi," she goes. "It's okay." But I know she's just waiting for the day she can get away from me.

ROSARIO: Me voy, hermana. Nos vemos mañana.

HORTENSIA: 'Stá bien. Buenas noches. (*They embrace.* RO-SARIO *exits upstage.* MANUEL *enters, still mumbling to himself. He doesn't notice* HORTENSIA *until she speaks.*) Manuel. (*He stops.*) Touch me. (*Pause.*) Yo existo. (*Pause.*) Manuel, yo existo. Existo yo. Existo yo. (MA-NUEL *walks past her, stands with his back to her.*) Nothing's changed, has it? I look at your back and it tells me nothing's changed. A back doesn't cry, ni tiene sonrisa, ni sabe gemir, gritar. But this is what I get to look at day in and day out.

MANUEL: Everywhere I go, everybody sees it. The girls, they see it. They're laughing at me all the time. The people I work with, the patrón ... he sees it. He's laughing, too.

Nobody knows our secret, but they all know and they're
all laughing at what they see inside my head.
HORTENSIA: (*Approaching him.*) You know how good I know this
back? I know it mejor que tú. (*She touches his back, he
freezes.*) ¿Sabes que tienes una herida aquí? (*Touching the
place on the wound.*) ¿Y un lunar allí? (*Touching him.*) ¿Y
otro acá? (*She pounds his back.*) ¡Mírame, cabrón! Why
don't you look at me? ¡Mírame! (*He spins around, grabs
her by the wrists.*)
MANUEL: Pues, take a good look because it's the last time you'll
see my face. (*She grabs him, tries to stop him.*)
HORTENSIA: Manuel. ¿Manuel, qué te pasa?
MANUEL: I don' need this. I got friends. I don' need none of
this! (*He pushes her away violently. She goes to him.*)
HORTENSIA: Manuel! (*He throws her to the floor, then pulls her
up by the hair.*)
MANUEL: (*Sobbing.*) Me das asco, ¿sabes? I can't stand the touch
of you. (*He drops her to the floor, grabs his jacket and the
bird and exits. HORTENSIA sobs, starts crawling on the
floor to the bathroom. Her face is bruised. LUPE enters.*)
LUPE: (*Running to her.*) Mami, ¿qué pasó? Did Papi hurt you,
Mami?
HORTENSIA: Estoy sucia. My body smells bad. Apesto. Apesto.
LUPE: No, Mami.
HORTENSIA: (*She looks up at LUPE, her eyes glazed. Beat.*)
Vente, mi bebita. I have to give you a bath, m'ijita.
LUPE: What, Mami? I don't need a bath.
HORTENSIA: (*Pulling at LUPE's clothes.*) I have to take off your
piyamita and your little diaper.
LUPE: No, Mami.
HORTENSIA: I'll put you in the water.
LUPE: ¿Qué 'stás diciendo, Mamá? (*She keeps trying to drag LUPE
to the bathroom.*)
HORTENSIA: Vente, m'ija. Don't worry. I'm gonna test the water
first con el dedito. (*She pulls on her.*)
LUPE: Stop, Mami. You're hurting me. (*She suddenly catches the
fear in LUPE's eyes.*)
HORTENSIA: Don't look at me like that! ¡No puedo soportarlo!
(HORTENSIA *grabs* LUPE, *covers her eyes.*) Conrado ...
You got his eyes. Why you got to have his eyes? (LUPE
begins to cry. She buries LUPE's *face into her lap, holds
her down, covering her face and mouth.* LUPE *struggles.*)
I have to turn off the sound. No llores más, bebita. (*She*

smothers LUPE's *cries.*) I cover your little head with my
hand and push it down into the water. (*She pushes* LUPE's
head further into the floor. LUPE *stiffens.*) Your pierni-
tas stop kicking. Your skin goes white and still. (LUPE
goes limp.) Sí. Eso. Everything is quiet. (*Beat. Seeing*
LUPE *limp on the floor,* HORTENSIA *screams.*) ¡Dios
mío! ¡Qué he hecho! I killed her. ¡Para qué! For him?
¡Qué he hecho! ¡Qué he hecho! (LUPE *gradually stirs,*
coming out of her shock. She sits up. Seeing this, HOR-
TENSIA, *hysterical, rushes to the bathroom. She grabs*
a douche bag and a bottle of vinegar. LETICIA *enters.*
LUPE *runs to her.*)
LUPE: Lettie, it's Mami. (HORTENSIA *climbs into the tub. She*
   starts to pour the vinegar into the bag, her hands shaking.
   LETICIA *goes to her.* LUPE *stands back, horrified.*)
LETICIA: Mamá, what are you doing?
HORTENSIA: ¡Estoy cochina! Filthy!
LETICIA: Did he hit you, Mamá?
HORTENSIA: ¡Me tengo que lavar! ¡Me voy a bañar! (*She aban-*
   dons the bag, pouring vinegar directly all over herself. LE-
   TICIA *tries to get the bottle from her.*)
LETICIA: No, Mamá. ¡Dámela!
HORTENSIA: ¡Déjame sola! ¡'Stoy sucia! ¡Desgraciada!
LETICIA: Mamá, you're gonna hurt yourself. Let it go.
HORTENSIA: Tu padre thinks I stink, pues now I stink for sure!
LETICIA: Give me it! (*She grabs the bottle from her.* HORTEN-
   SIA *slumps into the tub, holding her bruised face.*)
HORTENSIA: ¿Por qué no me mata tu papá, por qué no? It's
   better if he kill me!
LUPE: (*Softly.*) No llores, Mami.
LETICIA: Let me see your eye.
HORTENSIA: No me toques. 'Stoy sucia. (LETICIA *gets a wash-*
   cloth, puts it to her mother's bruise. She resists.)
LETICIA: C'mon, Mamá. Now, hold it there. (HORTENSIA *does.*
   LETICIA *starts to unbutton* HORTENSIA's *robe.*) God,
   you're drenched in the stuff.
HORTENSIA: (*In tears, spying* LUPE.) ¡Dile que se vaya! I don't
   want her to see me!
LETICIA: Lupe, go get her other robe. (LUPE *doesn't move.*)
HORTENSIA: (*To* LETICIA.) ¡No quiero que me vea!
LETICIA: (*To* LUPE.) Now! (LUPE *runs out.* LETICIA *helps*
   HORTENSIA *off with the robe. She wears a bra and*
   panties.)

HORTENSIA: I'm sorry you gottu see me así, m'ija.

LETICIA: It's okay, Mamá. It's not your fault. (*She dries HOR-TENSIA's shoulders, her back.*)

HORTENSIA: I guess all my girls are grown up now.

LETICIA: Yeah. (*She unties HORTENSIA's hair, drying it. Moments later, LUPE enters with the robe.*) Sabes qué, Leticia. Tu hermanita es una señorita now.

LUPE: Ay, Mami.

LETICIA: I know, Mamá. (*LUPE gives the robe to LETICIA. LETICIA drapes it over her mother's shoulders. LUPE takes the washcloth and dabs HORTENSIA's forehead.*)

HORTENSIA: (*To LUPE.*) No, ya no eres baby. You gottu behave a little different now, m'ija. Tú sabes ... con más vergüenza. You can' go jumping around all over the place con los chavos like before.

LUPE: (*Soberly.*) Sí, Mami.

HORTENSIA: I got no more babies. (*LUPE strokes her mother's hair.*) You got good hands, hija. (*Pause.*) Now, I'm your baby, no m'ija? Now you have to clean my nalguitas jus' like I wipe yours when you was a baby.

LUPE: Ay, Mami.

HORTENSIA: (*After a pause.*) You girls are all I got in the world, you know.

LUPE: (*Sadly, gently dabbing the bruise.*) Sí, Mami. Sí. (*LETICIA sits on the edge of the tub and watches her mother and sister. The lights gradually fade to black.*)

ACT TWO
A few months later.

.... SCENE ONE ....

Sunset. ROSARIO sits on the porch. She fans herself. LUPE sits on the step below her. LETICIA lies on top of the bed reading a book, radio next to her. "Evil Ways" by Santana plays in the background.

LUPE: Papi keeps talking to himself all the time. Maybe he's a saint.

ROSARIO: Tu papá no es un santo, m'ija.
LUPE: He could be. He suffers inside like the saints.
ROSARIO: Maybe he'll die and it'll be our sin because we didn't
    know he was a saint.
ROSARIO: Don' say that. Some peepo suffer because they want
    to.
LUPE: I don't wanna.
ROSARIO: So don't. But your papi wan's to suffer.
LUPE: He doesn't. He has something inside ... that hurts him.
ROSARIO: What?
LUPE: I dunno.
LETICIA: (*From the bedroom.*) Lupe!
LUPE: What!
LETICIA: Are you gonna do my toenails?
LUPE: Yeah. (MANUEL *enters the kitchen from upstage center,
    moving his lips, talking silently to himself. An orange color
    washes over the scene.* ROSARIO *looks into the horizon.*)
ROSARIO: Mira, ya se pone el sol. (*They all observe the sunset for
    a moment.*) This is the best time of all the day. ¿Ves las
    sombras?
LUPE: It's so clear.
ROSARIO: En esta hora, just before the sun sets, you see the shad-
    ows more clear than anytime of the day. (*The sunset col-
    ors deepen, then fade as the sun descends into the horizon.
    LUPE goes to the kitchen, pulls a chair out for her father
    to sit.* ROSARIO *exits.* LUPE *sits at his feet, rubs some
    dirt off his shoe.*)
MANUEL: When my compadre, Conrado, was a little boy, he used
    to shine shoes for a living. He was never ashamed of it
    because, like he said, it was about making a buck any-
    way you could. He constructed the little shoe shine box
    with his own hands. I watched him do it. He sawed six
    perfectly even rectangles of wood and hammered them to-
    gether. He made the top piece so it could flip open and
    shut. Like this. (*He demonstrates.*) And then he sanded it
    con una piedra. He painted the box black because most of
    the shoes he shined were black, he said, and that way the
    box would never look dirty. But the Tucson streets were
    very dirty in those days and the polvo would seep into the
    cracks of the box anyway. (*Pause.*) You don't know him,
    Lupita, but my compadre is an American success story.
    He use to live here ... near us. But then, he went back to
    Arizona to make it big.

LETICIA: Lupe!
LUPE: Yeah! (*Standing.*) I'm coming. (LUPE *goes to the bedroom. Distraught,* MANUEL *exits upstage, talking to himself.* LUPE *gets a bottle of nail polish, sits by the foot of the bed and starts applying polish to* LETICIA'*s toenails.* LETICIA *keeps reading.* LUPE *singing along with the radio.*) "Oh you've got to change your evil ways, baby ... " (*The music fades.*) What name did you choose for your confirmation, Lettie?
LETICIA: Cecilia.
LUPE: Why Cecilia? Saint Cecilia was burned at the stake.
LETICIA: I liked the name.
LUPE: I was thinking of Magdalena for me ... Naw, cuz then people call you, Maggie. That's Maggie O'Connel's name. I can't stand her.
LETICIA: They could call you Lena. Anyway, nobody calls anybody by their confirmation name. It's just on paper.
LUPE: Yeah, but I love the story about her.
LETICIA: Who?
LUPE: Mary Magdalene. (*She rises, begins to dramatize the story.*) I loved how she jus' walked right through all those phony baloney pharisees, right up to the face of Jesus. An' there they were all looking down their noses at her like she was not'ing but a ... tú sabes, a fallen woman.
LETICIA: Well, she was a prostitute.
LUPE: She doesn't look to the right or to the left, jus' keeps staring straight ahead. The pharisees try to stop her, but Jesus tells them, "Let her come forward." (*Returns to the toes.*)
LETICIA: Make sure you get it all the way down to the cuticle.
LUPE: I am. (*She paints one toe, then returns to the story of Magdalene.*) So the crowd opens up and makes a path for her. And then she kneels down in front of him an' jus' starts crying and crying for all the sins she's done. (*Sobbing dramatically at the feet of Jesus.*) An' y'see his feet are dusty from all those long walks in the desert ... She's crying up a storm, it's coming down in buckets all over Jesus' feet ... (*Sob, sob, sob.*)
LETICIA: Are you finished?
LUPE: In a minute. But suddenly the tears become like bathwater, real soft an' warm an' soothing-like. She's got this hair, y'see, this long beautiful dark hair, an' it's so thick she can make a towel out of it. It's so soft, it's almost like velvet as she spreads it all over Jesus' feet. (*She pours her*

hair over Jesus' imaginary feet, then returns to LETICIA*'s toes.*)

LETICIA: Blow on 'em a little so they can dry faster, will you? (*She does, then goes over to* LETICIA.)

LUPE: Can you imagine what it musta felt like to have this woman with such beautiful hair wiping it on you? (*Plays with the strands of* LETICIA*'s hair.*) It's jus' too much to think about. And then Jesus says ... (*Pulling up* LETICIA *as "Magdalene."*) "Rise woman and go and sin no more." (*After a beat.*) Now that's what I call forgiveness. That's ... relief.

MANUEL: (*Offstage.*) Lupita! Lupe!

HORTENSIA: Lupe! ¡Tu papá te 'stá llamando!

LUPE: (*Putting the polish away.*) God, I'm everybody's slave around here. (LUPE *exits. "Evil Ways" rises in the background. The lights and the music gradually fade out.*)

.... SCENE TWO ....

MANUEL *is talking to the caged canary in the garden left. He drinks from a bottle of tequila. It is dusk.*

MANUEL: I am a lonely man. I bring the bottle to my lips and feel the tequila pour down behind my tongue, remojando the back of my throat. Corre down la espina, until it hits my belly and burns como madre in there. For a minute, I am filled up, contento ... satisfecho. (*Pause.*) I look across the table and my compadre's there y me siento bien. All I gotta do is sit in my own skin in the chair. (*Rises, goes into the kitchen, sits at the table.*) But he was leaving. I could smell it coming. I tried to make him stay. How did I let myself disappear like that? I became nothing, a ghost. I asked him, "You want her, compa?" He said, "Yes." And I told him, "What's mine is yours, compadre. Take her." (*Rises, walks to the upstage wall.*) I floated into the room with him. In my mind, I was him ... And then, I was her, too. In my mind, I imagined their pleasure ...

and I turned to nothing. (*Fade out.*)

.... SCENE THREE ....

MANUEL, LETICIA *and* LUPE *are seated at the kitchen table.*
LUPE *wears a Catholic school uniform.* HORTENSIA *is making
breakfast.* LUPE *and* LETICIA *are eating.* LETICIA *puts the food
to her mouth, without lifting her eyes from the college textbook she
is reading.* MANUEL *is writing a letter.*

HORTENSIA: Leticia, if you read while you eat, the food doesn't
    set right in your stomach.
LETICIA: I'm all right.
LUPE: You got a test, Lettie?
LETICIA: A mid-term.
LUPE: Is college hard?
LETICIA: Uh-huh.
HORTENSIA: Don't bother your sister, hija. Tiene que estudiar.
LUPE: I wanna go to college, too.
LETICIA: You should try to get a scholarship. Go to Harvard or
    something.
LUPE: What's Harvard?
LETICIA: The best. (HORTENSIA *puts a plate of food down for*
    MANUEL. *He ignores it.*)
HORTENSIA: (*To* MANUEL.) What are you doing?
MANUEL: Writing a letter.
HORTENSIA: You're not goin' to eat? (*He doesn't respond. They
    all look at him. After a beat,* LUPE *takes a slip of paper
    and a pen from the book bag on the floor next to her, goes
    to* HORTENSIA.)
LUPE: Mami, I need my confirmation form signed.
HORTENSIA: Dásela a tu padre. (*She puts the form down in front
    of him.*)
LUPE: Will you sign this for me, Papi? (MANUEL *ignores it.*
    LUPE *points to the signature line.*) Right here. (*He con-
    tinues writing the letter.* LUPE *brings it back to* HORTEN-
    SIA. HORTENSIA *looks over at* MANUEL, *then signs the
    form.*)
LETICIA: (*Taking her plate to the counter.*) You ready, Lupe?
LUPE: Yeah. (*They gather their things to leave. They kiss their
    mother, then their father.* MANUEL *does not respond.*)
LETICIA: See ya, Dad.

LUPE: Bye, Papi.

LETICIA: (*Exiting.*) 'Bout the time you're in college, lots of Chicanos will be going to Harvard, you'll see.

LUPE: (*Following her.*) Where's it at?

LETICIA: Cambridge, Massachusetts.

LUPE: Too far.

LETICIA: (*From offstage.*) I'll be home late. Gotta work tonight.

HORTENSIA: Okay, m'ija.

LUPE: Bye, m'ija.

LUPE: Bye, Mami.

HORTENSIA: Que les vaya bien. (HORTENSIA *clears off the
table.* MANUEL *is addressing an envelope. She brings
him a cup of coffee. He pushes it away very slowly, the full
length of his arm. Beat.*) Why are you writing him?

MANUEL: Because he's my compadre.

HORTENSIA: ¿Y quién soy yo?

MANUEL: You're my wife.

HORTENSIA: Sí, soy tu esposa. Cuando tienes hambre, I put
the food in front a you. When you're sick, I force the
medicine into your mouth. I iron your pantalones and
put out clean pijamas for you each night. Everytime you
take a bath, I wash out the ring in the tub. (*He tears the
page from the tablet.* HORTENSIA *takes a letter from her
apron and tosses it onto the table in front of him.*) You ask
him to come back. ¿Por qué, Manuel? Why you wanna
do this to us? (*He grabs the letter, bolts up.*)

MANUEL: You read this? You read my letter?

HORTENSIA: Sí, la leí.

MANUEL: You had no right. (*Putting the envelope in her face.*)
Do you see your name on this sobre?

HORTENSIA: No.

MANUEL: Pues, until my compadre puts your name here, you got
no right to read what he writes to me.

HORTENSIA: Whatcha got to say to that man?

MANUEL: Nada que te importa a tí. My compadre's coming back
and when he does, we ain't never gonna talk about you.
Ni una palabra. We're gonna talk about the track or the
weather or my new grandson or cualquier chingada cosa
que queremos, but we ain't gonna talk about you. And
we ain't gonna talk about my son neither. I had a compadre before you went and messed it all up. So you can
forget any other ideas you got, 'cause everything's gonna
go back to normal. Todo está bien arreglado. Y cuando te

digo que my compadre's coming for dinner, you're gonna make his favorite chile verde. I don't care what you feel, m'entiendes? Me vas a obedecer. And you'll put the plate of food in front of his face and you'll pretend that you feel nothing, menos que antes. Becuz' if I see you give him, even a little sign, like your face gets a little red o demasiada pálida or your hand shakes a little when you pour el café into the taza, recuerdas que you're gonna pay porque te estoy watchando, mujer. And it's gonna to be like the old times and you're not going to mess it up again. (*He stuffs the letter he has written into an envelope and seals it. He puts both letters into his pocket and exits.* HORTENSIA *watches him. After a beat, she sits, drops her face into her hands. Fade out.*)

.... SCENE FOUR ....

LUPE *is on the porch, shining* MANUEL'*s shoes.* ROSARIO *approaches, sits on the step.*

ROSARIO: Tu papi's getting all spruced up, eh?
LUPE: Really.
ROSARIO: Dáme uno. Yo te ayudo.
LUPE: Thanks, tía. (*She hands her a shoe to polish.*)
ROSARIO: He's going out?
LUPE: Uh-huh.
ROSARIO: ¿Adónde?
LUPE: To see that man.
ROSARIO: Who?
LUPE: Conrado.
ROSARIO: How do you know?
LUPE: I heard Papi telling Mami. She's getting his clothes ready. She's been singing all day, so she won't say nothing mean to him.
ROSARIO: She's singing?
LUPE: She's mad inside, so she sings. That way only nice things come out of her mouth.
ROSARO: Tu mamá es una buena mujer.
LUPE: I know. (HORTENSIA *enters the kitchen singing to herself, with underlying irritation. She puts a pair of* MANUEL'*s dress pants and a suit coat over the back of a chair. Upstage stands an ironing board. She begins pressing his dress*

shirt.)

MANUEL: (*Offstage.*) Lupe!

LUPE: ¡Allí voy! (ROSARIO *and* LUPE *rise, go into the kitchen.*)

ROSARIO: If they di'nt take the license from me, we could all go out and paint the town ourselves tonight.

LUPE: In that car! Forget it, tía! It's got fins sharp enough to kill somebody.

ROSARIO: Pues, we got protection then. (LUPE *exits with the shoes.* ROSARIO *pours herself a cup of coffee and sits at the table.*)

ROSARIO: Conrado's back?

HORTENSIA: Sí. I don't know what it is ... It's like he wants to jump right into the heart of the herida and bury himself in there. I'm his wife, but I'm not goin' to jump in there with him. (MANUEL *enters in his underwear, moving his lips, talking to himself silently. He wears a hat and holds his shoes and two ties.* HORTENSIA *hands him the shirt and he puts it on. They watch him dress in silence. He then puts on the pants, examining the creases. He licks his fingers and runs them down the edge of a crease. He sits down, then stands up, checking the crease again.*)

MANUEL: The crease doesn't stay in them. (*He looks distraught. He holds up the two ties.*) La azul or the yellow one?

HORTENSIA: La azul. (MANUEL *chooses the yellow one instead, stuffing the blue one into his pant pocket. He sits down and puts on his shoes with a shoehorn. The women continue watching him dress, their eyes never leaving him.*)

ROSARIO: Sometimes a man thinks of another man before he thinks of anybody else. He don' think about his woman ni su madre ni los children, jus' what he gots in his head about that man. He closes his eyes and dreams, "If I could get inside that man's skin, then I'd really be somebody!" But when he opens his eyes and sees that he's as empty as he was before, he curls his fingers into fists and knocks down whatever stands in his way. (*He stands, buttons his coat. He looks at* HORTENSIA.)

HORTENSIA: If you go, Manuel, you won't find me here when you get back. I don't know where you'll find me, but I won't be here.

MANUEL: (*Starting for the door.*) Fine.

HORTENSIA: I'll take the girls, Manuel. You'll have a empty house to come home to. No 'stoy jugando. The minute you walk out that door ... (*He turns, then slowly ap-*

proaches her. He bends and kisses her cheek, begins to exit.) No puedo aguantarlo. No puedo. (*He stops in the doorway, turns.*)

MANUEL: You'll do as I say. Things will get better now. You'll see. (*He dips his hat slightly over one eye and runs his fingers over the rim of it. He imagines himself in Conrado's image, muy suave.*) Adiós, mujer. (*He exits. There is a pause.*)

HORTENSIA: (*Still staring at the door.*) I don' wan' Lupita here when Manuel comes home tonight.

ROSARIO: Sí, hermana. I'll take her. (*LUPE enters upstage. RO-SARIO looks at her. The tension frightens her.*)

LUPE: ¿Tía?

HORTENSIA: (*Brusquely.*) You're goin' to go with your tía tonight, m'ija.

LUPE: But ... (*HORTENSIA doesn't look at her.*)

HORTENSIA: Lettie will bring your pijamas later. (*ROSARIO puts her arm around LUPE. LUPE watches her mother's back.*) You be a good girl now.

LUPE: Sí, Mami.

ROSARIO: Good night, hermana. (*They go to the door.*)

HORTENSIA: Good night.

LUPE: Mami ... ? (*HORTENSIA goes to her, kisses LUPE.*)

HORTENSIA: Nos vemos por la mañana, m'ija ... muy tempranito. (*They exit. After a few moments, HORTENSIA goes out onto the porch, lights a cigarette, waits.*)

.... SCENE FIVE ....

It is the wee hours of the morning. HORTENSIA *still waits on the porch.* LETICIA *enters wearing a miniskirt and boots.* LETICIA *doesn't notice her until* HORTENSIA *speaks.*

HORTENSIA: It's two o'clock in the morning. (*She stops.*)

LETICIA: I know. (*LETICIA goes into the kitchen. HORTENSIA follows her.*)

HORTENSIA: ¿Crees que eres mayor ya?

LETICIA: No.

HORTENSIA: Eres hombre, entonces. (*LETICIA sits.*) Tha's what you want, isn't it? To be free like a man.

LELTICIA: That wouldn't be so bad.

HORTENSIA: (*Sitting.*) Pues, no naciste varón. If God had wanted you to be a man, he would of given you somet'ing between your legs.

LETICIA: I have something between my legs.

HORTENSIA: But you're not a woman yet. In this house you're not a woman, you're my daughter ... a daughter I can't control. I know what you're feeling and I can't stop you. You walk in that door and I can smell the woman coming out of you.

LETICIA: What's wrong with that?

HORTENSIA: I don' know what to tell you no more. Maybe there's nothing wrong with that. I marry un hombre tranquilo. A good man. And I watch his back bend, his belly blow up with beer and I see my daughter grow to look at him con desprecio and ... contempt.

LETICIA: It's not contempt, Mamá. It's pity.

HORTENSIA: That's worse ...

LETICIA: (*After a pause.*) Do you love him?

HORTENSIA: Maybe I don't love him. To be with a man so long, day in and day out, it's hard to know. Your head is on the pillow next to his. You feel his body, his weight, su aliento. I could know tu padre's breathing anywhere porque lo oigo hasta en mis sueños. Entra en el alma cuando uno duerme ... Funny, when a man is asleep, tha's when you really get to know him. You see the child's look on his face, before he wakes up and remembers he's a man again. In his half-dream, tiene la voz de un niño. But your husband really isn't your child. He di'nt come from your body. Y no matter cuántas veces le das el pecho, tu marido no es tu hijo. Your blood never mixes. He stays a stranger in his own home.

LETICIA: Do they ever really grow up, Mamá?

HORTENSIA: I don't think so. Maybe for you it'll be different. (*There is a pause.* LETICIA *goes upstage, stands with her back to* HORTENSIA.)

LETICIA: I thought of you tonight. I thought of no longer being your daughter, that what I was gonna do ... would turn you away from me.

HORTENSIA: I don' wanna know.

LETICIA: There they were, the Raza gods with their legs spread, popping beers, talking revolución and those things, each with its own life, its own personality and I wanted to taste them all. Each and every fruta. "Una joya," you would say. (*Pause.*) So, I opened my legs to one of them, Mamá. The way a person opens her arms to take the whole world in, I opened my legs.

HORTENSIA: Is that what you call love?

LETICIA: (LETICIA *turns to her.*) It's not about love. It's power. Power we get to hold and caress and protect. Power they drop into our hands, so fragile, the slightest pressure makes them weak with pain.

HORTENSIA: Why, m'ija? Why you give your virginidad away for not'ing.

LETICIA: I was tired of carrying it around ... that weight of being a woman with a prize. Walking around with that special secret, that valuable commodity, waiting for some lucky guy to put his name on it. I wanted it to be worthless, Mamá. Don't you see? Not for me to be worthless, but to know that my worth had nothing to do with it. (*Pause.*)

HORTENSIA: You protect yourself, hija? (HORTENSIA *goes to her.*)

LETICIA: Yeah. I'll be all right. (*They embrace.* HORTEN-SIA's *face over* LETICIA's *shoulder holds an expression of loss. After a beat,* LETICIA *exits upstage.* HORTENSIA *watches her. Moments later,* CONRADO *appears in the garden. He walks up the porch steps. He is well-dressed in a suit and wears a hat, dipped over one eye. He removes the hat, combs his hair with his fingers, replaces the hat. The lighting shifts to a surreal quality. Facing upstage,* HOR-TENSIA *removes her bathrobe, she wears a dark evening dress. She turns to* CONRADO.)

HORTENSIA: Where's Manuel?

CONRADO: He's not here yet?

HORTENSIA: No. (*He enters the kitchen.*)

CONRADO: Te ves igual.

HORTENSIA: After thirteen years?

CONRADO: You look the same.

HORTENSIA: And you? Are you the same?

CONRADO: Pues, dime. Am I?

HORTENSIA: You've changed.

CONRADO: I'm older. (*He laughs. They both sit.*)

HORTENSIA: (*After a beat.*) Why did you come back?

CONRADO: To see Manuel. (*Pause.*) He wrote me.

HORTENSIA: He told you?

HORTENSIA: Sí.

CONRADO: He said you wanted me to come back.

HORTENSIA: And you believe that?

CONRADO: No sé. (*Pause.*) I'm broke.

HORTENSIA: That's why you came back?

CONRADO: Pues ...

HORTENSIA: (*Smiling.*) So, you didn't make it big?

CONRADO: No, 'mana. (*They both laugh.*)

HORTENSIA: So, here you are. (*Pause.*)

CONRADO: You remember one morning, I was standing on a
    street corner. It was First and Figueroa. I was with a
    woman, una güera, muy alta. I was talking to her when I
    heard the streetcar pass behind me. I turned around and I
    saw you looking at me through the window. The sun was
    just coming up into your eyes. And I turned to la güera
    and I kissed her on the mouth.

HORTENSIA: I remember.

CONRADO: I did that to let you go ... so that you would go to
    him. (*Pause.*) One month later, you married Manuel. He
    never knew what he had.

HORTENSIA: He's been good to me.

CONRADO: I used to watch Riguito and Leticia circling around
    you in the kitchen, two little satellites in your orbit. I
    watched the way you moved inside your apron. I wanted
    you, Tencha.

HORTENSIA: No me digas más. (*Stands, tango rises softly in
    background.*) When we first met, you and Manuel and me
    ... we had a good time, the three of us. He was the one I
    was with, but I was proud of you both, tan guapos en sus
    uniformes. Manuel danced a few numbers with me and
    then he'd say, "This one's for you, 'mano. Dance with
    Tencha." (CONRADO *walks up to* HORTENSIA. *They
    dance.* MANUEL *appears in back. He stands in the dark,
    watching.* CONRADO *dips* HORTENSIA *and is about to
    kiss her. She turns her face away. They stop, hold their
    dancing postures.* CONRADO *sees* MANUEL.)

CONRADO: Compadre. (HORTENSIA *backs away.* CONRADO
    removes his hat.)

MANUEL: (*To* CONRADO.) You never have enough. What I gave
    you was never enough.

CONRADO: Nothing happened.

MANUEL: There she is waiting for you, compadre. Isn't that what
    I said? I'll give you the shirt off my back. You want my
    shirt? (MANUEL *starts unbuttoning his shirt.*)

CONRADO: Stop it, compa.

MANUEL: You want my hat? (*He shoves* CONRADO *into a chair and sticks his hat on* CONRADO's *head.*) How about la waifa! (*He grabs* HORTENSIA *and throws her onto* CONRADO's *lap. She crawls from his lap, away from the men.*) After you left her like a rag in the bed, how could I go to her? Wipe up the little that was left of her. She walked around the house like she was something special, like she got a piece of you. (*He grabs* CONRADO *by the balls, then slumps into the chair.*) You know how that feels? To have your own wife holding something inside her that's not yours. She made me feel like I was nothing. (*Turning to him.*) I loved you, man. I gave you my woman. But that meant nothing to you. You just went and left. I gave you my fucking wife, cabrón. I gave you my woman. What does that make me? (*Pause.*) And all these years she looks at me like she knows something I don't know, like she's got something I don't got.

HORTENSIA: Manuel, you can't blame me. You were there that night. I heard you coming in. You were laughing and crying. Conrado was leaving. The whole house suddenly goes quiet y veo esta sombra in our room. (CONRADO *approaches* HORTENSIA *from behind.*) You stand there in the dark sin decir nada, jus' staring at me. You come and lay down next to me. (CONRADO *puts his arms around her. She continues addressing* MANUEL.) You put your hand around my waist and your touch is different. You speak ...

CONRADO: Hortensia.

HORTENSIA: ... And it's not your voice. I tell you que te vayas, tha' we can't do what you're thinking ... Y me respondes ...

CONRADO: No te apures. Manuel knows. This is what he wants.

HORTENSIA: And I close my eyes ... y me entras ... and nothing's the same after that. (*After a beat.*) Leave us alone now, compadre. (CONRADO *hesitates, looking at them for a moment. Then he grabs his hat and exits. There is a long pause.* HORTENSIA *does not remove her eyes from* MANUEL. *She reaches out her arms to him. He turns his face away. She recoils, bringing her arms back into her chest. She exits.* MANUEL *sits in a stupor. He slowly rises, takes out a fresh fifth of tequila and a bottle of pills. He swallows half the pills, washing them down with the tequila. He puts the tequila on the table.*)

MANUEL: Lupita ... (*He goes toward the bedroom.*) She's waiting for me ... (*Enters the bedroom. He becomes frightened, looking for her inside the bedding.*) Lupe? ... Lupita? (*He rushes back into the kitchen.*) She's gone. ¡M'iji-i-i-ta! (*He falls onto the chair, crying. It's the labored sobbing of a man unable to reach the core of his despair.*) She took everything from me. (*He weeps until he is empty of tears. Moments later, his face hardened, impassive, MANUEL grabs the bottle of tequila and goes out onto the porch. The sun is beginning to rise. He sits, a silhouette against the dawn's light. He swallows the remainder of the pills and raises the bottle to his lips. He drinks it down, his head thrown back. Black out. In the dark, the sound of his body hitting the floor. Moments later, the lights rise to reveal MANUEL in a heap on the floor. HORTENSIA enters, rushes to him, putting her ear to his chest. She looks up in horror. Fade out.*)

.... SCENE SIX ....

The day of MANUEL*'s funeral. The* WOMEN *and* DAUGHTERS *enter ritualistically in single file. They wear black.* ROSARIO *sits, a black rebozo on her lap.* HORTENSIA *holds two black dresses.* LETICIA *carries a suitcase. She sets it down.* LUPE *and* LETICIA *stand upstage in their slips.*)

ROSARIO: Bueno ... somos puras hembras now. A house full of women, no más. (*They look at one another, as if noticing for the first time.*)

HORTENSIA: (*After a pause.*) Ándale, m'ijas. You better get dressed. Your brother will be here para llevarnos purty soon. (HORTENSIA *hands* LETICIA *a dress.*) Toma. (*She hands* LUPE *a dress. They put them on.* HORTENSIA *zipping up* LETICIA*'s dress.*) Después de tantos años, es difícil decir, "He dug his own grave, let him lie in it." (*Zipping up* LUPE*'s.*) Did I kill him? When you let go your child's hand and they go off to meet la Muerte in the street, ¿es tu culpa? ¿O es el destino? (CONRADO *appears at the door. He holds a note in his hand. He removes his hat, combs his hair back with his fingers. Knocks, waits.*)

ROSARIO: Es él. (HORTENSIA *goes to the door with the suitcase.*)

CONRADO: (*Referring to the note.*) You wanted me to get his things?

HORTENSIA: Aquí 'stá su ropa. (*She hands him the suitcase.*)

CONRADO: What should I do with them?

HORTENSIA: Wear them. Burn them. (CONRADO *exits.* HORTENSIA *comes back inside. Sounds of car pulling up.*)

ROSARIO: Ya es hora. Ha llegado Rigo. (*They all begin to file out,* ROSARIO *stops.*) Lupita, cover up el espejo. (ROSARIO *hands her the rebozo.*) We don't want your papi to come back and try an' take us with him.

LUPE: Sí, señora. (HORTENSIA, ROSARIO, LETICIA *exit upstage.* LUPE *pauses for a moment, centerstage. She spies* MANUEL*'s hat on a chair. She picks it up, fingers its rim, pauses again. She goes into the bathroom, approaches the mirror, still holding the hat. After a beat.*) I've decided my confirmation name will be Frances 'cuz that's what Frances Pacheco's name is and I wanna be in her body. When she sits, she doesn't hold her knees together like my mom and the nuns are always telling me to. She jus' lets them fly an' fall wherever they want ... real natural-like ... like they was wings instead of knees. (*Pause.*) An' she's got a laugh ... a laugh that seems to come from way deep inside herself, from the bottom of her heart or somet'ing. (*Fingering the hat.*) If I could ... I'd like to jus' unzip her chest and climb right inside there, next to her heart, to feel everyt'ing she's feeling an' I could forget about me. (*Pause.*) It's okay if she doesn't feel the same way ... it's my secret.

HORTENSIA: (*Offstage.*) Lupe ... !

LUPE: Ya voy. (*As she covers the mirror with the rebozo, the lights fade to black.*)

End of Play

Miriam's Flowers

Migdalia Cruz

CHARACTERS

MIRIAM NIEVES: a Puerto Rican girl of sixteen.
DELFINA NIEVES: her mother, thirty-six.
PULI NIEVES: her seven year old brother.
ENRIQUE ROJAS: her boyfriend, a grocer, thirty-five.
NANDO MORALES: Delfina's lover, Puli's father, thirty-seven.

PLACE

The South Bronx. The set should be simple and dark. On stage should be the home altar, in the Nieves' apartment with a statue of San Martín de Porres; the church altar with a white plaster "Pieta"; and the funeral home altar, with simple red candles. The candles in the church should be blue and the candles on the home altar can be many colors. The candles should be lit from the beginning of the play and burn throughout. The bathtub must appear in the same place in which the white coffin appears.

This play moves through various locales in a neighborhood in the South Bronx. Just a suggestion of the place is all that is necessary except, as I mentioned before, for the altars. They need to be as detailed as possible.

TIME

Summer to Winter, 1975.

.... SCENE ONE ....

In the dark is heard the first verse of "I Wanna Be Where You Are" by the Jackson Five. Then, a scream from MIRIAM *who has awakened from a nightmare. Her scream stops the music.* DEL-FINA *runs in, turns on the light, holds* MIRIAM *and rocks her.*

DELFINA: Sssh, ssh, sssh ... It's okay, baby. Mami's here. Mami's here. Sssh, ssh, ssh ... It's over now. (*Pause.*) Sssh ... sssh. (*Lights fade to candlelight.*)

.... SCENE TWO ....

MIRIAM *and* DELFINA *on the sofa in the Nieves' apartment.* MIRIAM *examines the newspaper article about* PULI'S *death.*

DELFINA: I always wanted to look like somebody else.
MIRIAM: Who?
DELFINA: Somebody famous.
MIRIAM: Castro?
DELFINA: Stupid! Why would I want to look like that ugly man?
MIRIAM: He's famous. He runs a whole country.
DELFINA: I wanna be beautiful, like Sophia Loren. Yes, Sophia Loren. She's very beautiful.
MIRIAM: Isn't she dead?
DELFINA: Stupid! She's not dead.
MIRIAM: What are you gonna wear?
DELFINA: To be Sophia Loren I have to wear a very tight dress with big polka dots and big buttons.
MIRIAM: I mean to the funeral.
DELFINA: I ain't going to no funeral. Nobody dead. Nobody in this house is dead! You understand me? Nobody.
MIRIAM: I'm going.
DELFINA: You're not going anywhere.
MIRIAM: Please, Ma.
DELFINA: You go in that room, Miriam, and pray that your brother gets better.
MIRIAM: Puli's dead, Ma. He was chasing after a baseball and got snagged on the tracks. He di'nt have no arm, remember? The train cut it right off and we couldn't find it. They had

to pin up his sleeve like a little cripple boy in his little box ... I've never seen such a little box.

DELFINA: You stupid girl! You didn't see nothing like that. You got bad dreams in there. (*She knocks on* MIRIAM's *head.*) What did I tell you about those dreams? I'm gonna tie your head to that door over there and slam it a few times. Maybe you'll get some sense then.

MIRIAM: Ma, you saw it, too. It was small and white, like a little bathtub. (NANDO *enters and stares at* MIRIAM.) And he's in the paper, too. He always wanned to be in the paper like ... like Roberto Clemente.

DELFINA: Shut up!

MIRIAM: And ... and they show him, Ma. How he was. All in pieces. I di'nt wanna look at it, but ... he's the first one of us ever been in the paper. (*Fade out.*)

.... SCENE THREE ....

In the park, PULI *and* MIRIAM *are playing.*

PULI: Why you always take so long? I been waiting two monfs already!

MIRIAM: You woulda been dead by hunger now, if you been here two months.

PULI: Maybe I am. I'm a ghost, Miree. An' you better gimme a quarter or I scare you to death.

MIRIAM: You don' scare me no how.

PULI: I scared Ricky.

MIRIAM: Nobody scares Ricky.

PULI: I did. He was shooting up in the yard and then he went crazy and he chased me out of there and then he scared me. I ran fast.

MIRIAM: Stop lying, Puli!

PULI: It's true. I swear, it's very true.

MIRIAM: It's true or it's not true, it can't be very true.

PULI: Why not?

MIRIAM: Because.

PULI: I saw Lisette's ombleego yesterday. It's wrinkled up and ugly, jus' like her. And it had dried-up blood on it. It looked like a piece of tree. And she put it by her belly button and it still fit there—like perfect. Like when she was still tied to her mami's stomach.

MIRIAM: Why should I care about Lisette's ombleego? I got one
of my own.

PULI: You do? Show me.

MIRIAM: No way, baby. That's my own personal thing. If you got
your ombleego and you pray on it, then you get everything
you pray for.

PULI: How come Mami di'nt keep mine?

MIRIAM: She said boys' ombleegos bring roaches in the house
because they sweet.

PULI: Yeah ... There's sugar in everything. I seen that on T.V.

MIRIAM: You hear a lot of shit on T.V. Didn't I tell you already
the only thing you can believe is me? What do you think
big sisters are for anyway? For the truth! For telling you
the truth.

PULI: Miree, you think I'm gonna be a baseball player—a good
one?

MIRIAM: You're gonna be great, baby. Very great. And there's
gonna be statues of you in all the parks in the Bronx.

PULI: The whole Bronx?

MIRIAM: Yep. Every bit of the Bronx.

PULI: Pick me up.

MIRIAM: You're not my baby.

PULI: But I wanna be your baby.

MIRIAM: You're too fat.

PULI: Please ... (*He tries to jump up on her.*)

MIRIAM: Shit! Let me sit down first.

PULI: Now?

MIRIAM: Okay. Sit down, little baby.

PULI: Mami. Mami! I want some milk!

MIRIAM: No milk today, baby. How about some ... Ombleego!

PULI: Yuck!

MIRIAM: Get up. I'm tired of this game.

PULI: Let's go on a trip.

MIRIAM: Where to?

PULI: Heaven. I wanna see if everybody there is yellow like Pa-
pabuelo was. He looked like Lisette's ombleego.

MIRIAM: All dead people look like ombleegos, that's why we
got'em. So we don' get no surprises.

PULI: Oh ... (*Fade out.*)

.... SCENE FOUR ....

The action of this scene is simultaneous with Scene Three. The statue of San Martín is turned away from the scene. NANDO is going down on DELFINA. His head is under her skirt. He speaks from there.

NANDO: When I reach the top of your head, to kiss your eyes, I have my tongue tucked between your legs.

DELFINA: You're disgusting.

NANDO: Love can't be disgusting.

DELFINA: Your's is. I always gotta wash after. Like five or six times. With soap.

NANDO: You shouldn't wash too much, Fina. All your juices will dry up. That's how you get old. (*He comes up from under her skirt and wipes his entire face with a handkerchief.*) I love that. But it gets hard to breathe sometimes.

DELFINA: You shouldn't do it for so long. You're not so young yourself.

NANDO: (*Holding the handkerchief to his nose.*) Aaahh! Smell that. It's us. Together. (*He holds it out to DELFINA.*)

DELFINA: ¡Ay! ¡Fo! ¡Pendejo! ¡Saca eso! Get out of here! I know what I smell like. Guava jelly. You tole me that two hundred times now.

NANDO: I think you taste more like the paste. Not so sweet like the jelly, but solid, secure. And like I imagine you—you're jelly on a cracker with goat cheese. I can't think of anything I would rather eat.

DELFINA: You love me too much. (PULI *and* MIRIAM *enter giggling from outside; they catch* DELFINA *and* NANDO *kissing.* PULI *and* MIRIAM *continue to laugh. Fade out.*)

.... SCENE FIVE ....

PULI *exits.* NANDO, DELFINA *and* MIRIAM *dress for the funeral.* NANDO *whistles a Spanish children's song. When they are dressed, they move into Scene Six.*

.... SCENE SIX ....

MIRIAM *and* DELFINA *at the funeral.* DELFINA *rocks back and forth.* MIRIAM *talks to the corpse of her brother,* PULI. *They kneel by the coffin.* NANDO *stands still, behind them.*

MIRIAM: I wanna be a singer. I listen to the radio all the time and I tell people's fortunes. I mean, I sing wif the radio and it's like telling a fortune 'cause I can look into somebody's face and know exactly what song to sing at them and like it helps them ... I can do that for you, too. Gimme your hand. (*She takes his hand and holds it against her cheek. She sings "I'll Be There" by the Jackson Five.*) "I'll be there ... I'll be there. Just call my name, and I'll be there ... Look over your shoulder, honey. Oooh, ooh. I'll be there. I'll be there. Just call my name ... and I'll be there ... " I'll be wif you soon, Puli. Don' be scared of God or nuffin'. He's old, but he's okay. You like that song? You liked those Jackson Five, di'nt you? Yeah ... (*She puts his hand back in the casket.*) I'll keep listening to 'em for you. I'll tell you all about 'em. Yeah. As long as one of us is listening ... Ain't I a good singer though? That's one thing my papi give me. When he cut me that time when he was having that nightmare and he thought my bobo was chokin' me and he cut it in the dark, but it was my neck. You remember? I tole you this story before. He made my voice better, anyway. He cut it just right. Did me a favor. Only good thing he ever give me. (DELFINA *faints. We hear a verse of "I'll Be There." Fade out.*)

.... SCENE SEVEN ....

DELFINA *pretends to read from a children's Bible to* MIRIAM, *who is in bed, shaking.*

DELFINA: Miriam lived in the desert. She had a very big heart. She had ten brothers. She followed Moses around and he would have married her except he couldn't get into the promised land. So she married somebody else. (*Closes the book firmly.*) Go to sleep now!

MIRIAM: Mami!

DELFINA: You're almost sixteen years old, Miriam. The only thing you should be scared of is outside—on the street. Go to sleep.

MIRIAM: Why di'nt Miriam marry Moses? It seems like a good match and everything.

DELFINA: Because he was ugly. And short. A short, ugly, dark man.

MIRIAM: Like Nando.

DELFINA: Nando is beautiful. Didn't you ever look at his lips. They are ... they are like chocolate baby twins.

MIRIAM: He's short, though. Do he ever act funny around water?

DELFINA: What do you mean?

MIRIAM: Do he do Moses-like things?

DELFINA: No.

MIRIAM: He don't talk much.

DELFINA: He's only got half a tongue.

MIRIAM: What do you mean? Like somebody cut it out?

DELFINA: Yeah. When he was a little boy.

MIRIAM: No shit! That's somefin' ... He probably don' kiss too good then.

DELFINA: He kisses great.

MIRIAM: Moses couldn't a been as short as Nando.

DELFINA: Why not? Everybody was shorter then. They had to run around and carry stuff across the desert, so they had to be low to the ground.

MIRIAM: Shit. I'm glad I don' live in those times. I like tall guys.

DELFINA: Go to sleep! (DELFINA *turns off the light and exits to the kitchen.*)

MIRIAM: Shit! I like 'em tall. With dark, wavy hair and no hair on their backs or shoulders, 'cause I want to vomit when I feel that kind of hair. (*A loud whisper.*) And with dicks that you can see when they're walking—the kind that gets in their legs' way and they gotta keep shifting it around because it bothers them. I love those kind, 'cause they need somebody to take care of it for them. Why do she always gotta turn off the light? (*Fade out.*)

.... SCENE EIGHT ....

NANDO *whistles a Spanish children's song as he bounces a baseball off the side of* PULI's *gravestone. Then he speaks.*

NANDO: Men have to work. You can't be home all the time when you're a man. You unnerstan' me? (*Pause.*) And ... and I taught you the same. When you're the man of the house, you work. I work. I know you unnerstan'. Women don't unnerstan'. They expect you to be there all the time, watching over everything. I can't be in two places at the same time, Puli. I know you know that. I'm not no fockin' magician. (*Pause.*) And it's a good job I have for the kind of brain I got. I can always remember numbers. That's important in a post office ... I put numbers together in my head and they come out like a picture. Like the number seven, I see it and it's a big wooden arrow pointing out. (*Pause.*) So ... when you got a family, you make money. You watch out for your sisters. And you don't let nobody look at your wife. You don't let other men look at what's yours. You ... take care of it. (*Pause.*) Men don't get scared. Not of other men. If you get scared of other men, you hide it. It helps if you hit them ... yeah, when you feel their bones cracked against your fist, that's a good feeling. We keep it under control. My papi used to tell me that the only people you respect are the people who can beat you ... (*He bounces the ball off the gravestone in silence.*) Puerto Ricans are good at baseball. That's another thing women don't unnerstan'. If you play good baseball, you can be good at everything else because nothing else means anything ... I wasn't ever really good at it, but my papi wanned me to be. I know he did because he beat the shit outta me whenever I missed a catch. He tole me only faggots like carving things outta wood. Men play sports. And that's right. You don' get nowhere making things. I mean, if you wanned to make things, I woulda let you, but that's because you got a great arm. When you're good at baseball, people leave you alone. (*Pause.*) People woulda loved you, Puli. You woulda been something. (*Fade out.*)

.... SCENE NINE ....

We hear Eddie Palmieri's "No Pienses Así" as the lights come up on NANDO *who is kneeling on the ground, packing* PULI's *clothes into a box. He folds what is clean, and what is not he places to the side.* MIRIAM *enters quietly. She has made herself up to look like* DELFINA. *She wears one of* DELFINA's *black slips. She stares at him for a moment.*

MIRIAM: What are you doing? (*No response.*) What are you doing, Nando?

NANDO: What does it look like I'm doing? (*He sees how she is
dressed. She goes to the box and unpacks what NANDO
has packed.*) Hey, hey, hey. Don't do that! The church
needs ... these things.

MIRIAM: (*Like a hiss.*) You motherfucker. (*She throws herself
on NANDO, pummeling him.*) I hate you, you motherfucker! I hate you! (NANDO *puts his arms around*
MIRIAM *and holds her tight, kissing her forehead.*) Let
go of me! You don' care about me! All you ever cared
about was stickin' yourself inside my mami, you stinkin'
ball of shit! (MIRIAM *spits into* NANDO's *face. He slaps
her so hard that she falls to the floor.*)

NANDO: Oh, God. Oh, Miree, baby, I'm ...

MIRIAM: Don't. I can't hear you. You can say anything you
want, but I can't hear you. You got those ugly, dead eyes
... the eyes of a fuckin' statue. The kind of eyes wif
no color, no eyelashes. Dirty, black eyebrows sunk smack
into your head, wif hair that don' never move. I can't hear
nuffin' comin' out of a fuckin' stone. (DELFINA *enters,
returning from church. She has a veil over her head. She
sees the box of* PULI's *clothes, goes to it, stares into it and
pulls out a pair of worn-out shoes.*)

DELFINA: (*To* MIRIAM, *without looking at her.*) Take off my
clothes. (MIRIAM *stares at* DELFINA *for a moment, then
very deliberately strips as the lights go down. Fade out.*)

.... SCENE TEN ....

DELFINA *in the living room ironing* PULI's *clothes. She
speaks to* NANDO, *who is asleep on the armchair. He holds* PULI's
baseball glove.

DELFINA: He only wore his suit once before ... to Pepe's wedding. I said it was stupid to buy a suit. Kids in suits look
like midgets, especially boys. Or like monkeys. They always put monkeys in suits for T.V. shows. I didn't want
my boy to dress like a monkey, but the bride wanted it
like that—real formal. The shirt I had to borrow because
the shirt he had didn't have no buttons and, you know, I

couldn't find no buttons in the house to fix it, so a lady
from the church gave me her son's old shirt, but it didn't
even look old. It looked new. I think her son, Cholo, was
always too fat for it. So Puli got it. The bow-tie I got for
him to wear on the first day of school. He wanted to wear
a t-shirt, though, so he put his bow-tie on the belt loop of
his pants. He wore that almost all the time. When he fell
asleep with all his clothes on, I could wake him up by un-
clipping that tie. He'd shoot up like an arrow, pull it out
of my hands, and go back to sleep with that tie safe under
his pillow. The socks are Miree's. All his socks had holes,
and even though we had to fold them over twice, I think
it's better, socks without holes. Especially since the shoes
are new. He wanted those shoes for a long time—white,
Converse All-Star hi-tops. Everybody said sneakers are
disrespectful, but who was wearing them? Puli, and he
knew what he wanted. I made Miree go to the church
and ask for money. She hates me now. But Puli got his
sneakers. They looked good on him, I bet. I ... I couldn't
look. Or maybe when I looked I just couldn't see. They
did a good job on his face. They had to rebuild his head
up again because mostly it—a good job is what everybody
told me. Miree put a rose on top of him before they closed
him up. That's supposed to be only for women, but you
can't tell Miree what to do about nothing. I wish ... I
wish they had just showed his face. I didn't like seeing
his arm like that, it gave Miree nightmares. She's not
strong, like me. (*Fade out.*)

.... SCENE ELEVEN ....

MIRIAM *holds a library book as she kneels before the altar of
San Martín. She speaks to the saint.*

MIRIAM: I got an idea from this book I got from the library. It tells
all about how when saints bleed, they smell like violets.
And I thought, shit, that's weird. So I thought I should
ask you about it. Is that true? Does your blood smell like
flowers, San Martín? (*She takes out a razor and carves
gently into the statue's arm. Then she smells the spot.*)
Hmm ... I don't know. (*She then cuts into her own arm
and sniffs.*) Nope. Just plain ole blood ... (DELFINA

enters.) Ma!

DELFINA: What! What you so surprised about? I live here, too. Remember?

MIRIAM: Mmhmmm.

DELFINA: What'sa matter?

MIRIAM: Nothing.

DELFINA: I'm too tired for games. (*Pause.*) What's that?

MIRIAM: What?

DELFINA: That. What you're hiding behind you back. What's that?

MIRIAM: I'm going to the store. You want somefin'?

DELFINA: You're not going nowhere until you show what you got.

MIRIAM: Why are you so fucking nosey?! (DELFINA *slaps* MIRIAM *on the backside and pulls her arms in front of her.*)

DELFINA: How'd you do that?

MIRIAM: I don' know. (*Long pause.*)

DELFINA: Was you trying to shave? I remember I did that when I was your age and my mother beat the shit outta me. She said nice girls keep all their hairs—everywhere. (*Pause.*) You should be more careful.

MIRIAM: Yep.

DELFINA: You better wash it out with peroxide before it gets infected.

MIRIAM: When it's infected, what happens?

DELFINA: All kinds of things. Sometimes, if it's real bad, you gotta cut it off ... or sometimes it gets red and ugly and it stays on you forever.

MIRIAM: Oh ...

DELFINA: Got any mail today?

MIRIAM: Yeah. It's from them.

DELFINA: Open it for me, will you baby?

MIRIAM: No, Mami. I don' wanna ... I gotta go wash my hand. (*Fade out.*)

.... SCENE TWELVE ....

Lights rise on PULI *playing catch with* NANDO, *who is offstage.* PULI *wears a first baseman's glove. The type of throws alternate between flys and grounders. On the seventh throw the ball rolls between* PULI's *legs. He runs off after it. Fade out.*

.... SCENE THIRTEEN ....

MIRIAM *in the grocery store talking to* ENRIQUE, *the grocer, who is sweeping.*

MIRIAM: We got eight thousand dollars for Puli. That's how much the judge figures he's worth. Who can fight wif a judge? He must be right. And I was right, too. To spend it. We got a big color T.V. and a big antenna. And I got new coats for me and mami. And I went out in the street ...

ENRIQUE: You gonna buy something?

MIRIAM: I went out wif jus' my coat on and I showed all the men all I got. I showed my pussy and spread my lips for them. I let them fuck me and it feel good to be fucked that way, fucked to death. I wanned men pounding into me. Splitting me open. They know where to come. They all come inside me. Inside my house. Every time one of them slipped his dick inside me, I felt that train running over Puli's face—crushing him, beating him down into the dirt between the rails. I imagined my body was Puli's being smashed into the tracks, smearing the tracks wif his blood. I smeared those mens. I shit when they fucked me. I shit outta my mouf. They pumped so hard I felt their dicks coming outta my mouf. I wanned to choke on their dicks. I wanned to be split in half. That's the only way I saw to make it happen.

ENRIQUE: Why are you telling me this?

MIRIAM: We got eight thousand dollars. I cut my pussy sometimes wif a nail clipper. I jus' clip off little parts and then I pump and pump until I come so there's blood on my pillow—so I know somefin' fuckin' happened. He only got hurt once, but I hurt all the time for him. I take his hurt from him so he don' feel it no more. My pussy is his little brain being smooshed between metal. That red was blood and rust. The purple's his brain.

ENRIQUE: I gotta close now. You gotta go. I can't do nuffin' for you.

MIRIAM: His brains were soft. I'm soft too. Feel me. I'm soft too. Feel me and you won't ever haf to say goodbye. It's so hard to say goodbye to people who make you smile.

ENRIQUE: You don' mean that. You don' know me.

MIRIAM: Feel me.

ENRIQUE: You don' mean that.

MIRIAM: I wanna buy some razors—the blue kind, with the swords on 'em.

ENRIQUE: I don' got no more of those. Go home.

MIRIAM: Bring me home. (MIRIAM *and* ENRIQUE *cross into Scene Fourteen.*)

.... SCENE FOURTEEN ....

"Daddy's Home" by the Jackson Five plays. Lights rise on the street. NANDO watches MIRIAM walking with ENRIQUE. He watches until they disappear into the building, then he sits on the stoop, as the song and the stage lights fade, leaving him in candlelight. Fade out.

.... SCENE FIFTEEN ....

MIRIAM *and* ENRIQUE *in the Nieves' apartment.* ENRIQUE *is on top of her. A large T.V. looms in the background.*

MIRIAM: Dead animals are very interesting. I mean, unless you're a scientist or somefin', you don' get to see an animal's insides like that. You know what's interesting? How crows eat other crows. What's the matter wif those crows? Or are they right? Are we supposed to go off eating all our dead relatives?

ENRIQUE: I don't know ... I don't think so.

MIRIAM: You don't think so? I don' either. Birds are weird things. They got those weird toes and those weird beaks. I don' like the looks of them at all. It's not natural.

ENRIQUE: That's for sure. My mother keeps birds.

MIRIAM: What kind?

ENRIQUE: Six parakeets and one parrot and the parrot don't fly.

MIRIAM: What's he do, then?

ENRIQUE: He walks. Mostly backwards. And if you let him out of the cage, he crawls along the side of the wall like a spy or something. And gets into the cracks in the wall and wedges himself behind the sofa. He stayed back there for three days once.

MIRIAM: It's a miracle he di'nt die.
ENRIQUE: Ma said he lived on roaches. She seen him go after
    them when they're inside his cage. He likes them ... I
    mean, I don't understand it, but I'm not no bird.
MIRIAM: No, you're not no bird, all right.
ENRIQUE: Not no fucking bird.
MIRIAM: Roaches, huh? You ever actually seen him swallow one?
ENRIQUE: Sure.
MIRIAM: Did it make you want to throw up?
ENRIQUE: No.
MIRIAM: It makes me sick even to think about it ... but you
    know, I bet they taste kind of sweet.
ENRIQUE: Yeah?
MIRIAM: You know why I think that? Because they are always in
    the sweets, walking around in sugar, trying to get into the
    sweet grease in the gas holes of the oven ...
ENRIQUE: Yeah ...
MIRIAM: And when you turn on the oven, you hear that crackling
    sound, but not all of them die. Their little asses are burn-
    ing, but they made it out. (*Pause.*) It's like this dream I
    had about these alligator women. They was coming here,
    to the Bronx to get me out ... And I almos' went wif
    'em too, but they wouldn't let me take my statue of San
    Martín de Porres. And I don' go nowhere wifout him.
ENRIQUE: Is that all you got for me? Your stupid dreams? C'mon.
    Let's do ... you know, it.
MIRIAM: Who's stopping you?
ENRIQUE: I know all about you. About what kind of girl you are.
    You take your panties off for everybody else—why not for
    me?
MIRIAM: I can't spread my legs no more ... I'm too tired to hold
    them apart.
ENRIQUE: I'll hold them open for you.
MIRIAM: Go home. You have a wife.
ENRIQUE: She's dead—down there I mean.
MIRIAM: You don' even know what to call it.
ENRIQUE: Papaya ... sweet guava ... honeyed tropical fruit. The
    kind that pulls out your fillings. So sweet it hurts.
MIRIAM: You shouldn't do nuffin' that makes you hurt.
ENRIQUE: I'm hurting now. (*He takes her hand and puts it on his
    crotch.*) See?
MIRIAM: (*Pulling her hand away.*) Shit. It fells like a blackjack.
ENRIQUE: Wanna see?

MIRIAM: Go home.

ENRIQUE: You'll never have to pay for razors again. I'll order the kind you like—blue with the swords.

MIRIAM: I'll paint you a picture. Close your eyes. (*He does and she takes out a razor and begins to cut lightly into his arm.*)

ENRIQUE: Are you crazy?!

MIRIAM: It'll only hurt a little bit.

ENRIQUE: I don't care how much it hurts! You're not cuttin' into my arm.

MIRIAM: What are you scared of? (*She begins to unbutton her blouse.*)

ENRIQUE: You shouldn't do that. You're gonna get sick. You could poison your blood like that. What do you do that for?

MIRIAM: For fun.

ENRIQUE: Fun? We was having fun before you cut me.

MIRIAM: You like me, don't you? (*She takes off her blouse.*) It's gonna be a real pretty picture.

ENRIQUE: Oh, God! You're so beautiful. (*She takes his hands and puts them on her breast.*) You're so soft, baby. Let me taste you. Let me put my tongue inside you …

MIRIAM: It'll hurt really good. Close you eyes. (*He closes his eyes and nervously hands her his arm.*)

ENRIQUE: Just a little bit, okay. (*She carves a heart into his arm.*)

MIRIAM: It's like the sacred heart of Jesus. Look at it.

ENRIQUE: Lydia's not gonna like this.

MIRIAM: Sure. I'll just put her name though the middle of it … then she'll love you forever.

ENRIQUE: (*Gasping as she cuts into his arm.*) Ay! Uhhh, maybe just an L, okay? (*Fade out.*)

.... SCENE SIXTEEN ....

In church, by the statue of Mary holding the crucified Jesus. MIRIAM has a hand on one of Jesus' wounds.

MIRIAM: I bet you bled a lot more than I do. Look. (*She shows the statue her arm.*) I don' bleed hardly at all. See? (*She carves into her arm with a razor, allowing the cut to bleed onto the statue.*) See? You remember how it is, now? To be alive? (*Fade out.*)

.... SCENE SEVENTEEN ....

We hear a slow Eddie Palmieri tune as the lights rise on DEL-
FINA, *who is holding* PULI *in a tight, slow-dance embrace. She
places an orange between them, in the center of the embrace.*

PULI: What's that for?
DELFINA: That is so you don't get fresh with me.
PULI: Oh ... What's fresh?
DELFINA: What's fresh? You know what's fresh.
PULI: No, Mami. What is it?
DELFINA: It's when, you know, how boys can be.
PULI: Huh? Like if I hit you?
DELFINA: You hit me, baby, and you're in trouble.
PULI: (*Smiling broadly.*) Oh, yeah?
DELFINA: (*Squeezing his cheeks.*) Look at that face! Okay. So
        back. One, two. One, two. Back and forth. Back and
        forth. Now, step on the middle of your foot. Like, bounce.
        That's it. That's good. We're dancing now.
PULI: What's this dance called?
DELFINA: I call it serious dancing. Because you only do it with
        people you're serious with. Like somebody you want to
        marry. Okay?
PULI: Okay ... (*They dance a while in silence.*) I think I got it
        now.
DELFINA: Yeah ... you got it all right. You like this dance?
PULI: Yeah. But I don't like the orange. How come an orange?
DELFINA: That tells you how close to get to the girl. If you get
        any closer than that, something could happen.
PULI: Like you'd make a baby?
DELFINA: Who tole you that? Miriam?
PULI: Noooo ...
DELFINA: You can't believe nothing your sister tells you, baby.
        She's pretty but she knows a lot of bullshit.
PULI: Wait. (*He pulls away from her and puts the orange under his
        chin.*) This is more fun. You gotta try and take it from
        me without hands, Ma. Just your face.
DELFINA: Your face?
PULI: Yeah. You scoop it up under your face. Like ... (*He moves
        his head and neck as if he's grabbing something under his*

chin.)

DELFINA: You look like a chicken.

PULI: Mami, just try it, okay?

DELFINA: Okay ... (*She takes the orange from* PULI.) Ha! I did it! (*She drops it.*) Oh, shit!

PULI: That's okay. You're just starting. I used to be like that, too.

DELFINA: You did? So you don' think your mami's a dummy?

PULI: No. You just gotta keep trying. Like when I was just a little kid, Papi was teaching me how to catch grounders and they just kept flying between my legs until Papi tole me that to do something good, you gotta think that you are good. So jus' keep thinkin', Ma.

DELFINA: I'll do that.

PULI: Let's do it again. (*They pass the orange back and forth between them several times laughing as each one scrambles to keep the orange off the ground and still between them. Finally, it falls.*)

DELFINA: You always make me do weird shit, kid.

PULI: I'm not no kid.

DELFINA: Oh, yeah? (*She tickles him. He laughs hysterically and tickles her back. They both laugh as the lights fade. Fade out.*)

.... SCENE EIGHTEEN ....

NANDO *stands behind DELFINA, trying to get her to respond to his lovemaking. She does not.*

NANDO: Why are you always so mean to me?

DELFINA: You make me mean, baby. How come you never say nuffin' to Miriam?

NANDO: She looks at me with those eyes and I can't.

DELFINA: What eyes? She's got my eyes ...

NANDO: You got way prettier eyes than her.

DELFINA: I do?

NANDO: Yeah. Your eyes don't stare like that. She always stares like that. It gets on my nerves.

DELFINA: You're the one who stares at her ... I seen you do it.

NANDO: It's just ... I just don't know what to say to her. (*He enters her roughly from behind.*)

DELFINA: I love you. (*Fade out.*)

.... SCENE NINETEEN ....

In the Nieves' apartment, MIRIAM *enters from outside.*

MIRIAM: It smells good in here.
DELFINA: You want some soup?
MIRIAM: Pigeon soup is disgusting.
DELFINA: Oh, you're gonna be very sorry you said that because
　　　　　one day when you are lying sick in the hospital and the
　　　　　only thing that will make you feel better is a bowl of my
　　　　　soup, I won't bring it to you because I'll think you hate
　　　　　it, and when I get there and you tell me you want it, I'm
　　　　　gonna have to come all the way back home to pick it up,
　　　　　and by the time I get back, you'll be dead.
MIRIAM: Why do you always talk about those things? Don't you
　　　　　like me?
DELFINA: I'm just realistic. Everybody dies.
MIRIAM: Why don' you talk about you dying?
DELFINA: I sewed all the buttons back onto your yellow blouse.
MIRIAM: Oh ...
DELFINA: How'd you lose all your buttons at once?
MIRIAM: I don' know ... Maybe people who lose buttons all the
　　　　　time have bigger hearts than other people.
DELFINA: Oh. How pretty! Big hearts and no brains. You are
　　　　　like a stuffed animal, Miree.
MIRIAM: What kind of animal?
DELFINA: Something very small with no lips. (*Fade out.*)

.... SCENE TWENTY ....

In church, MIRIAM, *talking to the statue of the Virgin holding
the crucified Christ.*

MIRIAM: I'm the invisible girl, Mary ... always searching for a
　　　　　hole in the wall to pull myself through to get to the other
　　　　　side. The other side is only for me, I could see myself
　　　　　then. I could feel my fingertips then and the pointy pieces
　　　　　of skin being torn down the sides of my fingers. I could
　　　　　see the scars then, on the bottom of my thumbs from the
　　　　　Wilkinson Swords—I write on myself with them. I carve

myself into my hands. And for Lent, Mary, I'll cover them with purple cloth. I keep my gloves on in the church, until everybody leaves and then I come to you. To show you. (*She takes off her gloves.*) See? I show you mine and then I can touch yours ... (*She places her hands on the carved wounds of Jesus.*) They feel so fresh, Jesus. Like mine. I can smell the blood on them. Smells like violets and sweet coffee with five sugars, like Ma takes it ... (*Pause.*) I'm never gonna die—not from my wounds anyway. I never go in deep and I don't make them long. I make little points that add up to a picture, a flower picture. And sometimes they're so pretty they make me cry, and I like that, 'cause when I get those tears on my hands and on my arms, they sting, and then I know I'm alive, 'cause it hurst so bad. Does that happen to you, too? (*Fade out.*)

.... SCENE TWENTY-ONE ....

In the grocery store, ENRIQUE *and* MIRIAM *argue.*

ENRIQUE: I can't do it anymore ...

MIRIAM: Yes, you can. (*She throws open her coat. She is naked.*)

ENRIQUE: Not here!

MIRIAM: Why not?

ENRIQUE: Shit! Close your coat.

MIRIAM: (*Dropping her coat on the floor and leaning casually against the shelves.*) You know what I want.

ENRIQUE: We don't carry them no more.

MIRIAM: Give 'em to me now.

ENRIQUE: I don't got them to give.

MIRIAM: GIVE THEM TO ME! GIVE THEM TO ME!

ENRIQUE: You got such pretty arms, baby. I'm not letting you do that anymore, Miriam.

MIRIAM: Why do you want to kill me? Why do you want to drink my blood? Where do all these groceries come from? Look at all those cartons of milk. I look like milk. I taste like it too. You can put me in your refrigerator and I can dance around and get people to buy stuff.

ENRIQUE: Stop.

MIRIAM: It's too late. You love me, don't you?

ENRIQUE: Shit, yes. (*Lights fade to candlelight.*)

.... SCENE TWENTY-TWO ....

MIRIAM, *talking to the statue of San Martín de Porres in her mother's altar.*

MIRIAM: I saw what I thought I would never see today! My own mother in the bathtub. She's the only person I know who keeps her underwear on to the very last minute in case she dies in there, in case the police have to come and take her away—or the firemen. (MIRIAM *speaking to* DELFINA *who is drunk.* DELFINA *is in the tub,* MIRIAM *stands outside the bathroom door.*) Are you still in there?

DELFINA: I don't feel so good, baby. I feel very bad.

MIRIAM: You been in there for two hours already. That's why you feel so bad. You gonna turn into a prune.

DELFINA: Wash my back?

MIRIAM: No, Mami. You're making yourself sick in there.

DELFINA: You afraid to see your mami naked.

MIRIAM: You ain't naked.

DELFINA: Come on in here. (MIRIAM *enters the bathroom.*) What's the big deal? You spend almost all your time in here wifout me. Why not wif me? What do you do in here alone?

MIRIAM: Nuffin'. You want me to wash your hair?

DELFINA: No more shampoo.

MIRIAM: I could use the soap.

DELFINA: I don't like that soap in my hair. Nando says my hair feels like fried pork skin when I wash it with that soap.

MIRIAM: Nando's a fool, Ma.

DELFINA: Yeah ... He's buying me a bird for my birthday.

MIRIAM: What kind of bird?

DELFINA: Pink. (MIRIAM *begins to wash* DELFINA's *hair with the soap.*)

MIRIAM: There ain't no pink birds except flamingos. And he don't got the money for one of those.

DELFINA: Or blue. I don't mind a blue bird, as long as it don't bite.

MIRIAM: You gonna teach it to talk?

DELFINA: What for?

MIRIAM: So you got company when I'm out.

DELFINA: Birds shouldn't talk. You teach a bird to talk and the devil gets into it. That's the devil talking—making fun of everything—making fun of me. I don't play with the devil. You shouldn't either. Don't you every talk with birds.

MIRIAM: I won't. Dip back. (DELFINA *dips her head back into the tub.*)

DELFINA: Soap don't never come outta my hair. (*Lights fade to candlelight.*)

.... SCENE TWENTY-THREE ....

NANDO *speaks to* PULI*'s grave. He holds a birdcage made of ice cream pop sticks. It is* DELFINA*'s birthday.*

NANDO: It started with these shoes. They're the first ones I got that make my feet look like I always thought they should look. Like I used to think my feet didn't deserve nothing on them. Nothing good. Because they was so big—like monster feet. Nobody could love feet like that ... so, I don't blame her. She keeps me off, but I don't blame her ... but she won't keep me off no more. I know who I am because when I look down there I can see myself and I like what I see ... sometimes. That's what give me the idea. I was walking with these fine, high-tone shoes and I stepped on a pile of dogshit. I mean, that's what I thought. So, I was standing there cursing it out, screaming at the street, Hey, fucking street with the fucking shit on it! I wanna kill you, you fucking street. Fucking assholes, I said. Fucking stupid people with stupid fucking dogs! But then, from the bottom of my shoes came this perfume. I hadda close my eyes a minute because it was so sweet ... it almost made me fall over. And then I figured out it was ice cream. Somebody left this whole pile of ice cream smack in the middle of the street. Chocolate. Dark. And it had these sticks sticking out of it. Like a porcupine or something. It was a pile of ice cream pops all melted together and put out on the street. (*Pause.*) I took those sticks home because they made me think of Fina. She's like a stick for me that I don't ever wanna be without, like the ones people use when they're pulling themselves up mountains. Ever since then, everytime I saw one—in

the garbage or on the street—I picked it up and saved it.
And if I passed a candy store, sometimes I'd buy one and
eat it real, real, real slow. I smell like chocolate now. I
can see when she sees me how her nose opens up ... those
two little holes calling to me. She really likes chocolate—
and with my spit all over it, it's gonna make her think of
me. I'm gonna be inside her all the time now. It's like
magic. (*Lights crossfade to the stoop of the building where
the Nieves' live. MIRIAM suddenly appears at a window
as* NANDO *moves to the stoop.*)

MIRIAM: What the fuck are you doing here? Huh? Did your
mother die or somefin'? Mami's not here. She don't
wanna see you no more, neither. She's got another
boyfriend, Nando. That's where she is, stupid fuck-face
Nando. She's wif her other man. He's a beautiful man.
And she has a real fine time wif him. I hear 'em sometimes. (NANDO *sits on the stoop, his back to* MIRIAM.)
Get off my fucking stoop, asshole! We don' want you here!
Stupid! Everybody! Hey, everybody! Look at this hole.
(MIRIAM *disappears into the apartment for a moment,
returns with a bucket of water. She looks down at him
for a moment, then dumps the bucket of water over him.
NANDO hunches over but doesn't move.*) Look at you!
You jus' sit there like a fucking fool. (*Pause.*) And what's
that piece of shit you got wif you? It better not be nuffin'
for me, I don' like shit from you. That's for Mami, right?
Man, you are so fucking cheap you can't even buy her
somefin'. You just go and make some cheap shit. What
is it, dummy? A box? You made her a box. Oooh ...
she's gonna like that. We can put our garbage in it! Just
right for garbage. Oh ... oh, wait a minute. (*She goes
in and returns with some eggs. As she speaks she throws
them one by one at* NANDO *who puts his coat over the
cage.*) Here's some birds for you, fuckface. Here you go!
Here! And one—for good luck. (*Silence.*) You're scared
of me, ain't you? I ain't scared a you, you fuckin' killer
... (*Pause. She goes in and returns with a small table,
which she throws at the cage. NANDO moves to protect
the cage, but the impact of the table on his back makes
him fall onto the cage, crushing it.*) That's the thing, hole.
You don't ever know what's gonna come falling from the
sky. (DELFINA *appears on the stoop.*)

DELFINA: Miriam! (MIRIAM *goes back in and slams the window shut.* DELFINA *goes to* NANDO *to help him up. He doesn't let her. He motions violently for her to go away.* DELFINA *runs into the house. Fade to candlelight.*)

.... SCENE TWENTY-FOUR ....

DELFINA *in the dark, teaching an imaginary bird to talk.*

DELFINA: (*In a bird-like voice.*) Hello. Say hello, beautiful. Hello beautiful. (*Silence.*) Hello, beautiful. Who loves you? Who loves you, beautiful? (MIRIAM *enters, turning on the lights.*) Turn off the lights! (*Fade out.*)

.... SCENE TWENTY-FIVE ....

MIRIAM *and* ENRIQUE *in the tub with the statue of San Martín.*

MIRIAM: Rub my legs.
ENRIQUE: Like this? (*He rubs them softly.*)
MIRIAM: Harder.
ENRIQUE: Like this?
MIRIAM: Harder.
ENRIQUE: Like this?
MIRIAM: That's pretty good.
ENRIQUE: I love you.
MIRIAM: No, you don't. I just got nice, big legs. Like tree trunks.
ENRIQUE: They're the biggest ones I've ever touched.
MIRIAM: How do they feel?
ENRIQUE: Strong. Hard. Like ... tree trunks.
MIRIAM: Don't do that. Don't repeat exactly what I say into my face. I hate that.
ENRIQUE: I love you. (*Fade out.*)

.... SCENE TWENTY-SIX ....

NANDO *enters in candlelight. He moves to the gravestone. He bounces a ball against it seven times, then he places the baseball on the grave and exits. Fade out.*

.... SCENE TWENTY-SEVEN ....

ENRIQUE, *staring up at the bottom of the Cross Bronx Expressway which is lined with pigeons. He carries a homemade net. He is stalking pigeons.*

ENRIQUE: I'll get you soon. You'll have a good house to live in for the rest of your life and you will never be lonely. Miriam's mother will turn you into soup for her cousin, Nereida, who's pregnant again, but before you go, you'll be mine—and I'll keep you well and you can drink from my beer and maybe I'll let you wear my hat. (*He tries to capture a pigeon. He scares most of them away, but there is one that is lame and walks up to him. He scoops it up and leaves.*) I'm going to call you Mary, because of your blue eyes. Or maybe Marilyn. (*Fade out.*)

.... SCENE TWENTY-EIGHT ....

In the Nieves' apartment. ENRIQUE *holds the pigeon gently in his hands.* MIRIAM *looks out the window.* DELFINA *enters from the kitchen.*

ENRIQUE: I caught a good one for you. (DELFINA *comes to him, pulls the pigeon out of the bag, holds it by its neck, turns it around, checks it out and slams it against the wall.*) So fast? Why'd you have to do it so fast? I liked her. (DELFINA *twists the pigeons head.*) Jesus ... (DELFINA *exits into the kitchen with the pigeon.*) Jesus. I liked her. I called her Marilyn.

DELFINA: (*Offstage, sings.*) "Amor divino, ven búscame, que estoy perdida, yo bien lo sé. Amor divino, ¿por qué será que yo estoy perdida en la soledad? Amor divino, ¿por qué será que yo estoy perdida en la soledad?"

MIRIAM: Love's never gonna find you, Ma. (DELFINA *continues to sing;* ENRIQUE *joins her.*) Not Christ neither. (MIRIAM *puts her arm on the windowsill and slams the window down onto it.*)

ENRIQUE: Jesus! (ENRIQUE *runs out. Fade out.*)

.... SCENE TWENTY-NINE ....

MIRIAM *stands over* DELFINA, *who is lying in the tub.*
MIRIAM *is slowly and methodically tearing pages out of the yellow
pages. As she speaks she takes each page and tears it up into as
many pieces as possible, then she moves to the next page.*

MIRIAM: I gotta tear them all out. Take all those numbers and
waste them on the floor. Walk over all those businesses.
All those places run by people wif money. I do it so I
don' do it to my eyes. I was getting an infection. The
doctor at the clinic said he never seen nothin' like it. He
never known nobody who tore out their eyelashes like I
do when I get bad dreams ... I fight wif myself in my
sleep. (*Pause. She continues to tear.*) Now, I just tear
paper. (*Long silence.* MIRIAM *scrubs* DELFINA*'s back
and arms.* DELFINA *is so drunk, she can hardly move.*)
DELFINA: Wash my hair.
MIRIAM: No, Ma. I got a lot to do today.
DELFINA: What? What you got?
MIRIAM: Mami ...
DELFINA: Please wash my hair. I love when you do it.
MIRIAM: Just a little bit. Then I gotta clean the house.
DELFINA: There's papers everywhere.
MIRIAM: Yeah, I ...
DELFINA: There's papers everywhere, Miree.
MIRIAM: I know, Ma. I put them there.
DELFINA: There's so many papers ... did my bird get loose or
somthing? Maybe it's not paper, maybe it's feathers.
MIRIAM: No, Ma. I did it.
DELFINA: You did it?
MIRIAM: Yeah, Ma. I needed somefin' to do.
DELFINA: You don't still do that, huh? You got such pretty arms,
baby. They're just like mine.
MIRIAM: (*Stroking* DELFINA*'s arms.*) Yeah ... you do got pretty
arms.
DELFINA: You don't still do that?
MIRIAM: Tell me a story, Ma.
DELFINA: I don't know no stories. (*Pause.*) Don't look at me like
that.

MIRIAM: Like what?

DELFINA: You're blaming me, aren't you?

MIRIAM: No, Ma.

DELFINA: You're still blaming me, you bitch. And you're the one shoulda been there. You should always watch out for your baby brother.

MIRIAM: Dip it back. (DELFINA *puts her head back into the tub and* MIRIAM *finishes rinsing her hair in silence. Fade to candlelight.*)

.... SCENE THIRTY ....

NANDO *enters. He puts money on the home altar, stops at the altar looking at each item. Then we hear footsteps. He listens.* MIRIAM *enters. They stare at each other.*

MIRIAM: Take a fuckin' picture ... it'll last longer. (NANDO *exits. Lights fade to candlelight.*)

.... SCENE THIRTY-ONE ....

DELFINA, *alone in the living room. She wears a red, velveteen robe, slippers that match and a short, rabbit fur jacket.*

DELFINA: Shit! (*She walks back and forth, pacing manically.*) I'm so cold I can't think. (*She goes to the window.*) She's not coming back this time. (*Resumes pacing; hears something at the door.*) Bitch. (DELFINA *runs to the sofa and sits casually;* MIRIAM *opens the door and is startled to see* DELFINA.) Don't stand there like a dummy! Go out or come in. (MIRIAM *comes in.*)

MIRIAM: You should be sleepin'. It's late.

DELFINA: I know Get me a blanket. (MIRIAM *gets her a blanket;* DELFINA *snatches it from her hands.*) Thank you.

MIRIAM: I'm gonna go to sleep now.

DELFINA: Take off your coat.

MIRIAM: No.

DELFINA: You been showing it again, haven't you?

MIRIAM: No ...

DELFINA: Your coco is gonna dry up, you keep it out in the air like that.

MIRIAM: So!

DELFINA: Why you keep doing that?

MIRIAM: I don' know. I like to. I like it when men stop and stare. Sometimes they turn red too, embarrassed, I like that.

DELFINA: Why that boyfriend of yours don't stop you?

MIRIAM: I ain't got no boyfriend. You took care of that.

DELFINA: Good. Good. Without a man you're gonna go crazy. You're gonna get put in a crazy house soon and don' look at me to visit you.

MIRIAM: When I go to one of those houses, I want you to bring me some Brown Cow soda and raspberry jelly bars. I love them.

DELFINA: Me, too ... when I go to the old people's house, I want you to bring me pound cake and chocolate ice cream. And maybe some pigeon soup, because the food's gonna be bad there for sure. (*Pause.*) Go put on some clothes under that coat, Miree.

MIRIAM: Okay, Mami. (MIRIAM *exits to the bedroom;* DEL-FINA *takes out a pound cake and cuts a big piece for herself. Fade out.*)

················· SCENE THIRTY-TWO ·················

MIRIAM *enters the house wearing her long coat. She goes directly to the statue of San Martín and prays silently.* NANDO *follows close behind, bloodied from fighting.* MIRIAM *ignores him as he speaks and continues to pray.*

NANDO: I fixed it for you. They don't say nothin' about what's mine. They look at girls and say bad things. Anybody looks at you, you tell me. You tell your papi, and I'll kill them. Nobody looks at my baby girl like that. I see them looking at little girls and touching themselves. I showed them my knife. They won't look at you no more ... LOOK AT ME, MIRIAM! (*He grabs her by the back of her coat and drags her away from the altar. Fade out.*)

················· SCENE THIRTY-THREE ·················

DELFINA *is on the floor and* MIRIAM *is trying to undress her in order to bathe her.*

DELFINA: No!

MIRIAM: C'mon. Lift up your arms.

DELFINA: Nooo! Not today. I don' want one.

MIRIAM: Ma!

DELFINA: How can you do this to me? I don' gotta take a bath
if I don' want to. I'm older than you, so you don' tell me
what to do.

MIRIAM: You stink, Ma. Nobody's gonna talk to you no more if
you stink.

DELFINA: No. (*She sits in a puddle of water.*) This is clean water,
my friend. Very clean. It's very true. How can I stink if
I am in clean water, stupid?

MIRIAM: I don' know. But you do. Did you pee in your pants or
somefin'?

DELFINA: (*Quietly.*) No.

MIRIAM: Ma ...

DELFINA: Not a lot. I tried to make it to the bathroom, but the
door didn't work.

MIRIAM: Oh, Ma. Get up offa there. (MIRIAM *drags* DELFINA
up and undresses her as much as DELFINA *will let her
and helps her into the tub.* DELFINA *still wears all of
her underwear including stockings and a slip.* DELFINA
grabs a towel and wraps it around her head like a turban.)

DELFINA: Don't I look like something? I feel like something with
this towel wrapped around my head. I bet Nando would
like me like this.

MIRIAM: Yeah, Ma. You're somefin' all right, but how are you
gonna wash? If you leave on those wet clothes 'til they
dry, you gonna be covered with all the dirt from the tub.
So what's the fuckin' point of that? You can't get clean
with dirt on yourself.

DELFINA: It's sexier. Men like when women have strong smells.
They make all those jokes about tunafish and catfish and
... other fish, but they really like that smell. It's a warm,
freshly cooked food smell. Your father loves that smell.

MIRIAM: He's dead.

DELFINA: Don't say that!

MIRIAM: In this house, he is. I'm not letting him come here no
more. He comes here and talks shit. His brain is dead,
Ma.

DELFINA: You should be more like him. Then men would find
you more attractive.

MIRIAM: I do okay.

DELFINA: Don't you dare ever say that about your father again.

MIRIAM: He ain't my fuckin' father!

DELFINA: He's the kind of man who ain't never gonna die. He's too good.

MIRIAM: Good people are always the first to kick ... look at Puli.

DELFINA: He wasn't always so good. He used to want me to read to him all the time. I hate kids like that. (*Fade out.*)

.... SCENE THIRTY-FOUR ....

PULI, NANDO *and* MIRIAM *in the park. They have a small tape recorder.* NANDO *puts on a tape and* MIRIAM *races into position behind* PULI *as the music comes up. It is "I Want You Back" by the Jackson Five. They do an elaborate lip synch routine to the song as* NANDO *watches. Toward the middle of the song,* DELFINA *enters and joins* MIRIAM *as back-up.* PULI *imitates little Michael Jackson.*

ALL: "Uhnuhhuhuhuhahah, let me tell you now, huhuhuhuh ... When I had you to myself, I didn't want you around. Those pretty faces always make you stand out in a crowd. Then someone took you from the bunch, one glance was all it took. Now it's much too late for me to take a second look. Oh, baby, give me one more chance ... to show you that I love you. Won't you please let me back in your heart. Oh, darling, I was blind to let you go, let you go, baby. But now since I've seen you in his arms ... I want you back. Yes, I do now. I want you back. Oooh, ooh baby. I want you back. Yeah, yeah, yeah, yeah. I want you back. Naah, naah, nahn, nah ... Trying to live without your love spent most sleepless nights. Let me show you, girl, that I know wrong from right. Every street you walk on, I leave tear stains on the ground, following the girl, I didn't even want around. Let me tell you now, oh baby, all I need is one more chance, to show you that I love you. Won't you please let me, back in your heart. Oh, darling, I was blind to let you go, to let you go, baby, but now since I've seen you in his arms ... I won't spare any cost, for getting what I lost. I want you back ... "
(*Toward the end of the song,* DELFINA *pulls herself out of*

the memory and enters Scene Thirty-five. Fade out.)

.... SCENE THIRTY-FIVE ....

In the Nieves' apartment. DELFINA *sits by the stove, cooking her last pot of pigeon soup, like a ritual.*

DELFINA: When I'm not cooking pigeons, I'm not really alive. I can sit on the ledge and watch everybody walking by, but if I see a pigeon—in the air—I feel my heart pump like a son-of-bitch. Pigeons are what make living in New York worthwhile. In Puerto Rico, we had to go to the mountains to catch them. Here, they come to you. And the soup they make—it's like ice cream. Pigeons eat good in New York. They eat meat. In Puerto Rico, the pigeons eat vegetables, not enough fat on them to make a good sauce. Fat makes the sauce. Fat things taste the best. I know because I been fat all my life and the mosquitoes love me. They bite me up—it's because my sweat tastes sweet and smells sweet and they like that. But I don't like them. When I was a little girl, a cow in my neighborhood got drained dry by mosquitoes. It was the saddest thing I ever saw. I was so upset, my mother had to make me pigeon soup to calm me down. It still works on me like that. It's a calm food. (*She takes* PULI*'s shoes from underneath the stove and places them on the home altar. Lights cross to the bathtub as* DELFINA *moves to it, taking the rosary from the altar with her. When she gets to the tub, she ritualistically takes off her shoes, loosens her hair, makes the sign of the cross and enters the tub. Light cross to the church altar of Scene Thirty-six.*)

.... SCENE THIRTY-SIX ....

Lights rise on NANDO *in the church. He lights two candles, one for* PULI, *one for* DELFINA. *Prays silently. Fade out.*

.... SCENE THIRTY-SEVEN ....

We hear MIRIAM *singing softly to* DELFINA *the song of*

"ABC" by the Jackson Five. Lights up on DELFINA, *who is dead and dripping wet, laid out on the sofa in her best clothes.* MIRIAM *sits over her, carving flowers into* DELFINA's *arms with a razor.*

MIRIAM: (*Sings softly*) "A,B,C ... it's easy as 1,2,3 ... Ah, simple as do-re-me ... A,B,C, 1,2,3, baby, you and me, girl ... " (*Pause.*) You're gonna like you flowers, Mami. I'm trying to make them roses, but they ain't looking like roses. They look like tulips, but that's good 'cause it's almost spring and tulips always come up first. That's what it says in this book I got from the library about how to draw flowers, and they give you a little story about each one. And like tulips start it all up again. You know, like after everything's been sleeping with snow on top of it, there comes cutting up from the middle of it, a tulip. And if you look at one, you see it really looks like a pair of lips stretching up to kiss heaven. You don' bleed the way I do. That's good, so I can see what I'm doing better and I don' waste so many tissues. Tissues are gettin' so expensive ... you gonna like these, Mami. You're gonna open your eyes and the first thing you're gonna see are these flowers climbing way up your arm and you're gonna be so happy. They gonna make you feel like spring inside. And they'll remind you of me. We'll always be the same now. We got so much together. (*She continues to carve* DELFINA's *arm, softly humming "A,B,C." The sound of an ambulance.*) I think they're here now, Mami. (*She dabs at* DELFINA's *arm and then puts a blouse on her and buttons it up.*) You gotta keep warm now. You gotta keep your clothes buttoned up or you'll get into trouble. (*There's a loud knock at the door.* MIRIAM *puts* DELFINA's *hands together as if she were praying, and places a black veil over* DELFINA's *face.*) Now, they'll treat you like a saint. (*Another loud knock. For a moment, lights rise on the church altar, the home altar and* MIRIAM *as the other lights fade out; then blackout.*)

End of Play

Gleaning/Rebusca

Caridad Svich

CHARACTERS

BARBARA OTAÑO: a lively Cuban-American woman in her mid-twenties.
SONIA PALACIOS: Barbara's best friend and roommate. A romantic but practical Cuban-American woman also in her mid-twenties.

PLACE

Hialeah, Florida. The beautiful prairie. In the background, an unusually curved palm tree ensconced in a flat landscape of sand, as if seen through a sliding glass door. In the foreground, an oval area representing Barbara and Sonia's place. The only furniture pieces seen are a white kitchen table, a straight chair and a small coffee table or cube with its adjoining cube or low chair. Prop items visible are a small pile of magazines, a stack of mail including a newspaper or two, and an open coconut, an unopened coconut and a bowl on the table. The ironing board is off to one side. No walls, no doors.

At the beginning of the play, the place is as above: neat, relatively uncluttered. As the play progresses and the domestic activities occur, things begin to accumulate.

TIME

Takes place over six months at Barbara and Sonia's place.

.... SCENE ONE ....

BARBARA *is ironing a shirt.* SONIA *is grating the white pulp of a coconut into a large bowl.*

BARBARA: If I told you a thousand and one times ...
SONIA: You've told me everything.
BARBARA: You know what it is? I spend the nights like this, like a zombie looking at the ceiling to see what I'm going to do ...
SONIA: What you need are vacations. Long ones.
BARBARA: A rest. That's all I ask. Those people, I see them, they sit there, shuffle a few papers, have some coffee, go to lunch, talk on the phone, leave the office like new—not a wrinkle. And me? I look like a tornado hit my hair, a porquería, my clothes comoquiera and a pain in my feet, not pulsating, just an ache.
SONIA: You work too hard.
BARBARA: If I'm not working, I go crazy. Remember that summer?
SONIA: Don't remind me.
BARBARA: (*Pause.*) So you think Orlando and I should breakup?
SONIA: You've been going for so long. You've talked about marriage. I don't see why not.
BARBARA: "Why not" what?
SONIA: You should stay with him, unless you're not happy.
BARBARA: He's so dull.
SONIA: He's a good man. What do you want, another Rudy? All fire.
BARBARA: Yeah, but no ice.
SONIA: You think about him.
BARBARA: He was crazy. You can't beat that. (*Pause.*) I'm starving.
SONIA: You wanna get something?
BARBARA: No, I'm fine. I'll just listen to my stomach.
SONIA: We'll go get something.
BARBARA: If I eat something now, I'll never go to sleep.
SONIA: What you need is a bit of tilo.
BARBARA: I'm not nervous. I'm just in space.
SONIA: Then leave Orlando.

BARBARA: He has nothing to do with it. As you said, he's a good man. He loves me. You see the bracelet he bought me the other day? Gold. Fourteen carats.

SONIA: What do you need it for? You got a hundred pulseras.

BARBARA: For my colección. ¡Qué va! I wear them all. You have to make an impression. Besides, I like the way they sound así, "ching ching," it feels great. (*Pause.*) If I could close my eyes.

SONIA: (*Referring to her ironing.*) Take a break.

BARBARA: I think I will go on vacation this year.

SONIA: See it to believe it.

BARBARA: Just because I didn't go last ...

SONIA: Any year.

BARBARA: Well, you watch. This year I'm going. And not to the Everglades. But to a real place.

SONIA: Why don't you go to Rome?

BARBARA: It's so far away.

SONIA: It'd be great.

BARBARA: No. It's bad enough here. We have to put up with comments we don't want to hear.

SONIA: Orlando doesn't do that.

BARBARA: I don't let him.

SONIA: The way you treat him.

BARBARA: Me? You know what he had the nerve to tell me? Iron his shirts. How do you like that? As if I don't do enough already. I always look good. Even when I'm tired like a mule I get dressed up for him. And now I have to iron his shirts? No. (*Slight pause.*) Iron his shirts, shine his shoes. He's a parasite. He's a parasite and I'm a slave.

SONIA: Don't have to be.

BARBARA: That's right. Blame it on me.

SONIA: I just ...

BARBARA: What? You just what? (*Pause.*) When Sonia falls in love ... it's gonna be the end of the world.

SONIA: Stop!

BARBARA: Baby, you're so particular, I don't know.

SONIA: If he's out there, I'll find him.

BARBARA: Nobody's going to discover you at home. You got to get out there, make yourself seen.

SONIA: But it's so much effort. Just to think I have to put on make-up and clothes ... I'd rather stay home. At least here I can wear whatever I want, look like I look, and eat cookies after touching my cunt. Going out is such a production.

BARBARA: It's only temporary. When you come home, you take off your shoes and you're yourself again, nothing lost.

SONIA: (*Pause.*) Oye, you think he'll call?

BARBARA: Who?

SONIA: Polo.

BARBARA: Why would he call? Besides, if he's anything like his cousin Rudy ...

SONIA: Maybe he'll call. Don't you think?

BARBARA: It could happen.

SONIA: (SONIA *stops grating.*) My nails are a mess.

BARBARA: (BARBARA *stops ironing.*) My eyes are falling. (*Fade out.*)

.... SCENE TWO ....

Three weeks later. Evening. Box filled with old make-up. BAR-BARA is sorting, keeping those she wants in one area, and those she doesn't in another. SONIA is clipping items from the newspaper.

SONIA: So, it's official?

BARBARA: We're engaged. (*Pause.*) That's it.

SONIA: That's something.

BARBARA: (*Another pause.*) Until we have a ring ...

SONIA: Gotta have a ring.

BARBARA: Or else what's the point? (*Pause.*) I think it'll be good. Don't you?

SONIA: At least you'll have something.

BARBARA: It'll be good.

SONIA: (*Pause.*) He loves you.

BARBARA: I can't wait to marry him.

SONIA: Then what?

BARBARA: We'll be together.

SONIA: (*Pause.*) You could live with him.

BARBARA: No. I want a wedding. I want it to be permanent. It's the only way.

SONIA: I'll be lucky if I see you.

BARBARA: Huh?

SONIA: Nothing. (*Pause.*) You've thought about the dress?

BARBARA: I don't have a ring yet.

SONIA: The tailors around here are super busy. You go waiting
    around taking your time and ...
BARBARA: I'll make an appointment.
SONIA: You better make it soon.
BARBARA: I'll make an appointment.
SONIA: If you don't make it soon ...
BARBARA: Sonia!
SONIA: (*Pause.*) I haven't said a word.
BARBARA: I told you I'd do it.
SONIA: If you mess up, you mess up.
BARBARA: (*To herself.*) And you keep on and on.
SONIA: If it's a disaster, it's a disaster. It's not my business.
    (*Pause.*) You're gonna do pink or white? Don't tell me
    one of those strange colors like peach or blue que va a
    look like los carnavales.
BARBARA: White. I'll do white.
SONIA: (*Pause.*) Babi, Orlando's a treasure. Thinking about Rudy
    won't help.
BARBARA: I'm not.
SONIA: Your eyes are doing something.
BARBARA: I'm thinking.
SONIA: About Rudy.
BARBARA: Just thinking. What are you, wound-up today?
SONIA: (*Pause.*) Every time I say something ...
BARBARA: It's too much! The engagement, the wedding, this,
    that. I don't have time to pee and now I have to think
    about these things? It's too much.
SONIA: ¡Ay!
BARBARA: What?
SONIA: A fly.
BARBARA: Where is it?
SONIA: Flew away. Una picazón ...
BARBARA: Don't scratch.
SONIA: It itches.
BARBARA: That's what they want. Damn flies want you to scratch,
    scratch, scratch 'til it swells up like a bowling ball. I'll get
    the Caladryl.
SONIA: I'm all right.
BARBARA: It's the best thing.
SONIA: I won't scratch.
BARBARA: Well, remind me to put some on you later. 'Cause if
    not ...
SONIA: I know.

BARBARA: (*Pause.*) I wonder who'll come visit. Didn't your
    mami used to tell you that? When a fly comes in, that
    means somebody will come visit?
SONIA: No.
BARBARA: Mine did. Whenever a fly came in, I'd spend the next
    day or two waiting. Somebody always showed up.
SONIA: Really?
BARBARA: Without fail.
SONIA: (*Pause.*) Sometimes I think no one's going to come along.
BARBARA: You got Polo.
SONIA: Yeah, he's intense, but I'm talking about someone. I'll
    see him, he'll see me, and I know he'll be someone. With
    Polo, I still feel like I'm waiting.
BARBARA: You don't see each other enough.
SONIA: We see each other plenty. But when we're in bed, it's like
    it's just me, me and what I'm thinking. (*Pause.*) We could
    be so good, we could be great. If only he were in the same
    bed with me.
BARBARA: There are other guys.
SONIA: I want to work it out with him. You worked it out with
    Orlando.
BARBARA: We're engaged.
SONIA: Exactly. You're going somewhere.
BARBARA: (*Pause.*) Doesn't hurt to look.
SONIA: If I look, I'll start touching.
BARBARA: So?
SONIA: So, what would Polo think?
BARBARA: He'll think you're hot.
SONIA: Yeah?
BARBARA: Candela. (*Fade out.*)

.... SCENE THREE ....

Two months later. Afternoon. As SONIA *sweeps the floor, she
weeps and sings the following Cuban nursery rhyme:*

SONIA:

    Amambrochato,
    matandile, dile, dile,
    Amambrochato,
    matandile, dile, do.

¿Qué quería usted?
Matandile, dile, dile,
¿Qué quería usted?
Matandile, dile, do,

Yo quería un ...

(SONIA *stops, thinks for a moment, smiles, and the idea
having cheered her up, continues the song.*)

... ice cream.
Matandile, dile, dile,
Yo quería un ice cream.
Matandile, dile—

BARBARA: (BARBARA *enters, unloads basket of clothes to the
floor, starts folding the laundry.*) Oye, how foul I am. I
have a stench under my arms ... I can't get rid of this
smell. And I bathe, but it doesn't help.

SONIA: You need a good soap. One of those Irish Spring. They're
huge.

BARBARA: They don't do me any good. There was an Avon thing
once. If I could find it again ... And last night, what a
stink. My vagina was like a manure deposit. No, I'm a
pig. Una pura puerca.

SONIA: (SONIA *sets broom down, joins* BARBARA *in the folding.*)
You don't look it.

BARBARA: It's the disguise, mi vida. I'm a lady on the outside,
but inside ... Oye, but when I'm with a guy? Perfume
city.

SONIA: I don't like perfume. You can't smell anything.

BARBARA: I hate it too, but ... Your eyes are horrible. Don't tell
me you've been crying.

SONIA: I need more sleep.

BARBARA: Don't we all. (*Pause.*) Help me fold this, will ya.

SONIA: What?

BARBARA: This sheet. I can't do it by myself. (SONIA *takes an
end of the bed sheet* BARBARA *is holding. They go about
folding it.*) Why do they always make bed sheets so ... ?

SONIA: So two people can fold them. (*They finish folding it.*)

BARBARA: I hate this sheet.

SONIA: Orlando picked it out.

BARBARA: (*Pause.*) I feel like I don't know what.

SONIA: Loves me, loves me not?

BARBARA: It's this marriage thing. It's a big step. And the more
it gets put off, the bigger it gets. (*Pause.*) My feet. They
stink, too. A smell así mustio. Like mothballs o no se
qué.
SONIA: You're obsessed.
BARBARA: I'm not used to these smells.
SONIA: You never noticed them?
BARBARA: Why didn't you tell me before?
SONIA: I didn't smell anything. (*Pause.*) When you get older
you start to smell things. Your nose starts to work. You
know how your nose never works and then one day there
it is? (SONIA *takes a tack of folded clothes and places it
in another area.*)
BARBARA: What are you doing?
SONIA: They're my clothes.
BARBARA: I folded them.
SONIA: I don't want them to get confused.
BARBARA: You always do that.
SONIA: What?
BARBARA: You always think I'm going to steal your clothes.
SONIA: I don't think that.
BARBARA: You move them. Every time.
SONIA: When you get married, you won't have to deal with it.
(*Silence.*)
BARBARA: My bladder is killing me. Since this morning I've been
trying to go to the bathroom.
SONIA: So go.
BARBARA: No. No. (*Pause.*) It's like a bomb.
SONIA: Will you go, for heaven's sake. Holding it in like that is
not good for you.
BARBARA: Maybe I don't wanna go.
SONIA: You said since ...
BARBARA: It may be a false alarm. I hate false alarms. You sit
there and nothing. Meanwhile your mind is telling you,
"Go, go." It's torture.
SONIA: I don't care. I don't care. I don't care. I don't care. I
don't care. I don't care.
BARBARA: (*Pause.*) I won't go, then.
SONIA: Do what you want, all right? You always do.
BARBARA: (*Pause.*) What happened?
SONIA: What happened? What would happen? Polo and I had a
fight.
BARBARA: Today?

SONIA: Yes. Today.
BARBARA: You didn't tell me.
SONIA: Ay, coño ...
BARBARA: Okay okay, you had a fight. What happened?
SONIA: Nothing.
BARBARA: Don't tell me nothing.
SONIA: He came up to me. His eyes were white, and strange.
I said, Baby, what's wrong with you? He looks at me.
His tie's all messed up, and his hair is wet. And he says,
"Sonia. Sonia, I love you, but I can't see you."
BARBARA: Same as his cousin.
SONIA: He is not Rudy.
BARBARA: What did Rudy say, huh? (*Pause.*) You think they'd
consult each other. To use the same line twice ...
SONIA: It wasn't a line.
BARBARA: What was it, then?
SONIA: I was scared for him. His eyes were so white. I could see
the grey in his pupils like a mirror. I could see myself.
BARBARA: They know how to do it, don't they? Twist you up
inside.
SONIA: You don't know what you're talking about.
BARBARA: You care for him. Hell, I care for Rudy. After all the
shit ... But Sonia, if you let him, he'll gnaw on you 'til
there's nothing left. No bones, nothing. Is that what you
want?
SONIA: I don't want an Orlando.
BARBARA: Orlando's a good man. You've said that a thousand
times.
SONIA: I don't want to settle.
BARBARA: I'm not settling.
SONIA: Then what are you doing? (*Pause.* BARBARA *starts to un-
fold the already-folded clothes, throwing them to the floor.*)
BARBARA: I'm not getting married.
SONIA: Come on.
BARBARA: I'm not.
SONIA: And the ring and the ...
BARBARA: I'll let him know.
SONIA: You're not getting married?
BARBARA: That's what I said.
SONIA: What will you do?
BARBARA: Go out. Have a drink.
SONIA: Rudy won't come back.
BARBARA: I know.

SONIA: You're really going to end it.
BARBARA: I said it. It's done. (BARBARA *finishes unfolding,*
    looks at the "new" pile of clothes.)
SONIA: You're my hero. You really are.
BARBARA: I'm just here. No better, no worse. Just here. And
    sometimes I don't like it very much. But I go on.
SONIA: You have to. (BARBARA *begins to fold clothes again.*
    Fade out.)

.... SCENE FOUR ....

A week later. Evening. SONIA *is collating and stapling doc-*
uments. BARBARA *moves about. She fans her crotch, picks up a*
magazine and barely flipping through it, sets it down, goes to the
phone as if it were about to ring, then moves away from it, hums to
herself, stops and checks her watch, fans herself again.

BARBARA: I looked at him and said to myself, "What was it that I
    saw in him?" One of those super indiscreet thoughts, but
    that was exactly what went through my mind; what was it
    that I saw in him? Thinking that and ashamed right away,
    no? It's too cruel, but sometimes clarity is like that—no
    mercy, as they say. (*Pause.*)
SONIA: He'll recover.
BARBARA: With Jacqueline or one of those.
SONIA: You mind?
BARBARA: She's a safe harbor. Everybody has one. For me it's a
    cup of hot chocolate and "chas," there I'm left ...
SONIA: Like an angel.
BARBARA: (*Pause.*) And you, what? Quiet, eh? Like an oyster.
SONIA: All goes well.
BARBARA: Rose-colored life.
SONIA: What do you want? Calamities I don't have, and romantic
    adventures? That's your department. I simply work in
    peace, come home and rest myself.
BARBARA: That pile of documents, that's rest. Real rest. (BAR-
    BARA *sets the fan down, skims through a stack of maga-*
    zines.)
SONIA: If I left everything at the office, it'd be the neverending
    pile. This way, it's one less thing I have to do when I go
    in.
BARBARA: They pay you for this?

SONIA: Not everything is about getting paid.

BARBARA: Ask the farts at the office, see what they tell you. Money and that's it, that's all they care about. You do the work for free at home? Terrific. The money stays in their pockets.

SONIA: Does not. I got a promotion.

BARBARA: Pennies.

SONIA: More than that.

BARBARA: So what? So they can pat you on the back and say "Sonia, you're now the office manager?" Look, they can stick their labels in their culo, 'cause they make you work and work and work and work, and one day you're stuck in a hospital with a million bills to pay, and nobody remembers you. (*Pause.*) They can convince you, but not me. I get paid for every minute. Even when I pee.

SONIA: If I don't do this, I'll be behind.

BARBARA: And your social life, what? Down the drain?

SONIA: I don't need a social life.

BARBARA: You need a social life like eating, breathing, or anything else. Unless you've given up on life. Have you given up on life? 'Cause if you have, I need to know.

SONIA: I don't have time.

BARBARA: 'Cause of that stupid promotion.

SONIA: It is not stupid.

BARBARA: It's running your life.

SONIA: (*Pause.*) I can't live with men twenty-four hours on my mind. It's impossible.

BARBARA: You think I ...

SONIA: It's not what I think, it's what I see.

BARBARA: Blind you are. (*Pause.*) Twenty-four hours. Wouldn't I like it.

SONIA: What about the train?

BARBARA: What about it?

SONIA: You miss it all the time. Miss it 'cause you're staring at all the guys.

BARBARA: I get distracted. Don't know what I'm thinking. (*Pause.*) Sometimes I think I'm in another world, that everyone else is there inside, and I'm outside, waiting for the train. Then I think, well, but they're the same. In their world. It's a miracle, a miracle we all walk around sane down the street and the world doesn't explode right now, because if you stop to think—it's a globe of crick-

ets. A true globe of crickets. (BARBARA *sets a magazine
down, starts fanning herself again.*)

SONIA: Oye, what would you do with three thousand dollars?

BARBARA: Where'd that come from?

SONIA: Thinking. (*Pause.*) If you had three thousand dollars,
what would you do?

BARBARA: I don't know.

SONIA: I'd buy an ice cream store.

BARBARA: I'd go to Chicago.

SONIA: That's less than three thousand dollars.

BARBARA: The rest I'd put in the bank.

SONIA: You've never been to Chicago?

BARBARA: No, and I always ... Why an ice cream store?

SONIA: So I can eat ice cream whenever I want. All the flavors,
and mix them with nobody looking at me like a strange
insect.

BARBARA: We're a pair of idiots.

SONIA: Why?

BARBARA: Other people would say a yacht or a stereo television,
and we, with ice cream and Chicago, would be content.
What a pair, no? (*Fade out.*)

.... SCENE FIVE ....

Three weeks later. Afternoon. SONIA *is ironing.* BARBARA
is cleaning out her handbag.

SONIA: I haven't felt like this about anyone since—never.

BARBARA: And Polo?

SONIA: Not even Polo. No. Romy is different. He makes my
heart race.

BARBARA: It's a crush.

SONIA: No. It's like I've been in a cave not communicating with
anyone for years and all of a sudden, there he is.

BARBARA: (*Pause.*) Someone.

SONIA: Someone. (*Pause.*) A little formal ...

BARBARA: He's shy.

SONIA: It's only been a week. He doesn't know what to do.

BARBARA: How old you say he was?

SONIA: Nineteen.

BARBARA: You gotta give 'em time.

SONIA: He can take as long as he wants.

BARBARA: No pressure. (*Pause.*)
SONIA: The phone's enough.
BARBARA: Waiting?
SONIA: It's agony.
BARBARA: And what, you have to be here holding a torch? Get
   out there. Those guys that are shy ... they got fires lit
   everywhere. And at nineteen? Pal carajo.
SONIA: You think he's too young.
BARBARA: Sonia, it's okay. We're not the same person, right?
SONIA: I love him.
BARBARA: As long as you're happy ...
SONIA: (*Pause.*) Like you with Orlando.
BARBARA: It doesn't mean I let him walk all over me. I throw
   fits. Not too big, but enough to let him know I exist.
SONIA: You think if I threw a fit with Romy it would help?
BARBARA: It's always good to show you got temper. Especially
   with these young guys. They wake up, así, like a lightning
   bolt.
SONIA: He may go for it, too.
BARBARA: You never know. (*Fade out.*)

························ SCENE SIX ························

A week later. Evening. BARBARA *is cracking and beating
eggs.* SONIA *is chopping celery.*)

BARBARA: I took him aside and said, "The next time you come
   back here, I'll show you a really good time." And then I
   let him have it.
SONIA: Why do you treat him like that?
BARBARA: He brings it out in me.
SONIA: Rabia.
BARBARA: Rabia. I'd like to take Orlando between my teeth and
   eat him with one bite.
SONIA: Then what?
BARBARA: Find somebody else. (*Pause.*) Even as a kid, I'd
   be very happy playing with my dolls and all of a sudden I would look at the boys and it would hit me like
   a thunderbolt—that kind of rage where you don't know
   what you're doing, all you know is that you're angry and
   you gotta release it somehow? Like that. And I would
   start throwing things or scratch myself.

SONIA: I would tear out my hair.

BARBARA: No.

SONIA: Until I heard the snap in my scalp. It was consuming. Mami thought I was epileptic.

BARBARA: Wouldn't she get it?

SONIA: She'd forgotten about rabia. When she got married, she buried it.

BARBARA: Maybe she never got it.

SONIA: She did. I would catch her. Except she wouldn't take it out on herself. It'd be the mop, the faucet ... She would hit the steak so hard I'd swear she was killing somebody. "Mami, is everything all right?" (*The chopping of celery and beating of eggs builds to a climax.*) "Just tenderizing the steak, mi vida. Tenderizing the steak." And she'd keep hitting it with the mortar. Poom! Poom! Poom! (*Pause.*) It was a sight.

BARBARA: (*Pause.*) I can't help myself. Even when I think of him
...

SONIA: Orlando's gonna get really mad one of these days, and it won't be because you brokeup with him either.

BARBARA: I'd like to see it. That was one thing you could say for Rudy—when he was angry, he was angry. When he was sweet, he was ...

SONIA: What rapture. (*Pause.*) Can I ask you something?

BARBARA: What?

SONIA: Was Rudy as good in bed as people ... ?

BARBARA: He was a sweetheart.

SONIA: So it's not true about ... ?

BARBARA: He's good, but he's a sweetheart. That's what people don't know. That's why he hates me. 'Cause I know. He can't stand it.

SONIA: (*Pause.*) You know what I'd like? I'd like it if Romy would take off his pants. Just once. He's so damn formal.

BARBARA: You need to move on to someone else.

SONIA: I've thought about it. But there's always the possibility he might loosen his fly and ... I'd hate to miss it.

BARBARA: You have a dilemma.

SONIA: An impending catastrophe. What if he breaks off with me? Then what?

BARBARA: Then you pull down his pants, and to hell with it.

SONIA: If I were you ...

BARBARA: "If I were you ... " You sound like a broken record. You're not me. And if you were, you'd be much smarter than to get into the messes I get—playing with this one and that one because inside you're breaking así in pieces of the heart. You? Never. You'd be still until he couldn't move. Then chaz! You'd grab him, and never let him go. And me? I'd still be swimming to see if a fish jumps, thinking always of the last one. It's an existence of torture. I wouldn't recommend it to anyone.

SONIA: Better stay where I am.

BARBARA: You shouldn't play the fool either, 'cause they take you for a comemierda, y pal carajo. (*Pause.*) It's gonna work itself out. You'll see. You're going to wake up Sunday morning and say, "How different I feel. Like a new woman." It's Saturdays that kill you.

SONIA: Why is that?

BARBARA: Because you go around with the same clothes you always wear around the house, and your snot falls so far your nose touches the ground. You ask me, "Why do I feel bad?" How can you not feel bad? In the house, in the dark on a Saturday night, the lights out, a candle lit, Emmanuel on the stereo, and crying like Mary Magdalene.

SONIA: It's that I love him.

BARBARA: Then screw him. Get it over with. (*Pause.*) You're not a nun.

SONIA: I'm ashamed to call him. It's true. I get a fear that grabs my head and stomach, and it's impossible.

BARBARA: You're in the throes of it, eh?

SONIA: Yes.

BARBARA: That changes things. (*After a slight pause,* SONIA *stops chopping.*)

SONIA: You give me a rub?

BARBARA: Your back?

SONIA: My whole body's spent.

BARBARA: (*Stops beating eggs.*) Lie down. I'll give you a Chinese massage.

SONIA: You're an angel.

BARBARA: That's how devils disguise themselves. (*Jokingly.*) Take off your clothes, here I come.

SONIA: (SONIA *lies face down on the floor.* BARBARA *steps onto her.*) But with your feet?

BARBARA: It's the only way. (*Fade out.*)

.... SCENE SEVEN ....

Two weeks later. Afternoon. BARBARA *is drying her wet fingernails in a large bowl of ice.* SONIA *is grating the white pulp of a coconut into a large bowl.*

BARBARA: I have never seen Orlando like that. It was como ira, that kind of anger you think God has in all those Bible movies, así, puro macho. Look how my arms get. Goose bumps and everything.

SONIA: Did he hit you?

BARBARA: No, although a slap would be the end. One thing's for sure, punches from a man I do not stand for, not even from the most beautiful of the species. Hands are for touching, not hitting.

SONIA: (*Pause.*) You brokeup for good, right?

BARBARA: It was about time. (*Pause.*) He kept trying to make up all day—"Hey, mami ... Hey, mami." That's one of those things that unnerves me, a man calling a woman who's not his mother mami. That makes me ...

SONIA: You broke up with the guy. What do you want?

BARBARA: You're always coming to the aid of men. If it were up to you, they'd be ready for their First Communion the second they're born.

SONIA: And if it were up to you, they wouldn't leave the belly. They'd stay there 'til they're fifty years old.

BARBARA: Seventy.

SONIA: Seventy. Especially los cubanitos.

BARBARA: The French can leave earlier.

SONIA: You and the French.

BARBARA: Everyone has their things.

SONIA: (*Pause.*) Are you going to get up from there or are you going to continue drying your nails?

BARBARA: Ay, I had forgotten completely about them. Why didn't you tell me before? I'm here like a parrot, chaca, chaca, chaca, and look at this, they almost froze.

SONIA: I was waiting to see what you'd do.

BARBARA: Perverse. Look at my hands.

SONIA: They're fine. You make a drama over everything.

BARBARA: (*To herself.*) I can't believe this.

SONIA: A little more time, now you have drier nails.

BARBARA: Now this job is really set.

SONIA: So get the nail polish remover, start over if you want. You think it'd be a crime.

BARBARA: It is. It's criminal. Look at that. (BARBARA *begins to remove the polish. She will re-paint her nails.*)

SONIA: (*Pause.*) So, you think I should shave?

BARBARA: What?

SONIA: My hair.

BARBARA: I wouldn't.

SONIA: But it doesn't do anything. It just sits there between my navel and my cunt.

BARBARA: Men like it. It's one of those zones. That little line of hair, that invitation below the navel—they can't resist it.

SONIA: I can't stand the way it looks.

BARBARA: Then shave it.

SONIA: Maybe I'll leave it.

BARBARA: Look, the important thing is to make sure it stays in a line, not messy, 'cause then it's not sexy at all. Nobody likes a jungle. (*Referring to nails.*) Red's a good color, no?

SONIA: It's bold.

BARBARA: Orlando hates it. (*Pause.*) They're not too red, are they?

SONIA: You brokeup, right?

BARBARA: You're right. Did I tell you I ran into him?

SONIA: Who?

BARBARA: Rudy.

SONIA: It's gonna start up again. I can see it already.

BARBARA: He said he was going to call me.

SONIA: You're going to see him?

BARBARA: Well, de puta I'm tired. All the guys who try to put the moves on me call me "puta" or "putica ... "

SONIA: And Rudy? What did he call you?

BARBARA: Sirena. "Mi sirena."

SONIA: What's the difference?

BARBARA: I was his mermaid.

SONIA: His putica mermaid.

BARBARA: What have you got today, matches under your ass? I ran into him. That's all. (*Pause.*) Give me some coco rayado, will ya.

SONIA: I'm not finished.

BARBARA: Just a little.

SONIA: No!

BARBARA: (*Pause.*) You better give me some later.
SONIA: I will.
BARBARA: You better. (*Pause.*) They could take away all the
    food on earth. As long as they leave coconut ... Mami
    says they used to eat it all the time when they were in
    Cuba. Stroll by the wharf, eat coconut ... What a life,
    huh? (*Pause.*) At least we got the mall.
SONIA: Big deal.
BARBARA: The problem is you don't like malls because you can't
    buy everything you want.
SONIA: It's a waste of time.
BARBARA: And strolling's not?
SONIA: Strolling is strolling. It's supposed to be a waste of time.
BARBARA: All I know is I go to a mall, and I can breathe again.
SONIA: I can breathe without it. (*Fade out.*)

.... SCENE EIGHT ....

Two weeks later. Night. BARBARA *is eating popcorn and
drinking wine as she listens to music on her Walkman.*

BARBARA: Coño. (*The cassette tape has stopped.* BARBARA
    takes off her Walkman headphones.)
SONIA: (SONIA *enters. She takes off one shoe, throws it.*) ¡Coño!
    (*Takes off other shoe, throws it.*) ¡Carajo! (*Throws purse.*)
    ¡Mierda! (SONIA *grabs bag of popcorn from* BARBARA,
    munches furiously.)
BARBARA: What happened?
SONIA: He lied. He lied to me.
BARBARA: I told you.
SONIA: He stood there fresh as a head of lettuce. (*Pause.*) After
    all this time, right?
BARBARA: I didn't want to tell you.
SONIA: I didn't want to hear. I was too busy thinking about
    whether he'd take his pants off or not.
BARBARA: At least he did that.
SONIA: For what it was worth.
BARBARA: You didn't care for it?
SONIA: Let's say I had bigger expectations.
BARBARA: Really? (SONIA *nods.*) Who would've thought, no?
SONIA: I just can't believe he would lie to me. He seemed so
    sincere. No lines, no bullshit.

BARBARA: He's young. What did you expect?

SONIA: He must've thought I was a complete idiot. I thought they'd be different. I thought young men would be different. I hate myself.

BARBARA: Don't say that.

SONIA: I do.

BARBARA: How could you know?

SONIA: I could've listened. I mean, he's a kid. I knew that. (*Pause.*) Asshole.

BARBARA: You feel shitty.

SONIA: These pantyhose ride down my ass. I've been holding them up all night trying to discreetly pull them up.

BARBARA: Take 'em off.

SONIA: Off they go. (SONIA *slips off her stockings.*)

BARBARA: Sometimes I think I work to buy stockings. You know how much I'd save if I didn't work?

SONIA: Yeah, but you'd be broke. Broke and unpresentable. Can't get a job like that.

BARBARA: Could always work in a factory.

SONIA: And get treated like dirt? I'd rather get treated like dirt and look good than get treated like dirt and look like I just got out of bed. 'Cause then you start to believe it. You start to believe you're nothing. (*Pause.*) Look at this. My eyelashes are falling off. Every day, another eyelash. (*Pause.*) I've been crying too much.

BARBARA: Well, then stop crying. You don't want to lose your eyelashes. They're one of your best features.

SONIA: It's because of Romy, and Polo, and who knows who else.

BARBARA: They're not worth it.

SONIA: They are worth it. Why else do we fall all over ourselves to be with them?

BARBARA: (*Pause.*) Make a wish.

SONIA: What?

BARBARA: On the eyelash. Make a wish. Press it to your chest like this and ... (BARBARA *mouths some words to herself inaudibly, then blows away an imaginary eyelash from her finger.*) ... the wish has more power.

SONIA: Really?

BARBARA: It's what Mami used to say.

SONIA: I've lost so many wishes already. What should I wish for?

BARBARA: Anything. (*Pause.*) Sonia, it always works, and even if it doesn't, it feels good.

SONIA: Well ... I wish ... (SONIA *mouths some words inaudibly.*
   Slight pause. Blows away eyelash from her finger.) It does
   feel good.
BARBARA: Didn't I tell you?
SONIA: You did.
BARBARA: Now what did you wish for?
SONIA: I can't tell you.
BARBARA: You wished Polo would come back, didn't you?
SONIA: No.
BARBARA: Romy?
SONIA: Don't talk about him.
BARBARA: I just ...
SONIA: It's over. We're over. ¡Se acabó!
BARBARA: What's wrong with your neck? ¿Tienes tortícolis?
SONIA: I don't know. I slept wrong last night or something. It's a
   sting and a crack every time I move my head.
BARBARA: What a pain.
SONIA: You're telling me.
BARBARA: I bet it happened when you were watching TV. Didn't
   I tell you, Sonia, you're gonna get something in your neck
   if you keep on like that.
SONIA: I always lie belly down to watch TV. It's not the first time.
BARBARA: Yes, but yesterday it was five hours with your head up
   like this watching one program after another like a nut.
SONIA: I was a TV mouse.
BARBARA: You were a viper.
SONIA: And all you wanted to do was sleep. Turn this way, turn
   that way.
BARBARA: You were watching cada paquetico. I didn't want to
   say anything, but what garbage.
SONIA: I had to distract myself.
BARBARA: That's what magazines are for, or even music. You
   put on a little salsa and that's it, you're distracted.
SONIA: If it were you, you'd call Orlando at four in the morn-
   ing and be chikee, chikee, chakee on the phone 'til your
   ears turned red. "Ay, my love. Ay, my heart." And me,
   aguantando la vela.
BARBARA: You don't have to wait for me to go to sleep.
SONIA: What am I going to do, put the sheet over my head and
   pretend I'm asleep? At least I eat my banana chips and
   listen to the eternal story of Barbara and Orlando, and
   Orlando and ...

BARBARA: You don't have to be so noisy. Every time you bite into a chip it's crunch, crunch, crunch. Orlando tells me, "Hey baby, is Sonia still awake? Tell her to go to bed 'cause those damn banana chips are driving me crazy."

SONIA: Liar. He likes to know someone's listening. At least with the chips, he has something to say.

BARBARA: You think?

SONIA: Listen, you may know men, but I know human beings. Orlando likes to have an audience, not a big one, but enough to feel he's worth something. Why else do you think he got back with you?

BARBARA: I don't think Orlando is that type of guy.

SONIA: You've been on-and-off with him so long you can't tell.

BARBARA: (*Pause.*) I'll get some alcohol for your neck.

SONIA: I don't need alcohol. (*Pause.* BARBARA *flips through a magazine.*) You know what I want?

BARBARA: What?

SONIA: A baby.

BARBARA: No.

SONIA: To feel it así pulling at me, letting the air in and out ...

BARBARA: So get married.

SONIA: I'm not talking about men.

BARBARA: Babies come from them, too.

SONIA: Not from their bodies they don't. (*Pause.*) I'm talking about in my arms, to feel a smaller body, a body without prejudice. You know what that would be?

BARBARA: So babysit.

SONIA: Everything's a joke to you.

BARBARA: (*Pause, referring to magazine.*) You think it's true?

SONIA: What now?

BARBARA: That a Frenchman's kiss is like love for a hundred years.

SONIA: Where'd you read that?

BARBARA: (*Displaying magazine.*) Réplica.

SONIA: Garbage. I read the horoscope and use the rest for toilet paper.

BARBARA: What are those sounds?

SONIA: My stomach.

BARBARA: What a symphony.

SONIA: It's been like this since dinner.

BARBARA: The food?

SONIA: No.

BARBARA: (*Pause.*) You'll get over him. (*Fade out.*)

.... SCENE NINE ....

Two months later. Night. BARBARA *is sleeping amidst a pile of unfolded clothes. She snores quietly.* SONIA *enters, singing softly to herself,* "*Cuando Calienta el Sol.*" *She takes off her sandals, so as not to disturb the sleeping* BARBARA, *and begins to cross.* BARBARA *wakes.*

BARBARA: ¡Ay!
SONIA: You all right?
BARBARA: What a dream.
SONIA: Didn't mean to wake you.
BARBARA: No, no. It's all right. (*Pause.*) God, what time is it?
SONIA: It's late.
BARBARA: Oh, God.
SONIA: You didn't have to stay up.
BARBARA: I didn't. I was ... (BARBARA *looks at clothes that lie around her.*) I don't know what I was doing. (*Pause.*) Look at you.
SONIA: What?
BARBARA: You look good. (SONIA *starts to fold clothes.*) What are you doing? Leave that. The clothes can wait.
SONIA: I want to do it.
BARBARA: Stubborn. Stubborn as an ox. (BARBARA *goes back to sleep.*)
SONIA: (SONIA *folds.*) How was your day?
BARBARA: (*After a pause,* BARBARA *snaps out of sleep.*) What?
SONIA: Your day. How was it?
BARBARA: It was Monday. Mondays are Father, Son and Holy Ghost. The Fox came, put everybody in line. Machismo, no?
SONIA: He put his hand on your ass today?
BARBARA: With me he doesn't get involved. I have an eye for the fresh. I smell them. I go down the street and sniff, sniff ... this one an asshole, this one not.
SONIA: You could leave.
BARBARA: (*Pause.*) Hot.
SONIA: Yeah.
BARBARA: We should go to the beach this weekend. First thing in the morning. Cool us off.

SONIA: I like it better in the afternoon.
BARBARA: Since when?
SONIA: Since always. Jorge loves the beach at night.
BARBARA: So that's what you've been doing.
SONIA: We walk, that's all.
BARBARA: Uh huh.
SONIA: I'm serious.
BARBARA: I watch the news and it's rape this, rape that ...
SONIA: I'll be fine.
BARBARA: You always say that, but one day something happens, and tremenda tragedia.
SONIA: You want me to call you?
BARBARA: Don't be absurd.
SONIA: I'll call you. That way you won't be so worried.
BARBARA: I'm not worried. (*Pause.*) Things are so crazy these days, you can't count on things. Went to the botánica, had such a scare.
SONIA: I don't know why you go there.
BARBARA: It used to be a nice neighborhood. Now, the nuts are loose, and the criminals are there, too, así que there's no salvation. Fíjate que a guy was peeing on the street. Así, with his zipper open and his thing hanging out. Now, I ask you, is that normal? Not even dogs. Dogs are more discreet. They go to a bush or a hydrant ...
SONIA: It's the neighborhood. Pretty soon that whole neighborhood is gonna be nuts and criminals.
BARBARA: What a combination. And where are we going to live? 'Cause they won't stay there. Nuts and criminals like nice places.
SONIA: If it gets bad, we'll move.
BARBARA: You may, but I can't. (*Pause.*) You're the one with the raise.
SONIA: Nothing I can do about that.
BARBARA: (*Pause.*) You wanna go out?
SONIA: Now?
BARBARA: I'm not tired. We could go to the club, check out the guys, dance ...
SONIA: No.
BARBARA: You got something better to do?
SONIA: Look, why don't you go out?
BARBARA: You don't wanna go out?
SONIA: I've been out. I'm tired.
BARBARA: Go to bed.

SONIA: I told you to go out.
BARBARA: I'm all right. I'll look at the stars or something.
SONIA: You can go. You don't have to ...
BARBARA: I know.
SONIA: (*Pause.*) Good night.
BARBARA: 'Night.
SONIA: We'll go tomorrow.
BARBARA: Get out of here. (SONIA *exits.* BARBARA *pulls a bed sheet from the pile, begins to fold it. Fade out.*)

.... SCENE TEN ....

Three weeks later. Morning. A cup of coffee on the table. Half-packed boxes strewn about the place. BARBARA *is sweeping.*

BARBARA: I explain everything and nobody listens to me. And I repeat things once, another time, and nothing. How do you explain that?
SONIA: (SONIA *enters with an armload and continues packing.*) You go too fast.
BARBARA: I go a thousand miles an hour. Qué rápido ni qué rápido, what it is is that they're stupid. Those stockboys have their heads in their feet. You think they're really listening? Qué va. They're looking at me with their eyes straight "uh huh, uh huh," and then they do what they want.
SONIA: You tell me things and I don't understand you either. Blaming those poor devils ... I don't know.
BARBARA: You don't understand me either? But in what language does one need to speak around here?
SONIA: All I know is that you start así with the ra-ta-ta-ta, and more than anything else it seems a string of nonsense than a conversation. Like they call those little drawings "doo-dles." Like that. Verbal doodles.
BARBARA: Doodles, eh? (*Pause.*) Next time I'm going to separate my words. Like Tarzan. "To-day the blah, blah, blah, blah, blah." Maybe then somebody will understand.
SONIA: You don't have to get like that.
BARBARA: How do you want me to get? (*Pause.*) I don't know how I'm going to afford this place by myself.
SONIA: You'll manage.

BARBARA: Yeah, I'll manage. I always do, right? (*Pause.*) Coño
...

SONIA: Barbara, if you want people to understand, you just go slower, check to see that they're understanding, that there aren't any spacy eyes.

BARBARA: They probably sent complaints to you-know-who, Mister Fox. And goodbye, goodbye for Barbara.

SONIA: They'd be doing you a favor.

BARBARA: No job? Some favor. You leaving, no job ... you want me to be really screwed, don't you?

SONIA: You could look for something better.

BARBARA: And if I don't find anything else?

SONIA: You keep looking. You keep looking until you do.

BARBARA: Look who's talking. Miss Raise, Miss Office Manager.

SONIA: You can do it.

BARBARA: (*Pause.*) I get itchy when I don't work.

SONIA: You have to stop working and take a breath. Listen to yourself. Listen to me.

BARBARA: (*Pause.*) ¡Coño!

SONIA: I won't say anything.

BARBARA: You never stop. Never, never, never stop. (BARBARA *cries.*)

SONIA: Babi?

BARBARA: What?

SONIA: It's not like I'm going to the end of the world. I'll still be here. I'll still be around. You can call me any time.

BARBARA: It's just I ...

SONIA: What? Tell me.

BARBARA: You won't understand me anyway.

SONIA: I understand you. Not all the time. Not now. But I understand. What is it?

BARBARA: (*Pause.*) I'm hungry.

SONIA: You want me to get something? I'll go get something.

BARBARA: Don't bother.

SONIA: What do you want to eat?

BARBARA: Some pastelitos wouldn't be bad.

SONIA: Guava or meat?

BARBARA: Guava. Something sweet, no?

SONIA: (SONIA *gets her purse, readies to go out.*) You're gonna drink the coffee?

BARBARA: It's hot.

SONIA: It's gonna be ice by the time you drink it.

BARBARA: (*Taking a sip.*) I'm drinking. See?

SONIA: Guava then. (*Heads out.*)
BARBARA: Sonia?
SONIA: What?
BARBARA: What are you gonna get?
SONIA: You know me.
BARBARA: Could you get me some of those little ...
SONIA: Biscuits.
BARBARA: Yeah. They're heaven. (SONIA *exits.* BARBARA
      remains. Fade out.)

End of Play

Simply María
or
The American Dream

Josefina López

CHARACTERS

Principals:

MARÍA: daughter of Carmen and Ricardo.
CARMEN: mother of María.
RICARDO: father of María.
JOSÉ: María's husband.
PRIEST

In order of appearance:

GIRL 1
GIRL 2
GIRL 3
MOTHER: Carmen's mother.
WOMAN
NARRATOR
IMMIGRANT 1
IMMIGRANT 2
IMMIGRANT 3
IMMIGRANT 4
STATUE OF LIBERTY
MEXICAN MAN
MEXICAN WOMAN
POSTMAN
PERSON 1
VENDOR 1
VENDOR 2
BAG LADY
PROTESTOR
MAN 1
DIRTY OLD MAN
CHOLO 2
VALLEY GIRL 1
VALLEY GIRL 2
CHOLO 1
PERSON 2
PERSON 3
PERSON 4
ANGLO BUYER
MYTH
MARY
MARÍA 2

REFEREE
ANNOUNCER
FLOOR MANAGER
HUSBAND
WIFE
SALESMAN
HEAD NURSE
NURSE 2
NURSE 3
NURSE 4
BAILIFF
JUDGE
PROSECUTOR
JUROR 1
JUROR 2

Note: Many of the above characters can be played by the same actor/actress.

PLACE

The play begins in an unspecified town in Mexico and moves to downtown Los Angeles.

TIME

Over a period of years chronicling the growth of María from birth to her womanhood.

······················ SCENE ONE ······················

There is a long thin movie screen on the top and across the stage that will be used to display slides of titles for a couple of seconds each. Lights rise. MARIA, *a young woman with a suitcase, enters. She goes to the center and remains still.* THREE GIRLS *enter and stand behind her.*

GIRL 3: (*Loud introduction.*) Romeo and Juliet elope. Or, where's the wedding dress? (*Lights slowly fade. Then dim lights slowly rise.* RICARDO, *a tall, dark and handsome young Mexican man enters. He tries to hide in the darkness of the night. He whistles carefully, blending the sound with the noises of the night.*)

CARMEN: (*From her balcony.*) Ricardo, ¿eres tú?

RICARDO: Yes! Ready?

CARMEN: Sí. (*She climbs down from her balcony, then runs to* RICARDO, *kissing and consuming him in her embrace.*) Where's the horse?

RICARDO: What horse?

CARMEN: The one we are going to elope on.

RICARDO: You didn't say to bring one. All we agreed on was that I would be here at midnight.

CARMEN: I would have thought that you would have thought to ...

RICARDO: Shhhh!!! ¡Mira! (*Points to* CARMEN's *room.*)

CARMEN: ¡Mi madre! Let's go! And on what are we going?

RICARDO: On this. (*Brings an old bike.*)

CARMEN: ¡Qué! On that? No! How could ... Everyone knows that when you elope, you elope on a horse, not on a ... Ricardo, you promised!

MOTHER: (*Discovering* CARMEN *gone.*) ¡Carmencita! Carmen! She's gone!

CARMEN: Oh, no! Hurry! Let's go!

RICARDO: (*Hops on the bike.*) Carmen, hurry! Get on!

CARMEN: We won't fit!

MOTHER: ¡M'ija! Where are you?

CARMEN: We better fit! (*Jumps on, and they take off. She falls and then quickly hops back on.*) Ricardo, marry me! (*Crickets *are heard, lights dim. Fade out.*)

.... SCENE TWO ....

THREE WOMEN *enter a church with candles. A fourth, much
older, enters with a lighted candle and lights the other candles. The*
THREE WOMEN *then transform into statues of the saints in the
church.* PRIEST *comes downstage, waiting for a wedding to begin.*
CARMEN *enters, pregnant.*

PRIEST: Will he be here soon?

CARMEN: Soon. He promised.

PRIEST: I was supposed to start half an hour ago.

WOMAN: (*Enters with a note.*) Is there anyone here named Carmen?

CARMEN: Yes ... Is it from Ricardo? (*Reading the note.*) "I
haven't been able to get a divorce. It will be some time
soon, believe me ... Just wait. I'm working hard so that
I can save money to buy a little house or a ranch for the
three of us. If you wait, good things will come." (*To*
PRIEST.) There won't be a wedding today. (*Exits crying
with* PRIEST. *The statues become* WOMEN *and they all
ad lib malicious gossip about the pregnant bride* CARMEN
enters again, holding baby. PRIEST *enters.* WOMEN *become statues again.*)

PRIEST: Will he be here? (RICARDO *enters.*)

CARMEN: He is here.

PRIEST: Good. Now we can start.

CARMEN: (*To* RICARDO.) I thought you wouldn't show up.

PRIEST: (*Begins his speech, which is more or less mumbled and
not heard except for:*) Do you, Carmen, accept Ricardo as
your lawfully wedded husband?

CARMEN: I do.

PRIEST: Do you, Ricardo, accept Carmen as your lawfully wedded
wife?

RICARDO: I do.

PRIEST: Under the Catholic Church, in the holy House of God,
I pronounce you husband and wife. (*Takes baby from*
CARMEN, *and sprinkles holy water on baby.*) Under the
Catholic Church, in the holy House of God, this child
shall be known as María. (*The* PRIEST *puts the baby
on the center of the stage.* CARMEN, RICARDO *and*

PRIEST *exit. On the screen the following title is displayed:*
THE MAKING OF A MEXICAN GIRL.)
NARRATOR: The making of a Mexican girl. (*The statues now transform into* THREE ANGELIC GIRLS *who begin to hum, then sing beautifully with only the word "María." They come center stage and deliver the following, facing the audience:*)
ALL: María.
GIRL 1: As a girl you are to be
GIRL 2: Nice,
GIRL 3: forgiving,
GIRL 1: considerate,
GIRL 2: obedient,
GIRL 3: gentle,
GIRL 1: hard-working,
GIRL 2: gracious.
GIRL 3: You are to like:
GIRL 1: Dolls,
GIRL 2: kitchens,
GIRL 3: houses,
GIRL 1: cleaning,
GIRL 2: caring for children,
GIRL 3: cooking,
GIRL 1: laundry,
GIRL 2: dishes.
GIRL 3: You are not to:
GIRL 1: Be independent,
GIRL 2: enjoy sex,
GIRL 3: but must endure it as your duty to your husband,
GIRL 1: and bear his children.
GIRL 2: Do not shame your society!
GIRL 3: Never,
GIRL 1: never,
GIRL 2: never,
ALL: Never!!!!
GIRL 1: Your goal is to reproduce.
GIRL 2: And your only purpose in life is to serve three men:
GIRL 3: Your father,
GIRL 1: your husband,
GIRL 2: and your son.
GIRL 3: Your father. (RICARDO *enters.*)
RICARDO: Carmen, I must go.
CARMEN: Ricardo, don't go. Not after all the time I've waited.

RICARDO: I don't want to leave you, but we need the money. There's no work here. I must go to el norte, so I can find work and send for you.

CARMEN: I don't want to be alone.

RICARDO: You have María. I'm going so that we can have the things we don't have.

CARMEN: I would prefer to have you and not the things I don't have.

RICARDO: I want something else besides a life on this farm.

CARMEN: María will not see you.

RICARDO: She will. When I am on the other side, I will send for you. She will be very proud of me.

CARMEN: You promise?

RICARDO: I promise.

CARMEN: Well, then I will wait; we will wait.

RICARDO: I will write. (*Kisses* CARMEN *on the forehead.*)

CARMEN: Ricardo, remember that I love you. (RICARDO *leaves.*) Don't forget to write. (*Fade out.*)

.... SCENE THREE ....

NARRATOR: Yes, write a lot; they will miss you. All who are in search of opportunity go to the same place: America. And America belongs to those who are willing to risk. (*A giant sail enters the stage brought on by* FOUR EUROPEAN IMMIGRANTS.)

IMMIGRANT 1: All for a dream.

IMMIGRANT 2: Ciao, mia Italia!

IMMIGRANT 3: Auf Wiedersehen, mein Deutschland!

IMMIGRANT 4: Au revoir, mon France!

IMMIGRANT 2: Hello, America! (*In the background "America the Beautiful" plays, the music growing louder. The* STATUE OF LIBERTY *enters.*)

IMMIGRANT 3: The Lady!

IMMIGRANT 4: Up high in the sky, incapable of being brought down.

IMMIGRANT 2: And like her ...

IMMIGRANT 3: ... we carry ...

IMMIGRANTS 2 & 4: ... a similar torch.

ALL: A torch of hope.

STATUE OF LIBERTY: Give me your tired, your poor, your huddled masses yearning to breathe free ... (*At the bottom*

of the STATUE OF LIBERTY *are* THREE MEXICAN
PEOPLE [RICARDO *is one of them*] *trying to go across
the stage as if it is the border.* *They run around hiding,
sneaking, and crawling, trying not to get spotted by the
border patrol.*)
RICARDO: ¡Vénganse! ¡Por aquí!
MEXICAN MAN: ¿Y ahora qué hacemos?
MEXICAN WOMAN: What do we do now?
MEXICAN MAN: ¡Vámonos! ¡Por allá!
MEXICAN WOMAN: ¡Nos nortearon!
RICARDO: Let's go back. (*They go to hide behind the* EURO-
PEAN IMMIGRANTS. *The* STATUE OF LIBERTY *com-
poses herself and continues.*)
STATUE OF LIBERTY: I give you life, liberty and the pursuit of
happiness for the price of your heritage, your roots, your
history, your relatives, your language . . . Conform, adapt,
bury your past, give up what is yours and I'll give you the
opportunity to have what is mine.
MEXICAN MAN: Pues bueno, if we have to.
MEXICAN WOMAN: Sounds good.
IMMIGRANT 4: Look, fireworks!
RICARDO: ¡Nos hicimos! (*"America the Beautiful" becomes over-
whelming; lights flash, representing the fireworks. A few
seconds later the same lights that adorn the celebration for*
EUROPEAN IMMIGRANTS *become the lights from the
helicopters hunting after the* MEXICAN PEOPLE. *Hound
dogs are also heard barking, and the* MEXICAN PEOPLE
scatter and try to hide.)
RICARDO: ¡La migra!
MEXICAN MAN: The immigration!
MEXICAN WOMAN: ¡Córranle! (*The* EUROPEAN IMMI-
GRANTS *and the* STATUE OF LIBERTY *all keep pointing at the* MEXICAN PEOPLE *so that they can be caught.
The* MEXICAN PEOPLE *run offstage, and with the sail
tilted down, they charge after them. Fade out.*)

. . . . SCENE FOUR . . . .

POSTMAN: (*Throwing in paper airplane.*) Air mail for Carmen
García.
CARMEN: (CARMEN *enters and reads letter.*) "Mi querida Car-
men, how are you? How is María? I've sent you some

more money. This is the last letter I write to you because
I am now sending for you. I fixed my papers with the
help of a friend, and I got an apartment where we can
live. Tell María I love her, and to you I send all my love
... " María! ... "Leave as soon as possible ... " Leave
as soon as possible ... María, ¡ven acá!

MARÍA: (MARÍA *enters.*) Yes, Mami.

CARMEN: María get ready; we're going.

MARÍA: Going where?

CARMEN: To join your father in the city of the angels.

MARÍA: Angels? (MARÍA *puts on her coat for the journey. Fade
out.*)

.... SCENE FIVE ....

On the screen the following title is displayed: **LOS ANGELI-
TOS DEL NORTE.** *The following is the making of a city. Actors
will take on many roles. It will be organized chaos. Noises of police
and firetruck sirens, along with other common city noises are heard.
The lights rise on* VENDORS *selling on the streets, and all sorts of
unusual and not so unusual* PEOPLE *found in downtown L.A. on
Broadway.* CARMEN *and* MARÍA *are engulfed in the scene, ap-
palled to see what they have come to.*

PERSON 1: Broadway! Downtown L.A.!

VENDOR 1: Cassettes, ¡cartuchos, dos dólares!

VENDOR 2: Anillos de oro sólido. Solid gold. Not plated.

CARMEN: Perdone, señora, could you tell me ...

BAG LADY: Get out of my way!

PROTESTOR: Homosexuality is wrong! No sex! No sex! ¡Se
va a acabar el mundo! The world is coming to an end!
(*Separates* CARMEN *from* MARÍA.)

CARMEN: María! María, where are you?! (*Searches frantically.*)

MARÍA: Mami! Mami! (*Cries for* CARMEN.)

WOMAN 1: Buy this! ¿Sombras para verte como estrella de cine?

WOMAN 2: Hair brushes, all kinds, a dollar!

WOMAN 3: You want to buy handbags?

WOMAN 4: ¡Vámonos! Here comes the police. (*All the* VEN-
DORS *on the street run away.*)

MAN 1: Jesus loves you! (*Hands* CARMEN *a pamphlet.*) He died
for our sins!

CARMEN: ¿Qué?

WOMAN 1: That RTD bus is late again!

DIRTY OLD MAN: Hey! Little girl! You want to get married? The world is coming to an end and you don't want to die without having experienced it.

CARMEN: María! María! ¿Dónde estás, hija mia?

CHOLO 2: East L.A.!

TWO VALLEY GIRLS: We love it!

CHOLO 1: Hey, bato!

TWO VALLEY GIRLS: Party and let party!

CHOLO 2: ¡Oye, mi carnal!

PERSON 2: ¡Viva la huelga! Boycott grapes!

PERSON 3: Chicano Power!

TWO VALLEY GIRLS: We love it.

PERSON 3: Chicano Power!

TWO VALLEY GIRLS: We love it.

PERSON 4: A little culture for the gringuitos. ¡Tostadas, frijoles!

ANGLO BUYER: How much? ¿Cuánto? ¿Salsa? ¿Cerveza?

CARMEN: María! (MARÍA *runs scared and bumps into* CAR-MEN. *They hug each other.* RICARDO, *dressed in a charro outfit enters and gives some yells as if ready to sing a corrido. All the chaos of the city stops, and all the city people recoil in fear.* RICARDO *becomes the hero rescuing* CARMEN *and* MARÍA *from their nightmare.*)

TWO VALLEY GIRLS: We love it!

CARMEN: ¡Ayyy! What a crazy city! It's so awful! People here are crazy! (*Almost about to cry, she embraces* RICARDO.) But Ricardo, I'm so happy to be here.

MARÍA: (*Trying to get attention.*) An ugly man chased me!

RICARDO: But you are all right?

MARÍA: Sí. Now that you are here.

RICARDO: Carmen, we are finally together like I promised.

CARMEN: Ricardo, where's our home?

RICARDO: Follow me. (*They leave the stage. Fade out. Props for next scene are set up quickly.*)

.... SCENE SIX ....

NARRATOR: They are going to the housing projects; Pico Aliso, Ramona Gardens, Estrada Courts. No one likes it there, but it's cheap. Es Barato. (*On the screen the following title is displayed:* **LITTLE HOUSE IN THE GHETTO.**) Little house in the ghetto.

RICARDO: Here we are.

CARMEN: ¿Aquí?

RICARDO: Yes, I hope it's all right. It's only for now.

MARÍA: (*Smiling.*) I like it! Look, Mami! There are swings and grass.

RICARDO: There are a lot of kids in the neighborhood you can play with.

MARÍA: Really, Papi? Would they want to play with me?

RICARDO: Sure. (*Noticing* CARMEN's *displeasure.*) What's wrong? You don't like it?

CARMEN: Oh. No, I'm just tired from the trip.

RICARDO: How was the trip?

MARÍA: (*Cutting in.*) It was great!

CARMEN: Great? You threw up on me the whole way here.

MARÍA: Except, I don't understand why the bus never got off the ground. Where are the angels? And where are the clouds? And the gate? And the music ... Like in the stories Mami used to tell me. I thought we were going to heaven. I thought you had been called to heaven because you are an angel. Are you an angel?

RICARDO: Yes, I'm your angel always.

MARÍA: So if this isn't heaven and you're an angel, what are we doing here?

RICARDO: María, I brought you to America so that you can have a better life. It wasn't easy for me. I was hiding in a truck with a lot of other people for hours. It was so hot and humid that people preferred to get caught by the migra than die of suffocation. But I was going to make it because I knew that I had a daughter to live for. I did it for you. In America, the education is great! You can take advantage of all the opportunities offered to you. You can work hard to be just as good as anybody. You can be anything you want to be! (*Pause.*) Carmen, let me show you the kitchen. (CARMEN *and* RICARDO *exit.*)

MARÍA: America, I don't even know you yet and I already love you! You're too generous. Thank you. I'll work hard. I can be anything I want to be! (*Starts changing clothes to end up wearing a casual shirt and pants when she finishes the following:*) America, I'm ready to play the game. I'm gonna show those boys in this neighborhood how to really play football! (*She makes some football moves. Then she runs out.* CARMEN *enters.*)

CARMEN: María, ¡ven aquí! (MARÍA *enters.*)

MARÍA: Yes, Mami.
CARMEN: La señora Martínez told me you were playing football with the boys.
MARÍA: Yes, Mami; I was.
CARMEN: I don't want you playing football with the boys. It's not proper for a lady.
MARÍA: But I'm good at sports. I'm better than some of the boys.
CARMEN: It doesn't look right. ¿Qué van a decir? (*In the background appear the* THREE GIRLS *who are only seen and heard by* MARÍA. *They whisper to her.*)
GIRL 1: Never shame your society.
GIRL 2: Never,
GIRL 3: never,
GIRL 1: never,
ALL: NEVER!!!
MARÍA: But my Papi said ...
CARMEN: You are not going to play with boys! (CARMEN *exits.*)
MARÍA: I don't understand. Papi tells me to compete, Mami tells me it doesn't look right. I like to compete, too. (MARÍA *exits to her room.*)
RICARDO: (*To* MARÍA.) María, ¡ven aquí! Who were you walking home with today?
MARÍA: A friend.
RICARDO: A boyfriend?
MARÍA: No, just a friend I have in my last class. He lives close by.
RICARDO: I don't want you walking home with or talking to boys. Study!
MARÍA: (*Dares to ask.*) Papi, why?
RICARDO: You're thirteen and you are very naïve about boys. The only thing on their minds is of no good for a proper girl. They tell girls that they are "special," sweet things, knowing that girls are stupid enough to believe it. They make pendejas out of them. They get them pregnant, and shame their parents ... Go to your room! (*The* THREE GIRLS *appear again and whisper to* MARÍA.)
GIRL 1: Never shame your society!
GIRL 2: Never,
GIRL 3: (*Does not continue, but slowly walks away from the two girls.*)
GIRL 1: Never,
GIRL 1 AND 2: Never!! (*Spotlight on* MARÍA. MARÍA *goes to the mirror,* GIRL 3 *appears in the mirror.* MARÍA *brushes*

her hair and so does GIRL 3. *Then* GIRL 3 *begins to touch herself in intimate ways, discovering the changes through puberty, while* MARÍA *remains still, not daring to touch herself. Finally, when* MARÍA *does dare to touch herself,* CARMEN *comes into the room and discovers her. Lights quickly come back on.*)

CARMEN: María, what are you doing?

MARÍA: Nothing.

CARMEN: María, were you ... (*Before* MARÍA *can answer.*) It is a sin to do that. Good girls don't do that. (GIRL 3 *goes behind* MARÍA.)

GIRL 3: (*Whispering.*) Why? Why? Why?

MARÍA: Why?

CARMEN: (*Somewhat shocked.*) Because it is dirty! Sex is dirty.

GIRL 3: Why is it dirty? What makes it dirty?

MARÍA: (*Suppresses and ignores* GIRL 3.) I'm sorry, I didn't know what I was doing.

CARMEN: María, I'm telling you for your own good. Women should be pure. Men don't marry women who are not unless they have to. Quieren vírgenes. It's best that way, if you save yourself for your wedding night. Be submissive.

GIRL 3: Why? Why? Why?

MARÍA: Yes, but ... Why?

CARMEN: That's the way it is. I know it's not fair, but women will always be different from men. Ni modo.

MARÍA AND GIRL 3: I don't understand. Why must a woman be submissive? Why is sex dirty? (GIRL 1 *appears.*)

GIRL 1: María, stop questioning and just accept.

GIRL 3: No, María! God gave you a brain to think and question. Use it!

GIRL 1: But it is not up to us to decide what is right and what is wrong. Your parents know best, María. They love you and do things for you.

GIRL 3: María, they are not always right ...

RICARDO: (*Interrupting the argument.*) María! Come and help your mother with dinner right now!

MARÍA: All right! (*She goes to the table and chairs.*)

RICARDO: What do you do in your room? You spend so much time in there.

MARÍA: I was doing my homework.

RICARDO: It takes you all that time? (RICARDO *has the mail and pulls out a letter from the pile.*)

MARÍA: Yes, I want my work to be perfect so that I can win an award ...

RICARDO: All for an award? How about if I give you a trophy for washing the dishes when you are supposed to, and for doing the laundry right? (*He begins to read the letter. MARÍA searches through the pile. She finds a letter, reads it and becomes excited.*)

CARMEN: (*To* RICARDO.) Who's the letter from?

RICARDO: My cousin, Pedro.

CARMEN: What are you going to tell him?

RICARDO: The truth. I'm going to tell him his Martita did pendejadita and is due in three months. (*To* MARÍA.) What do I tell you?

CARMEN: Ayy, ¡qué vergüenza!

RICARDO: ¡Tanto estudio y para nada! It's such a waste to educate women. How is all that education helping her now. She's pregnant and on welfare ... What's that smell? The tortillas are burning!

MARÍA: Ayyy!!!! (MARÍA *runs to the kitchen.*)

CARMEN: When you get married, what is your husband going to say?

MARÍA: I'm sorry; I completely forgot.

CARMEN: You can't cook, you can't clean ...

MARÍA: I try to do all the chores you ask.

CARMEN: You can't do anything right. Not even the tortillas.

MARÍA: I really try ...

RICARDO: No Mexican man is going to marry a woman who can't cook.

CARMEN: You're almost eighteen! (*Looks to* RICARDO.) I married your father when I was eighteen and I already knew how to do everything.

MARÍA: Mamá, papá, there are other more important things ... (*She holds the letter, but decides not to say anything.*) I just don't care for housework. (MARÍA *goes to her room. Spotlight on* MARÍA. *She looks at the letter and* GIRL 3 *appears. They look at the letter and* GIRL 3 *reads.*)

GIRL 3: "Congratulations! You are eligible for a four-year scholarship ... Please respond as soon as possible ... " (MARÍA *jumps up in excitement. She then gets a typewriter and begins to type her response. The typewriter is not working.*)

She goes outside to look for her father. Fade out.)

.... SCENE SEVEN ....

RICARDO *and* MARÍA *enter.*

MARÍA: Papá ... ¿Está ocupado?

RICARDO: I'm reading the paper.

MARÍA: Do you think ... well ... maybe when you have finished reading you can fix this for me? Here is the manual. (*She shows it to him. He pretends to look, but cannot understand it.*)

RICARDO: Go get my tool box. I'll do it my way. (RICARDO *begins to check the typewriter carefully.* MARÍA *looks attentively and also tries to think of a way to introduce the subject of college.* GIRL 1 *appears.*)

GIRL 1: There is no one who can take the place of my father, who loves me but cannot show it any other way. If I wasn't scared, I would hold you. I love you. (RICARDO *finishes fixing the typewriter and hands it to* MARÍA.)

CARMEN: ¡Ayy! ¡Qué huebona! Where is María?

RICARDO: She's in her room typing. I fixed her typewriter.

CARMEN: What is she typing?

RICARDO: I don't know. Ask her.

CARMEN: (*She goes to* MARÍA'*s room.*) María, come help me fold the clothes.

MARÍA: I'm busy!

CARMEN: Busy? Busy! Can't it wait? I have things to do, too.

MARÍA: All right. (*They start folding the clothes.* RICARDO *enters.*)

CARMEN: María, your birthday is almost here. Do you want me to make you a beautiful dress for your birthday? Maybe you can wear it for your graduation? Oh, our neighbor, la señora Martínez, told me today her daughter Rosario is graduating from a good business school. She says she already has a good job as a secretary.

MARÍA: Mamá, Papá, I don't want to be a secretary. (*Pause.*) I want to go to college.

RICARDO: What?

CARMEN: It's too expensive.

MARÍA: (*Quickly.*) I was awarded a big, four-year scholarship!

RICARDO: ¿Qué? College? Scholarship?

CARMEN: ¿Para qué?
MARÍA: I want to be educated ... (*Courageously.*) I want to be an actress.
RICARDO: You want to go to college to study to be an actress? ¿Estás loca?
CARMEN: Ayyy, María, you are crazy! You don't know what you want.
RICARDO: I didn't know you had to study to be a whore.
CARMEN: What have we done to make you want to leave us? We've tried to be good ...
MARÍA: Nothing. It's not you. I want to be something.
RICARDO: Why don't you just get married like most decent women and be a housewife?
CARMEN: That's something.
RICARDO: That's respectable.
MARÍA: I don't understand what you are so afraid of ...
RICARDO: I don't want you to forget that you are a Mexican. There are so many people where I work who deny they are Mexican. When their life gets better they stop being Mexican! To deny one's country is to deny one's past, one's parents. How ungrateful!
MARÍA: Papi, I won't. But you said that with an education I could be just as good as anybody. And that's why you brought me to America.
RICARDO: No. Get married!
MARÍA: I will. But I want a career as well. Women can now do both.
RICARDO: Don't tell me about modern women. What kind of wife would that woman make if she's busy with her career and can't tend to her house, children and husband.
MARÍA: And that's all a woman is for? To have children? Clean a house? Tend to her husband like a slave? And heat his tortillas?
RICARDO: ¡Qué atrevida! Why do you make it seem as if it would be some sort of nightmare? (*Sarcastically.*) Women have always gotten married and they have survived.
MARÍA: But surviving is not living.
CARMEN: María, listen to your father.
MARÍA: Papi, I listened to you. That's why! You encouraged me when I was young, but now you tell me I can't. Why?
RICARDO: (*Trying to find an answer.*) Because ... you are a woman.
MARÍA: Papi, you're not being fair.

RICARDO: (*Trying to keep face and control.*) You ungrateful
    daughter! I don't want to see you. Get out of my face!
    (MARÍA *runs to her room, crying.*)

CARMEN: Ricardo, why don't you even let her try, ¿por favor?
    (*She goes to* MARÍA*'s room.* RICARDO *stands, and then
    exits. Lights change to* MARÍA*'s room.*) María, don't
    cry. Don't be angry at us either, and try to understand us.
    ¡M'ija! We are doing this for you. We don't want you to
    get hurt. You want too much; that's not realistic. You are
    a Mexican woman, and that's that. You can't change that.
    You are different from other women. Try to accept that.
    Women need to get married, they are no good without
    men.

MARÍA: Mami, I consider myself intelligent and ambitious, and
    what is that worth if I am a woman? Nothing?

CARMEN: You are worth a lot to me. I can't wait for the day when
    I will see you in a beautiful white wedding dress walking
    down the aisle with a church full of people. This is the
    most important event in a woman's life.

MARÍA: Mother, we are in America. Don't you realize you expect
    me to live in two worlds? How is it done? Can't things
    be different?

CARMEN: No sé. That's the way your father is. Ni modo.

MARÍA: Ni modo? Ni modo! Is that all you can say? Can't you do
    anything? (*Gives up on her and just explodes.*) ¡¡Ayy!! Get
    out! Get out! (CARMEN *leaves and* MARÍA *continues to
    pound on her pillow with rage.* MARÍA *slowly begins to
    fall asleep. Fade out.*)

.... SCENE EIGHT ....

On the screen the following title is displayed: **THE DREAM.**
GIRL 2, *who will now portray* MYTH, *appears. She wears a spring
dress and looks virginal. She goes to* MARÍA.

MYTH: (*Shaking* MARÍA *lightly.*) María, get up and come see.

MARÍA: Who are you?

MYTH: I'm Myth. María, come see what can be.

MARÍA: What do you mean? What's going on?

MYTH: María, you are dreaming the American Dream. You can
    be anything you want to be. Follow me. (*The sound of a
    horse is heard.*)

MARÍA: Is that a horse I'm hearing?
MYTH: See ... (*A* PRINCE *appears and he and* MYTH *begin to dance to a sweet melody. Just as they are about to kiss, the fierce sound of a whip accompanied by loud and wild cries of the horse running off are heard.*)
PRINCE: (*In a very wimpy voice.*) My horse! My horse! (*Runs off to catch his horse.*)
MARÍA: What happened?
MYTH: I don't know. (*Another crack of the whip is heard, but now* GIRL 3, *who will portray* "MARY," *appears with the whip.*)
MARY: Sorry to spoil the fairy tale, but Prince Charming was expected at the castle by Cinderella ... Hello, María.
MARÍA: And who are you?
MARY: My name is Mary. It's my turn now, so get lost Myth! (*She snaps her finger and a large hook pulls* MYTH *offstage.*)
MYTH: You're such a meanie!
MARY: Control, that's the thing to have. So come along and follow me!
MARÍA: Where are you taking me?
MARY: To liberation! Self independence, economic independence, sexual independence. We are free! María, in America, you can be anything you want to be. A lawyer. A doctor. An astronaut. An actress!! The Mayor. Maybe even the President ... of a company. You don't have to be obedient, submissive, gracious. You don't have to like dolls, dishes, cooking, children and laundry. Enjoy life! Enjoy liberation! Enjoy sex! Be free! (GIRL 1, *who will portray* "MARÍA 2," *appears brandishing a broom.*)
MARÍA 2: You bad woman! You bitch!
MARY: I'm not!
MARÍA 2: You American demon. You are. You are. You just want to tempt her, then hurt her.
MARÍA: (*Throwing* MARY *her whip.*) Mary, catch!
MARY: Thanks! Now we will see! (MARÍA 2 *and* MARY *have a mock sword combat, until a man blows a whistle and becomes a referee for a wrestling match.*)
REFEREE: (*Taking away the broom and the whip.*) All right, c'mon girls. I don't want weapons. Give them. (*The women push him away and charge at each other.* MARY *tries some dirty tricks.*) I told you I wanted this to be a clean fight. What were you using?
MARY: Nothing! I'm so innocent.

REFEREE: Now come over here and shake hands.

MARÍA 2: (*Asking the audience.*) Should I? Should I? (*Gets* MARY*'s hand and twists it. They wrestle wildly, with* MARY *winning, then* MARÍA 2. *The* REFEREE *finally steps in.*)

REFEREE: Break! Break! (*He holds* MARY *and pulls her out.*)

MARY: (*Barely able to speak.*) María, before you are a wife, before you are a mother, first you are a woman! I'll be back. (*She's dragged out.* MARÍA 2, *who won the fight, acknowledges the cheers of the crowd, then gestures for* MARÍA *to kneel and pray.* MARÍA 2 *puts a wedding veil on* MARÍA.)

MARÍA 2: A woman's only purpose in life is to serve three men. Her father, her husband and her son. Her father. (RI-CARDO *appears. He picks up* MARÍA *and escorts her to the church. The bells and the wedding march are heard. The following title is displayed:* **WHITE WEDDING.** MARÍA *walks down the aisle; the groom enters.*)

MARÍA 2: Her husband. (*The couple kneels and a wedding lasso is put around them.*)

PRIEST: (*Same as first* PRIEST.) Dearly beloved, we are gathered here, under the Catholic Church, in the holy House of God, to unite these two people in holy matrimony. Marriage is sacred. It is the unification of a man and a woman, their love and commitment, forever, and ever, and ever; no matter what! Well, then, let's begin ... María, do you accept José Juan González García López as your lawfully wedded husband to love, cherish, serve, cook for, clean for, sacrifice for, have his children, keep his house, love him even if he beats you, commits adultery, gets drunk, rapes you lawfully, denies you your identity, money, love his family, serve his family, and in return ask for nothing?

MARÍA: (*Thinks about it and turns to her parents.*) I do.

PRIEST: Very good. Now, José. Do you accept María García González López as your lawfully wedded wife to support?

JOSÉ: I do.

PRIEST: Good. Well, if there is anyone present who is opposed to the union of these two people, speak now, or forever hold your truth. (RICARDO *stands up, takes out a gun and shows it to the audience.*) Do you have the ring? (JOSÉ *takes out a golden dog collar. The* PRIEST *gives it his blessings.*) Five, six, seven, eight. By the power vested in me, under the Catholic Church, in the holy House of God, I pronounce you husband and wife. (*The* THREE

GIRLS *take away* MARÍA' *s veil and bouquet. They place the dog collar around* MARÍA' *s neck. Then they get the lasso and tie it around her to make the collar work like a leash. To* JOSÉ.) You may pet the bride. (*The lasso is given to* JOSÉ. *He pulls* MARÍA, *who gets on her hands and knees. They walk down the aisle like dog and master. The wedding march plays, people begin to leave. Fade out.*)

.... SCENE NINE ....

A table and two chairs are placed in the center of the stage. MARÍA, *pregnant, walks in uncomfortably. She turns on the television, then the ensemble creates the television setting, playing roles of T.V. producer, director, make-up people, technicians, as if the actual studio is there. Brief dialogue is improvised to establish on-set frenzy.*

ANNOUNCER: And here is another chapter of your afternoon soap opera, "HAPPILY EVERAFTER." Our sultry Eliza Vásquez decides to leave Devero in search of freedom!

FLOOR MAN: Okay everyone, tape rolling, standby in ten seconds. Five, four, three, two ... (*He cues.*)

ACTRESS: Devero, I'm leaving you.

ACTOR: Eliza, why?

ACTRESS: I don't love you anymore. Actually, I never did.

ACTOR: Eliza, but I love you.

ACTRESS: I faked it, all of it. I did it because I had to. But now I must go and be free! (MARÍA *claps loudly in excitement for her.*)

FLOOR MANAGER: Cut! (*To* MARÍA.) What are you doing here?

MARÍA: This is my living room.

FLOOR MANAGER: Oh, sure it is. Well go into the kitchen, make yourself a snack; we'll have the carpet cleaned in an hour. (*Pushes her aside.*) I know, I'm sorry ... Standby. Five, four, three, two, one.

ACTRESS: ... But now I must go and be free!

ACTOR: You can't do this to me!

ACTRESS: Oh, yes I can!

ACTOR: But I've given you everything!

ACTRESS: Everything but an identity! Well, Devero, Devero, Devero, I've discovered I no longer need you. There are unfulfilled dreams I must pursue. I want adventure.

FLOOR MANAGER: And ... cut! That's a take. Roll commercial.
Five seconds. Four, three, two, one. (*The soap opera ends.*
MARÍA *claps approvingly. A commercial quickly begins,
with the ensemble creating a similar on-set frenzy. In the
commercial a man comes home with a bottle of Ajax as a
gift for his wife.*)
HUSBAND: Honey, I'm home! I brought you something. (*Hides
the can treating it as if he had flowers.*)
WIFE: Hi, darling! (*They give each other a peck on the mouth from
a distance.*) How was work?
HUSBAND: Fine ... Ta-Dah! (*Presents the can.*)
WIFE: You shouldn't have. Oh, thank you! I need all the cleaning
power I can get!
HUSBAND: I can smell you've been cleaning.
WIFE: Yes! I've mopped the floors, done the dishes, the laundry;
this house is spotless.
HUSBAND: What a wife! (*They give each other another peck on
the mouth from a distance.*) You're a good wife! (MARÍA
*goes to turn off the television. The doorbell rings. She goes
to answer the door. It's her husband who grunts at her and
comes in, asks for his dinner and sits at the table.*)
JOSÉ: María! María! I'm home. I'm hungry.
MARÍA: José, how was work? Dinner is ready. I made your favorite dish. Do you want to eat now? (JOSÉ *doesn't answer.*) Well, I'll serve you then. (MARÍA *places a plate on
the table.*) My mother came to visit today and she asked
me what we are going to name the baby. She thought it
would be nice to call her Esperanza. (JOSÉ *grunts.*) Of
course it isn't going to be a girl. It's going to be a boy, and
we'll name him after you. That would be nice, wouldn't
it? (MARÍA *feels pains.*) Ayyy! How it hurts. I hope after the baby is born, I will be better. I've been getting so
many pains, and I have a lot of stretchmarks ... I know
you don't like me to ask for money, but I need the money
to buy a dress that fits. I have nothing I can wear anymore.
JOSÉ: (*After a spoonful.*) My dinner is cold.
MARÍA: Oh, is it cold? Well, I'll heat it up right now. It will
only take a minute. (MARÍA *runs to the kitchen. JOSÉ
leaves the table and stares at the bed. The following title
is displayed:* **THE SEX OBJECT**.
JOSÉ: María! ¡Mi amor! Come here, baby! ... Come on, m'ijita.
I won't hurt you ... (*He continues to try to persuade her.*

> *Eventually he gets his way. There are sounds of lust and pain. Finally,* MARÍA *gives out a loud scream of pain.*)
JOSÉ: What is it?
MARÍA: The baby! (*Fade out.*)

.... SCENE TEN ....

The lights rise after the scream. MARÍA *spreads her legs wide open, covering herself with a white sheet.* THREE NURSES *run in. On the screen the following title is displayed:* **THE REPRODUCING MACHINE OR BE FRUITFUL.** *Dolls will be used as babies.*)

SALESMAN: Here we have it. Direct from Mexico. The Reproducing Machine. You can have one by calling our toll-free number. Get your pencil.
HEAD NURSE: Now, relax. Just breathe like this. (*Example.*) Ahhh!! All in good rhythm. Good! Don't worry, millions of women have children, especially Mexican women, they have millions. But you'll get used to it. After your fourth child, they'll just slide right on out.
MARÍA: 'Amá! Mamá!
HEAD NURSE: There's nothing I can do. I went through it myself. Now, isn't the pain great? You're giving birth! Why, it's the most satisfying feeling a woman can feel. Okay, I think it's coming! Push, Push, Push. (*A baby pops up, flying into the air. It is caught by one of the nurses. She presents the baby to the* HEAD NURSE.)
HEAD NURSE: Oh, it's a girl.
NURSE 2: (*Presenting the baby to* JOSÉ.) Here's your baby daughter.
JOSÉ: A daughter? How could you do this to me? Well, I'll have to call her Sacrifice. (MARÍA *screams again.*)
HEAD NURSE: What is it?
MARÍA: There's another one inside; I can feel it!
HEAD NURSE: Nahhh! Well, I'll check just in case. (*She peeps under the sheet.*) Well, I'll be! Yeah, there's another one. Push! Push! Push! (*Another baby pops into the air.* NURSE 3 *catches the baby.*)
NURSE 2: (*Presenting it to* JOSÉ.) Here's another lovely daughter.
JOSÉ: Another daughter? I'll have to call her Abnegation.

SALESMAN: (*Appearing from nowhere.*) Here we have this amaz-
ing machine. The world renowned Reproducing Machine!
(MARÍA *screams again.*)
HEAD NURSE: What is it?
MARÍA: There's another one!
SALESMAN: Ahh, but if you were watching earlier, you saw the
other amazing function. It can also be used as a sex object.
HEAD NURSE: Push! Push! Push! (*Another baby pops up.*)
NURSE 4: (*Catching baby.*) I got it.
SALESMAN: Yes siree! You can be the boss. It's at your disposal.
Hours of pleasure. And if it ever does go out of control, a
kick and a few punches will do the job and it will be back
to normal.
NURSE 2: Here's another one.
JOSÉ: Another girl? Why are you doing this to me? I'll call her
Obligation.
SALESMAN: It's made in Mexico. It's cheap! It cooks! It cleans!
(MARÍA *screams again.*)
HEAD NURSE: Push! Push! Push! (THREE BABIES *pop up into
the air. Some land in the audience. All the nurses are busy
collecting them.*)
SALESMAN: Its stretchmarks can stretch all the way from here to
Tijuana. Not even a Japanese model can beat this one.
NURSE 2: (*To* JOSÉ.) Guess what?
JOSÉ: No, don't tell me; another girl?
NURSE 2: Surprise!
JOSÉ: (*Sees babies.*) Three girls! I'll call them Frustration, Regret
and Disappointment.
SALESMAN: It delivers up to twenty-one children. It feeds on
beans, chile and lies.
HEAD NURSE: Are there any more babies in that Mexican oven
of yours?
MARÍA: I don't think so.
HEAD NURSE: See you in nine months for your next Mexican
litter.
SALESMAN: You can have your own reproducing machine! Call
the number on your screen now! (*Fade out.*)

.... SCENE ELEVEN ....

*Lights rise after a brief pause. On the stage is a table which
serves as a crib for the six crying babies. On the screen the following*

title is displayed: **THE NIGHTMARE.** MARÍA *tries to quiet the babies by holding each one at a time, then by the bunch.* CARMEN, RICARDO *and* JOSÉ *enter. They stand behind her like demons.*

JOSÉ: Shut those babies up!

CARMEN: You're a bad wife!

RICARDO: This house is a mess!

CARMEN: You can't cook, you can't clean!

JOSÉ: Where's my dinner?

RICARDO: The dishes?

JOSÉ: My tortillas?

RICARDO: You're a bad wife!

CARMEN: I did it all my life!

JOSÉ: Bad wife!

MARÍA: No! I'm not! I'm a good wife! I try. I really do! (MARÍA *goes to get the laundry and begins to fold it quickly, but nicely and carefully. Suddenly, the clothes begin to take on a life of their own. There is a giant coat, and a pair of pants surrounding* MARÍA. *They start pushing her around, then her wedding dress appears and heads towards* MARÍA's *neck. They wrestle on the ground.*)

CARMEN: Martyr! (MARÍA *manages to get away, and runs upstage. As she is running, a giant tortilla with the Aztec Calendar emblem falls on her, smashing her to the ground.*)

MARÍA: Help!

RICARDO: Martyr! (MARÍA *manages to get out from under the tortilla; as she escapes, she is attacked by a storm of plates.*)

MARÍA: Help!

RICARDO, CARMEN AND JOSÉ: Martyr!!! Martyr!!! Martyr!!!

MARÍA: (*Becomes uncontrollably mad.*) Enough! Do you want your dishes cleaned? I've got the perfect solution for them. (MARÍA *gestures. Sounds of dishes being smashed are heard.*) Now you don't have to worry. I'll buy you a million paper plates! Ohhhh! And the tortillas. Mamá! I'm going to show you how they should be done. (*She gets a bag of tortillas and begins tossing them into the audience like frisbees.*) Are these good enough? I hope so! I tried to get the top side cooked first ... or was it last? Anyway, who cares! Here are the tortillas! (*Attacks her mother with a couple of tortillas.*) I hate doing the dishes! I hate doing the laundry! I hate cooking and cleaning! And I hate all housework because it offends me as a woman! (*There is a piercing moment of silence.*) That's right. I am a woman

... a real woman of flesh and blood. This is not the life
I want to live; I want more! And from now on I am di-
recting my own life! Action! (*Lights come fully on.* TWO
GIRLS *grab and pull* MARÍA *harshly to take her to another place. The stage now becomes a courtroom.* MARÍA
is sat next to the JUDGE. *The following title is displayed:*
THE TRIAL. *The courtroom is filled with people who create a lot of commotion. The* JUDGE, *the* BAILIFF *and
the* PROSECUTOR *enter.*)

BAILIFF: Please rise, the honorable hang-judge presiding.

JUDGE: (*Bangs his gavel until everyone quiets down.* JUDGE *will
be done by same actor who does* PRIEST.) Quiet in my
courtroom! I am warning you, anyone who causes any
such commotion like this again will be thrown out! Is
that understood! Let's begin!

BAILIFF: We are here today to give trial to María who is being
accused by her husband of rebellion toward her implied
duties of marriage.

JUDGE: How do you plead?

MARÍA: Plead? Innocent! Guilty! I don't know!

JUDGE: Are you making a joke out of my question?

MARÍA: No ... Sir.

JUDGE: It sounds to me like you wish to challenge these laws.

MARÍA: I don't understand why I am on trial. What real laws
have I broken?

JUROR 1: She knows what she's guilty of.

JUROR 2: She knows what laws not to break!

MARÍA: Who are they?

BAILIFF: Your jury.

MARÍA: But they are women, Mexican, traditional ... They can't
possibly be objective.

BAILIFF: They are a good jury.

MARÍA: This is unjust! I must speak up to this ...

BAILIFF: You have no voice.

MARÍA: Where's my lawyer? I do get one, don't I? (*The courtroom
fills with cruel laughter, which quickly stops.*)

JUDGE: No, you defend yourself.

MARÍA: How do I defend myself when I can't speak?

PROSECUTOR: (*To* MARÍA.) You're dead meat, shrimp. (*To audience.*) This trial is meant to help preserve the institu-
tion of marriage. Ladies and gentlemen of the jury ... in
this case, ladies of the jury. A man's home is his castle.
Where he has his foundation. It is the place where he

comes home to his family, and he becomes the king of his castle. But this poor man comes home one evening and finds his children unattended, his house a mess, his dinner unprepared and his wife sitting back, watching soap operas!

MARÍA: I object!

JUDGE: You have no voice.

MARÍA: You said I was to defend myself.

JUDGE: Not now!

PROSECUTOR: What we are going to try to do is prove the guilt of this woman ...

MARÍA: I object!

JUDGE: Shut up!

MARÍA: I won't!

JUDGE: Mister Prosecutor, call your first witness!

PROSECUTOR: I call Ricardo García to the witness stand. (RICARDO *takes the stand.*) Tell us about your daughter.

RICARDO: She was very obedient when she was young, but when she came to the United States she began to think of herself as "American" ... She studied a lot, which is good, but she almost refused to do her chores because she thought herself above them.

PROSECUTOR: Could you tell us what happened that evening your daughter rebelled?

RICARDO: I'd rather not ... That evening María was hysterical. She threw dishes, tortillas ...

PROSECUTOR: Thank you, that will be all. My next witness will be Carmen García. (CARMEN *takes the stand.*) Tell us about your daughter.

CARMEN: She's really a good girl. She's just too dramatic sometimes. She's such a dreamer, forgive her.

PROSECUTOR: Could you tell us what you saw that evening?

CARMEN: Well, she was a little upset, so she did a few things she didn't mean to do.

MARÍA: No, Mamá! I meant it!

JUROR 1: She admits it!

JUROR 2: She's guilty!

ALL: Guilty!

CARMEN: No, she's just unrealistic.

MARÍA: I'm guilty then! (*The whole courtroom becomes chaotic. Everyone yells out "guilty." CARMEN becomes so sad she begins to cry.*)

MARÍA: Mami, don't cry! (*The lights go on and off and everyone disappears. Fade out.*)

.... SCENE TWELVE ....

MARÍA *begins to regain consciousness and wakes up from her dream. She is awakened by* CARMEN*'s actual crying, which continues and grows.* MARÍA *gets up and listens to* CARMEN *and* RICARDO *arguing in the kitchen.*

RICARDO: ¡Cállate! Don't yell or María will hear you.

CARMEN: Then tell me, is it true what I am saying?

RICARDO: You're crazy! It wasn't me.

CARMEN: Con mis propios ojos I saw you and la señora Martínez meet in the morning by the park. You have been taking her to work and who knows what! Tell me, is it true? If you don't, I'm going to yell as loud as I can and let this whole neighborhood know what's going on.

RICARDO: Okay. It was me! ¿Estás contenta?

CARMEN: ¿Por qué? Why do you do this to me? And with our neighbor? She lives right in front of us.

RICARDO: Look, every man sooner or later does it.

CARMEN: Do you think I don't know about all of your affairs before la señora Martínez? She is not your first! I never said anything before because I was afraid you would send us back to Mexico. But now I don't care! You break it with that bitch or ... I'll kill her and you. ¡Ayyy! Ricardo, I've endured so much for you. I knew you were no angel when we ran off together, but I thought you would change. You would change, because you loved me. I love you, Ricardo! But I can no longer go on living like this or I'll be betraying myself and I'll be betraying María.

RICARDO: Carmen, ¡ven aquí! Carmen, wait! (CARMEN *and* RICARDO *exit. The* THREE GIRLS *enter.* GIRL 3 *hands* MARÍA *a piece of paper and a pen.*)

MARÍA: "Dear Mamá and Papá. Last night I heard everything. Now I know that your idea of life is not for me—so I am leaving. I want to create a world of my own. One that combines the best of me. I won't forget the values of my roots, but I want to get the best from this land of opportunities. I am going to college and I will struggle to do something with my life. You taught me everything I

needed to know. Goodbye."
GIRL 1: Los quiero mucho. Nunca los olvidaré.
GIRL 2: Mexico is in my blood ...
GIRL 3: And America is in my heart.
MARÍA: "Adiós." (*Fade out.*)

End of Play

My Visits with MGM (My Grandmother Marta)

Edit Villarreal

CHARACTERS

MARTA GRANDE: fifteen through eighty years of age, a Mexican refugee.

MARTA CHICA: Marta Grande's daughter, present in play only as memory.

MARTA FELIZ: ten through thirty-two years of age, American born, Marta Grande's granddaughter, Marta Chica's daughter.

FLORINDA: thirteen through seventy-eight years of age, Marta Grande's sister, also a Mexican refugee (actor can be double cast as NURSE WITH WINGS).

JUAN: twenty through sixty years of age, Marta Grande's husband, American born.

FATHER ERNESTO: early twenties, a priest new to the parish.

Note: The play is written so that one actor can play all male roles. The play calls for the actors to play a wide range of ages, age need not be presented realistically. In fact, youth, age and death should be treated as temporary states.

TIME

The present.

PLACE

Texas.

Optional suggestions: If possible, the Spanish in the play can be translated on an overhead projection strip. The scene titles can be used, or not, depending on production concept.

Marta Grande's Poem

Yo salí.
Pero los otros se quedaron.
Candelaria y José María,
Mis Padres, ellos se quedaron.

I got out.
But the others stayed.
Candelaria and José María,
My parents, they stayed.

Pero yo salí.
No podría soportarlo.
Pero mis hermanos se quedaron.
Leopoldo se quedó,
Maclovio se quedó,
También Erasmo y Jafet,
Hasta Alfredo, se quedó.

But I got out.
I couldn't stay there any longer.
But my brothers stayed.
Leopoldo stayed,
Maclovio stayed,
And Erasmo and Jafet,
Even Alfredo stayed.

Pero yo salí.
Yo ya no me aguantaba.
Pero mis hermanas se quedaron.
Ella y Soyenda, y Flora,
Las tres se quedaron.

But I got out.
I couldn't take it any longer.
But my sisters stayed.
Ella and Soyenda, and Flora
The three of them stayed.

Pero yo salí.
Mándeme Dios, pero yo ya no me aguantaba.
Con Florinda, la más joven,
Con ella me salí.

But I got out.

Forgive me, God, but I just couldn't take it.
With Florinda, the youngest,
With her I got out.

ACT ONE

.... PROLOGUE ....

In the dark, sounds of fire rise. Fire engine sirens rise and fade.
Then silence. Lights rise on a burnt-out shell of a house. Here and
there unrecognizable objects can be seen. MARTA FELIZ, *in her*
late twenties, enters. As she searches through the rubble of the house
...

FLORINDA'S VOICE: (*Whisper.*) This house is mine, Marta.
¿M'entiendes? (*Pause.*) ¿M'entiendes? (MARTA FELIZ
frowns. A bad memory.)

FLORINDA'S VOICE: (*Whispers, then rises in anger.*) ¡Sinvergüenza! ¡Necesitas un palazo!

MARTA FELIZ: (*Discovers the remains of a Mexican morral or*
hemp bag, the bright striped colors still visible on the bag.)
¿'Amá? Where are you? ¿'Amá?

MARTA FELIZ: (*Light rises on* MARTA GRANDE, *holding a sim-*
ilar bag.) Look. It's one of the old ones, 'Amá. It survived
the fire.

FLORINDA'S VOICE: (*Whisper.*) You made a will? American
whore!

MARTA GRANDE: (*Smiling.*) Your tía! (MARTA FELIZ *and*
MARTA GRANDE *giggle at the old memory. Light dims*
on MARTA GRANDE.)

MARTA FELIZ: (*To audience.*) After my 'Amá, my grandmother,
died, I threw away clothes. And I stored away photos,
green cards, letters and bills. The only thing I kept for
myself was her coin purse. Fake leather from the five-
and-dime with a rusty hinge that still closed tight.

MARTA GRANDE: In Texas, everything rusts.

MARTA FELIZ: Inside the coin purse were fourteen silver pack-
ages. Bus fares individually wrapped in tin foil. Exactly
the right combination of nickels and dimes for one bus
ride to town and back.

MARTA GRANDE: Una semana. One week.

MARTA FELIZ: She never learned to drive. After she ran over a
dog learning to back up for the first time, my grandfather

wouldn't ever let her have the wheel. But, as she used to
        say ...
MARTA GRANDE: Ni modo.
MARTA FELIZ: Even in her eighties, she used to take the bus into
        town regularly. All the bus drivers knew her by name,
        Doña Marta. She'd make them stop for her mid-block,
        coming and going. (*Female figures in silhouette appear,
        all wearing large Mexican rebozos, or shawls, which cover
        their heads and bodies. A corrido of leave-taking rises,
        plaintive yet insistent.*) When she came here from Mexico,
        I guess she looked the part. (MARTA GRANDE *begins
        to fill her hemp bag with her belongings.*)
MARTA FELIZ: Quiet. Mexican. Patient. Mexican. Long-
        suffering. Mexican. Dependent. Mexican. But inside
        she was different. When she left Mexico she was only
        fifteen. And all she took with her was what she could
        carry in a few sturdy morrales or hemp bags. (MARTA
        GRANDE *steps forward, the archetypal Mexican refugee
        icon wrapped in her rebozo and carrying her morral.*)
MARTA GRANDE: (*As a young girl.*)

Yo salí.
Pero los otros se quedaron.
Candelaria y José María,
Mis padres, ellos se quedaron.

MARTA FELIZ: Her parents wouldn't go. They were too old, they
        said. But she left anyway.
MARTA GRANDE: ¡Pos, sí! No podría soportarlo.
MARTA FELIZ: She couldn't bear it.
MARTA GRANDE:

Pero mis hermanos se quedaron.
Leopoldo se quedó,
Maclovio se quedó,
También Erasmo y Jafet,
Hasta Alfredo se quedó.

MARTA FELIZ: Her brothers wouldn't go. It was the Revolution,
        they said. The Revolution of 1910. But she left anyway.
MARTA GRANDE: ¡Pos, sí! Yo ya no me aguantaba.
MARTA FELIZ: She couldn't stand it one minute longer.
MARTA GRANDE:

Pero mis hermanas se quedaron.

Ella y Soyenda y Flora,
las tres se quedaron.

MARTA FELIZ: Her sisters wouldn't go. Things will get better.
And, if not, they can't get worse, they said. But she left
anyway.

MARTA GRANDE: ¡Pos, sí! Mándeme Dios, pero yo ya no me
aguantaba.

MARTA FELIZ: And so she begged God's forgiveness. And came
to Texas.

MARTA GRANDE: Okay! ¡Estoy lista!

MARTA FELIZ: But not alone. She talked one sister . . .

MARTA GRANDE: ¿Florinda?

FLORINDA: (*One of the shawled silhouettes.*) ¿Mande?

MARTA FELIZ: . . . her little sister, into coming with her.

. . . . SCENE ONE . . . .

Exilio / Exile

MARTA GRANDE: Florinda? (FLORINDA, *a distinctly different
type from* MARTA GRANDE, *enters.*)

FLORINDA: (*Plaintive.*) ¡Ay, Marta!

MARTA GRANDE: You want to go to the United States? Or what?

FLORINDA: I don't know. Tengo miedo, Marta.

MARTA GRANDE: Ni miedo. Ni pedo.

FLORINDA: ¡Ay! No hables así.

MARTA GRANDE: ¿Y por qué no?

FLORINDA: (*Plaintive.*) Me da miedo.

MARTA GRANDE: Pos, ¿sabes qué?

FLORINDA: ¿Qué? (*Long pause.*) Qué, what?

MARTA GRANDE: Yo también tengo miedo.

FLORINDA: You're scared?

MARTA GRANDE: Sí.

FLORINDA: ¿Dónde?

MARTA GRANDE: Aquí. (*Points to her head.*)

FLORINDA: ¿En el coco?

MARTA GRANDE: Sí.

FLORINDA: ¿Miedo de qué, hermanita?

MARTA GRANDE: De chingarme . . .

FLORINDA: (*Disgusted.*) ¡Dios mío!

MARTA GRANDE: Aquí entre esta tierra desgraciada y el cielo
. . .

FLORINDA: Y tú, ¿qué sabes?
MARTA GRANDE: ¿Y tú, ¿qué sabes?
FLORINDA: Y tú, señora, ¿qué sabes?
MARTA FELIZ: (*To audience.*) Somehow, my grandmother convinced the Baptist Church into bringing her and her sister, Florinda, to Texas.
FLORINDA: ¡Ni modo! We had to convert.
MARTA GRANDE: We were the first Baptists in a Methodist family. You should have heard the screams. ¡Por toda la frontera!
MARTA FELIZ: In Texas, they were housed in the basement of the Baptist Church.
FLORINDA: ¡Ay, Marta! It's so dark in here. No hay nada aquí en Tejas. Quiero mi familia.
MARTA FELIZ: But Texas, for my tía Florinda, became a kind of torture chamber, I think.
FLORINDA: ¡Quiero mi 'Amá y mi 'Apá! ¡Quiero mis hermanos!
MARTA FELIZ: Some people can leave their families and get by. But for Florinda, things just got worse. One Sunday she switched from the Baptists to the Pentacostals.
MARTA GRANDE: Your tía, Marta Feliz, was always looking for a macho god.
MARTA FELIZ: One of those primitive types who has answers for everything and leaves nothing to choice. Especially yours.
FLORINDA: (*Tight lipped.*) Bueno.
MARTA FELIZ: But Florinda was not happy as a Holy Roller either. Living in the United States convinced her that here voodoo was necessary. Magic spells and potions. She used to put together some strange brews. My grandmother told me they were worse than piss.
FLORINDA: (*Offering cup of herbal tea to* MARTA GRANDE.) Estafiate, Marta—for your nerves.
MARTA GRANDE: No me engañes con esa mugre.
FLORINDA: Pos ...
MARTA GRANDE: I drink only café americano now.
FLORINDA: Okay!
MARTA GRANDE: Cuando me pones en el sanatorio ...
FLORINDA: Okay!
MARTA GRANDE: Me puedes soplar ...
FLORINDA: ¡Bueno!
MARTA GRANDE: Con esa mugre desgraciada.
FLORINDA: (*Desperately trying to cope.*) ¡Bueno! Okay! ¡Bueno!
MARTA GRANDE: (*To* MARTA FELIZ.) I didn't like it.

MARTA FELIZ: It's possible my grandmother ruined Florinda's life when she made her leave Mexico.

FLORINDA: (*Still upset.*) ¡Bueno! Okay! ¡Bueno!

MARTA FELIZ: But I'm glad they came to Texas. Because here, my grandmother met my grandfather. And after that, his life, too, was never the same.

JUAN: (*Offstage.*) ¡Marta! (JUAN, *dressed in World War I uniform with rifle, enters.*) ¡Ay, Marta! Where have you been?

MARTA GRANDE: Where do you want me, chulo?

FLORINDA: Este fulano no es mexicano.

JUAN: I'm Tex-Mex, honey. American. And proud of it.

MARTA GRANDE: (*To* FLORINDA, *indicating the cup of tea.*) Give him the junk.

FLORINDA: (*Giving* JUAN *the herbal tea.*) Estafiate—for your nerves.

JUAN: Ay—gracias. (*Drinks.*)

MARTA GRANDE: It tastes like piss.

JUAN: Marta, the whole world is at war. And I'm going to go fight. Mira mi uniforme. (JUAN *performs military rifle drills.*) You like it?

FLORINDA: Dile no.

MARTA GRANDE: No.

JUAN: Will you marry me before I go away?

FLORINDA: Dile no.

MARTA GRANDE: I won't get married, chulo, to a man who cannot dance. Pero Florinda ...

FLORINDA: (*Simultaneously with* JUAN. *Prudishly.*) ¡Ay, no!

JUAN: (*Simultaneously with* FLORINDA. *Passionately.*) ¡Ay, no! (*Continues.*) Pos, Martita, you're the one I want. Will you marry me after the war? (JUAN *does a complicated rifle drill.*)

FLORINDA: Dile no.

MARTA GRANDE: Pos, si regresas en un pedazo, payaso.

MARTA FELIZ: After the war, they picked up where my grand-mother had dropped him off. But she wanted proof that he had not been hurt.

MARTA GRANDE: He showed me his body.

JUAN: Pero everything?! Now will you marry me?

FLORINDA: Dile no.

MARTA FELIZ: His body was perfect. Except for a moon-shaped scar on his upper back, exactly the size of the shell that crashed into him in France.

JUAN: ¡Soy macho, Marta!

MARTA GRANDE: Pues ...

MARTA FELIZ: For the rest of his life, he made her laugh by flexing his arm and changing the scar from a moon into a smile.

JUAN: (*Flexing his arm.*) Now will you marry me? Marta?

MARTA FELIZ: Eventually, she said yes.

JUAN: But I have to convert?

MARTA GRANDE: ¡Pos, sí!

JUAN: To what, Marta?

MARTA GRANDE: To the Baptists.

JUAN: ¡Ay, no!

MARTA GRANDE: Pos, they brought me here to Tejas.

FLORINDA: Aquí se dice "Texas," Marta.

JUAN: But we have always been Catholics, Martita.

MARTA GRANDE: Ni modo.

JUAN: Pos. Okay. Yes!

MARTA FELIZ: I think he would have turned Hindu to marry her.

JUAN: ¡Siempre yes! ¡Por toda mi vida, yes!

MARTA FELIZ: The conversion took place in the Rio Grande. He felt happy falling backwards into the river.

JUAN: For you, Marta, anything!

MARTA FELIZ: But when the water from the river crashed against the moon-shaped scar, he felt a pain.

JUAN: The Germans practiced gas warfare, 'manito. In the trenches in France, 'manito. And I breathed it in. All the guys breathed it in. (*Beat.*) The war is over, Marta. Now will you marry me?

MARTA GRANDE: Pos ... sí.

MARTA FELIZ: And together, with Florinda, they began a new life.

MARTA GRANDE: (*Coquettishly pinning a large red paper rose on her dark shawl.*) ¡Ay Yonni!

MARTA FELIZ: She always called him Johnny. I guess she thought it was American, like in the movies.

MARTA GRANDE: Necesitan policías—for the bridge.

JUAN: You want me to become a cop, Marta?

MARTA FELIZ: He was a cop. Until he retired at seventy-five.

MARTA GRANDE: You just have to take the aguacates, bananas and oranges away from the people crossing the border ...

JUAN: Pues ...

MARTA GRANDE: After you get a job, we'll buy a house.

JUAN: Of course!

MARTA GRANDE: Con tierra—for my chickens.

JUAN: Chickens? Qué suave.

MARTA GRANDE: And six children ...

JUAN: ¡Dios mío!

MARTA GRANDE: Okay, Yonni?

JUAN: (*After a pause and hopelessly in love.*) Pos. Okay! Yes! Siempre, yes! ¡Por toda mi vida, yes! (JUAN *and* MARTA GRANDE *embrace.*)

MARTA FELIZ: But slowly, the pain that began when he crashed backwards into the river on the day of his conversion became stronger and stronger.

JUAN: I got it from the Germans!

MARTA FELIZ: A lifetime after the war, when his Army discharge papers were old and yellow, he was told he had developed cancer. All by himself.

JUAN: When you're in the Army, ¿sabes?, you can't even piss without their permission. But then when you get out, you're to blame for everything that ever happened to you. ¡Qué chingazo!

MARTA FELIZ: My grandmother said that in his casket he looked like the young man she had loved all her life.

MARTA GRANDE: We look so young, Marta Feliz, when we die.

JUAN: (*With a salute.*) After the war, Marta, our life! (*Exits.*)

MARTA GRANDE: I want six, Yonni. Six children.

MARTA FELIZ: And the first one was my mother. (MARTA GRANDE *reveals an infant from the depths of her shawl.*)

MARTA GRANDE: Florinda? Mira.

.... SCENE TWO ....

La familia / Family

MARTA GRANDE: My daughter. The first one.

FLORINDA: (*Cold.*) Está muy chula.

MARTA FELIZ: (*To audience.*) My grandmother named her after herself.

MARTA GRANDE: Marta.

MARTA FELIZ: Immediately, they became Marta Grande and ...

MARTA GRANDE: (*To baby.*) Marta Chica.

MARTA FELIZ: My grandmother always said my mother was a perfect child, with curly jet black hair ...

FLORINDA: ¡Dios mío! (*Exits.*)

MARTA GRANDE: Florinda? ¿Qué te pasa? Florinda?

MARTA FELIZ: ¿'Amá? Can I see her?
MARTA GRANDE: Florinda? Es tu sobrina. Florinda?
MARTA FELIZ: ¡'Amá! Can I take a look?
MARTA GRANDE: ¿Tú? (*Pause.*) Pos, sí. This is your mother. (*Shows* MARTA FELIZ *her mother as a baby.*)
MARTA FELIZ: She is perfect, 'Amá.
MARTA GRANDE: She will work hard, esta niña. (*Light on* NURSE WITH WINGS, *a vision in white. She's putting on an immaculately clean and starched nurse's hat.*)
MARTA FELIZ: My mother became a nurse.
MARTA GRANDE: Mira su cachuchita blanquísima—como harina.
MARTA FELIZ: Her hair is so curly, 'Amá. And her eyes ...
MARTA GRANDE: They are like chocolate. And she plays the piano.
MARTA FELIZ: Perfectly.
MARTA GRANDE: Como un ángel. ("Marta Chica's Theme" *is heard, played on a piano. Light on nurse bumps off.*) And she had children, too. (*Referring to audience.*) Tell the people.
MARTA FELIZ: My mother had four children and I'm the first.
MARTA GRANDE: Y otra Marta.
MARTA FELIZ: And, yes. I'm also named Marta. But since there was already a Marta Grande and a Marta Chica, I was named ...
MARTA GRANDE: Marta Feliz. The happy one.
MARTA FELIZ: To be honest, my life has been one crisis after another. Marta Crisis would have been a far more appropriate name.
MARTA GRANDE: Y tú, ¿qué sabes?
MARTA FELIZ: Actually, the whole family has been riddled with crises. I can't take any credit for starting it.
MARTA GRANDE: Y tú, ¿qué sabes?
MARTA FELIZ: The first crisis came before I was even born. My father died.
MARTA GRANDE: No sabes nada.
MARTA FELIZ: 'Amá, I'm telling the people. (*To audience.*) Can you imagine? A baby with no father and a mother who left me with my grandparents.
MARTA GRANDE: ¡No sabes nada, niña chistosa!
MARTA FELIZ: I was an orphan in one sense ... (*Lights rise on a Mexican living room, devoid, however, of religious objects, with a plain brown upright piano in one corner and an*

ornate bird cage in another.) But my grandmother always told me I was a special kind of orphan ...

MARTA GRANDE: You have two mothers.

MARTA FELIZ: She had a way of turning anything bad, orphanhood, even the Revolution, into something better. (*MARTA GRANDE takes off her large rebozo, or shawl, revealing a housewife's dress and kitchen apron.*)

MARTA GRANDE: Marta Feliz? Where are your glasses?

.... SCENE THREE ....

Luchando / Struggling

MARTA FELIZ: (*Now a young teenager.*) ¡Ay, 'Amá! Look at them. They're so thick. I'll look like a frog.

MARTA GRANDE: ¡Ay, manita! Póntelos.

MARTA FELIZ: (*Putting on glasses.*) There! Are you happy? I'm so ugly.

MARTA GRANDE: ¡Pos!

MARTA FELIZ: ¡Pos!

MARTA GRANDE: ¡Pos!

MARTA FELIZ: Pos, I'm ugly. And a teenager.

MARTA GRANDE: Y tú, ¿qué sabes? Yo vine de la Revolución ...

MARTA FELIZ: Oh, God! Every time anything bad happens to anyone, you think about the Revolution.

MARTA GRANDE: Pos, ¡sí! Yo vine con nada. I had nothing!

MARTA FELIZ: I'm talking about my looks, 'Amá. Not the Revolution.

MARTA GRANDE: Nothing. No clothes. No money. ¡Nada!

MARTA FELIZ: 'Amá, I wasn't at the Revolution, remember? (*Crowd sounds in Spanish rise interspersed with loud gunshots, screams and terrified shouts.*)

MARTA GRANDE: ¡Ay! Marta Feliz, tú no sabes ... (*Crowd sounds bump off.*)

MARTA FELIZ: Geeze, 'Amá, how can I, one plain teenager, compete with an entire Revolution?

MARTA GRANDE: You know what you need, m'ija? Besides ganas? You need a job.

MARTA FELIZ: Pos, jobs are very hard to get here, you know. Not like in Mexico where anybody can work for nothing.

MARTA GRANDE: ¿Y qué?

MARTA FELIZ: And all the good jobs go to gringo kids, you know that.

MARTA GRANDE: ¿Y qué?

MARTA FELIZ: And all the ones that they don't take are boring. And they pay nothing.

MARTA GRANDE: You are lazy.

MARTA FELIZ: No. I'm smart. I got the system down.

MARTA GRANDE: M'ija, you need a little job. (FLORINDA *dressed in black, enters, removes a statue of the Virgin Mary from her pocket, kisses it, places it in a prominent place, genuflects before it, then exits.*)

MARTA FELIZ: Maybe I should stay home all day like tía Florinda.

MARTA GRANDE: (*Pocketing the statue.*) ¡Ay, no! ¡Pero no!

MARTA FELIZ: Okay! You're right. It's too awful. I'll kill myself instead and go to Aztec heaven with birds all around me. (*We hear birds chirping.*)

MARTA GRANDE: Forget the pinche aztecas, m'ija.

MARTA FELIZ: I'll wear feathers and eat chocolate all day...

MARTA GRANDE: You have to fight before you can eat.

MARTA FELIZ: It'll be so easy! I won't need a job because I won't need money. Economics, ¿qué no?

MARTA GRANDE: You have to fight, m'ija ...

MARTA FELIZ: Right. The American way. Hi ho! Anchors away!

MARTA GRANDE: No! You have to fight like a Mexican. My first job, I was fifteen. Como tú.

MARTA FELIZ: You had a job? (*Chirping sounds rise. Light rises on the bird cage. A shower of confetti rains over it.* MARTA GRANDE*'s voice is heard, amplified.*)

MARTA GRANDE'S VOICE: ¡Fortunas! ¡Fortunas! (MARTA GRANDE *joins in with the voice as it fades out.*)

MARTA GRANDE: ¡Fortunas! ¡Fortunas! ¡Quién quiere fortunas! (*A* YOUNG MAN *enters.*)

YOUNG MAN: Una fortuna, por favor.

MARTA GRANDE: Un centavo, por favor. (YOUNG MAN *gives* MARTA GRANDE *a coin. She reaches into bird cage, removes a fortune from the bird's beak and hands it to* YOUNG MAN.)

YOUNG MAN: Gracias.

MARTA GRANDE: (*Extraordinarily polite.*) De nada. A sus órdenes. Dígame lo que quiere. Estoy presta a servirle.

YOUNG MAN: (*Reading fortune.*) ¡Híjole de la chingada!

MARTA GRANDE: (*To* MARTA FELIZ.) They were all pendejos in those days.

YOUNG MAN: ¡Voy a hallar mucho dinero en un pozo cubierto con agua negra!

MARTA FELIZ: 'Amá, did he ever find gold in a hole in the ground covered with murky water?

MARTA GRANDE: What do you think?

YOUNG MAN: ¡Válgame Dios! ¡Muchísimas gracias! ¡Ay Dios mío! (YOUNG MAN *exits thrilled, tossing the fortune on the ground behind him.* MARTA GRANDE *picks up the fortune, folds it carefully back into its original creases and places it back in the bird's beak. Chirping sounds fade out. Light bumps off, the bird cage looks ordinary again.*)

MARTA GRANDE: Everybody always wants something for nothing.

MARTA FELIZ: Nobody in their right mind would do a job like that today, 'Amá.

MARTA GRANDE: Pos 'Manita, I did it. For two years. You have to fight m'ija. You get a job. You work hard. And then you die.

MARTA FELIZ: Well ... I want a glamorous job.

MARTA GRANDE: You're fifteen, m'ija. Y además, with those glasses ...

MARTA FELIZ: Okay! I'll settle for dangerous then.

MARTA GRANDE: Why?

MARTA FELIZ: Why? Because I'm going to be single forever. Look at me! 'Amá, don't worry. People who like dangerous jobs always get work because other people keep dying on the job. (*Darkly.*) Economics.

MARTA GRANDE: Pos, somebody I know had a dangerous job.

MARTA FELIZ: Who? You?

MARTA GRANDE: No. Florinda.

MARTA FELIZ: The black manta ray worked?

MARTA GRANDE: Pos, sí. She had a very dangerous job. Right here in Tejas. (*Lights rise on* FLORINDA, *now a girl of thirteen, standing on a cardboard box, holding between her hands a large pair of men's boxer shorts.*)

FLORINDA: (*Achingly timid.*) Diez centavos. Calzoncillos por diez centavos. ¡Ay, Dios mío! ¡Me voy a morir!

MARTA FELIZ: That was her job?

MARTA GRANDE: You don't know what suffering is, m'ija.

FLORINDA: ¡Marta! ¿Dónde estás? ¿Marta? ¡Ayúdame, por favor!

MARTA GRANDE: (*To* FLORINDA.) Tienen que ver el otro lado, Florinda.
FLORINDA: ¡Ay, Dios mío! ¡No puedo soportarlo! ¡Ayúdame, por favor!
MARTA GRANDE: (*To* FLORINDA.) ¡El otro lado, idiota!
FLORINDA: (*Languidly flipping the boxer shorts over to reveal the back side.*) Diez centavos ...
MARTA GRANDE: (*To* FLORINDA.) ¡Así, no! ¡Dale con "gas", mujer!
FLORINDA: Por favor, hermanita, te lo ruego, Martita.
MARTA GRANDE: (*Disgusted.*) ¡Ay, qué desgraciada! (MARTA GRANDE *joins* FLORINDA, *pulling out her own pair of men's boxer shorts.*)
MARTA GRANDE: ¡DIEZ CENTAVOS, CABALLEROS! NO MÁS DIEZ CENTAVOS PARA CALZONCILLOS LIMPIOS. (*A soft sell.*) ¿Mc permiten, señores? ¿Por favor? Si ustedes se quieren casar, o al menos, se quieren enamorar ...
MARTA FELIZ: You sold men's boxer shorts by saying that clean underwear was the best way to get LAID?!
MARTA GRANDE: ¡No, no, no 'manita! Eso no es lo que dije. Si te quieres enamorar. ENAMORAR, m'ija.
MARTA FELIZ: Okay. If you want to "fall in love."
MARTA GRANDE: You need clean underwear, ¿qué no?
MARTA FELIZ: 'Amá, you were a marketing genius.
MARTA GRANDE: Ahora, Florinda. ¡El Otro Lado! (*They both flip their boxer shorts over at the same time.*)
MARTA GRANDE: ¡CALZONCILLOS!
FLORINDA: Limpios. (FLORINDA *freezes.*)
MARTA GRANDE: So ... now when you look for a job, m'ija, think of me. Fifteen years old. Selling men's shorts on the street. In Spanish. And a virgin.
FLORINDA: ¡Válgame Dios!
MARTA FELIZ: Well ... it took balls.
FLORINDA: (*Disgusted.*) ¡Dios mío! (*Exits.*)
MARTA GRANDE: Y ahora, where's your job?
MARTA FELIZ: Well ... I applied at the library, 'Amá. But, you know, they're all gringos over there.
MARTA GRANDE: ¿Pos, qué te importa?
MARTA FELIZ: Pos, you know, at the library you have to talk to people all the time.
MARTA GRANDE: ¿Y qué?

MARTA FELIZ: Well, when people talk to me in Spanish, you know, if I don't answer in Spanish perfectly, you know . . .

MARTA GRANDE: Te chingan.

MARTA FELIZ: But then when I speak English, the gringos put me down. 'Amá, at school, they think we're culturally deprived. How can you be culturally deprived with two languages? It's more like cultural overload to me.

MARTA GRANDE: (*Pause.*) Pos.

MARTA FELIZ: Yeah, "pos."

MARTA GRANDE: Pues.

MARTA FELIZ: Pues, what?

MARTA GRANDE: Así es la vida. (*Long pause.*) Un chingazo después de otro.

MARTA FELIZ: Yeah. In English, the gringos say you get fucked over everytime you turn around.

MARTA GRANDE: ¡Claro! Un chingazo después de otro. ¡A la madre!

MARTA FELIZ: 'Amá, did everybody in Mexico talk like you?

MARTA GRANDE: No. Only the women. (*Taking a letter out of her pocket.*) Ten. This came today. From the pinche library chingado.

MARTA FELIZ: From Mrs. Norris? I don't want to open it.

MARTA GRANDE: Everybody has to have a job, m'ija.

MARTA FELIZ: ¡'Amá!

MARTA GRANDE: (*A threat.*) Calzoncillos.

MARTA FELIZ: Okay. I'll open it. (*Reading letter.*) ¿'Amá?

MARTA GRANDE: ¿M'ija?

MARTA FELIZ: Mrs. Norris is giving me the pinche job.

MARTA GRANDE: (*Triumphant.*) ¡CALZONCILLOS!

MARTA FELIZ: I get to work with books, 'Amá. ("Marta Chica's Theme" *is heard.*)

MARTA GRANDE: A Mexican at the library. Why not?

MARTA FELIZ: Thank you, 'Amá.

MARTA GRANDE: De nada, m'ija. (*Beat.*) Pero, you should thank your mother, también.

MARTA FELIZ: Yeah.

MARTA GRANDE: She works hard, m'ija. She earns her own money.

MARTA FELIZ: Yeah. And she has checks with only her name on them. Like an individual, 'Amá.

MARTA GRANDE: Your poor mother, m'ija. One husband, y después another one.

MARTA FELIZ: It's okay, 'Amá. So she's gotten married a couple of times? It's okay.

MARTA GRANDE: Qué lástima. Her husbands, they die.

MARTA FELIZ: I guess she hasn't had too many good breaks, huh? (*The* NURSE WITH WINGS *enters and sits on the piano.*)

MARTA GRANDE: La vida desgraciada de tu mamá.

MARTA FELIZ: (*To audience.*) Funny, until that moment I always thought my grandmother was playing the piano. You always think the person who takes care of you can do everything. But even she was not immune to crisis. (MARTA GRANDE *looks at the* NURSE WITH WINGS *as lights dim on her.*)

MARTA GRANDE: Your mother always wanted you to be with her, Marta Feliz. Pero sometimes—¿sabes?—we have no choice. Like your mother and her husbands. La Muerte comes when he wants to come. And we have no choice, Marta Feliz, we have no choice.

.... SCENE FOUR ....

El casamiento / Marriage

JUAN *enters. It is after the war. His uniform is now muddied and torn, with a few tarnished medals on one pocket. His arm is in a sling.*

JUAN: Marta? I think we should get married now.

MARTA GRANDE: El soldado bien usado.

JUAN: No joking, all right? I've seen better days. So what? (*Beat.*) The cops want me, Marta.

MARTA GRANDE: ¿De veras?

JUAN: You know, there aren't that many Mexicans on the force, and now, after the war, more of us are eligible. You know, some people think the war was the best thing that ever happened to us. (*He spits into a handkerchief.*)

MARTA GRANDE: ¿Juan? ¿Qué es esto?

JUAN: It's just a little cough, Marta.

MARTA FELIZ: It was cancer.

JUAN: But I'm okay. I'm okay!

MARTA GRANDE: (*Spreading newspapers on the floor near* JUAN.) Mira. Papeles.

JUAN: For me, Martita? Ay, gracias. (*Spits on newspaper.*) Gracias.

MARTA GRANDE: (*Stunned.*) De nada, Yonni.
MARTA FELIZ: I remember the newspapers splotched with blood.
JUAN: Now will you marry me, Marta? Martita?
MARTA GRANDE: Okay, Yonni. Okay. (*Exits. JUAN takes off his soldier's jacket, revealing a policeman's gun and holster on his hip. He takes out the gun and plays with it.*)
MARTA FELIZ: When my grandfather became a cop, they put him on the International Bridge.
JUAN: Confiscating illegal fruits and vegetables from Mexico. They gave me a .45.
MARTA FELIZ: Every morning, after his night shift, he would drive home. I can see him now in his policeman's uniform ...
JUAN: ¡Buenos días!
MARTA FELIZ: Waving to the civilians, which is what he called everybody out of uniform ...
JUAN: ¡Qué les vaya bien!
MARTA FELIZ: He was the good cop. The Tex-Mex cop. With contraband avocados, oranges and bananas in the back of his pick-up.
JUAN: (*To audience.*) You know what? There's no difference between an apple from this side of the border and an apple from the other side of the border. And anyone who's afraid of Mexican bugs better forget it. And you know why? Because the pinche bugs all came over here BEFORE there was a border.
MARTA FELIZ: He'd come home in the morning ready for a good day's sleep. Everything upside down, his life, like ours, filled with crisis.
JUAN: ¡Qué vida loca!
MARTA FELIZ: I was tiny then. No more than ten.

.... SCENE FIVE ....

Cuando era joven / When I Was Young

JUAN: Martita? Marta Feliz? You want to earn some money, m'ija?
MARTA FELIZ: (*To audience.*) Everyday, before he went to sleep, he would ask me to pull out his white hairs.
JUAN: I want to be young, m'ija. Like before the war. (*Going to sleep.*) Find them all, m'ija. (MARTA FELIZ, *now a girl*

of ten, looks through his hair for white hairs.)
MARTA FELIZ: Okay, Papi. How much are you going to pay me,
    Papi?
JUAN: One penny, m'ija. For a hundred white hairs.
MARTA FELIZ: There! I did a hundred.
JUAN: ¿De veras?
MARTA FELIZ: ¡Sí! De veras.
JUAN: (*Giving her a coin from his pocket.*) Bueno. Here's a penny.
    And tomorrow I'll give you another one. (*He falls asleep.*
    Cross fade to MARTA GRANDE *with newspapers under*
    her arm.)

.... SCENE SIX ....

Asimilación / Assimilation

MARTA GRANDE: Marta Feliz?
MARTA FELIZ: ¿'Amá?
MARTA GRANDE: It started with the newspapers, ¿recuerdas?
MARTA FELIZ: What, 'Amá?
MARTA GRANDE: Forgetting your Spanish. Before you went to
    school, we talked Spanish all the time. Pero after school,
    it was Inglés, Inglés, Inglés.
MARTA FELIZ: 'Amá, that's not true.
MARTA GRANDE: Pos, sí. Tenías seis años. Only six years old
    and you came home and made circles—¿asina?—all over
    the front page. ¿Recuerdas? (MARTA FELIZ *transforms*
    into a girl of six.)
MARTA FELIZ: At school I speak English all the time now, 'Amá.
    I'm getting real good at it. I can read it, too. Let me
    show you. Look, 'Amá, I found every "the" on this page.
    (*Spelling.*) T - H - E. It's a very important word, 'Amá,
    because the gringos, they use it all the time. I'll teach you
    English, 'Amá.
MARTA GRANDE: And I'll teach you Spanish. Comenzamos. La
    silla.
MARTA FELIZ: "The" chair.
MARTA GRANDE: El retrato.
MARTA FELIZ: "The" picture on the wall.
MARTA GRANDE: El libro.
MARTA FELIZ: "The" book.
MARTA GRANDE: ¿Y ésto? El periódico.

MARTA FELIZ: "The" newspaper! Pretty good, huh? ¿'Amá? I know English pretty good.
MARTA GRANDE: Y ahora tú. En español.
MARTA FELIZ: No. I don't want to.
MARTA GRANDE: Mejor los dos idiomas, m'ija. Two languages.
MARTA FELIZ: No. I want English. They make fun of me.
MARTA GRANDE: Con español. ¡Dos!
MARTA FELIZ: No.
MARTA GRANDE: ¡Sí!
MARTA FELIZ: No!
MARTA GRANDE: Two!
MARTA FELIZ: No! Why do you speak Spanish all the time?
MARTA GRANDE: ¿Qué?
MARTA FELIZ: Why don't you speak English? Like everybody else?
MARTA GRANDE: I understand todo. All the English.
MARTA FELIZ: But you don't speak it. I SAID I DON'T WANT TO BE LIKE YOU, 'Amá.
MARTA GRANDE: ¿Qué dices, m'ija?
MARTA FELIZ: (*To audience.*) That day, my grandmother was mean to me, the only time in her life.
MARTA GRANDE: Somos gente especial, Marta Feliz. We are special people. We speak two languages. Two! ¡Dos! And as long as you live in this house, don't you ever forget it! (*Exits.*)
FLORINDA: ¡Malcriada!
MARTA FELIZ: But nobody was meaner than Florinda. (FLO-RINDA *enters, a large rosary around her waist, a large ornate scapular around her neck, and a large malicious-looking crucifix in her hands.*)

.... SCENE SEVEN ....

Florinda / Florinda

FLORINDA: Marta Feliz?
MARTA FELIZ: ¿Tía?
FLORINDA: ¿Ya comiste?
MARTA FELIZ: Yes. I ate some tortillas. I'm not hungry.
FLORINDA: ¿Y te bañaste?
MARTA FELIZ: Yes. Yesterday. I took a bath yesterday.
FLORINDA: ¿Pero hoy?

MARTA FELIZ: No. Not today.

FLORINDA: ¿Te bañaste hoy?

MARTA FELIZ: No. Yesterday. I took a bath yesterday.

FLORINDA: Your ears? Did you wash your ears?

MARTA FELIZ: Yes. Tía ...

FLORINDA: Your pants. Did you change your pants?

MARTA FELIZ: Yes. Tía ...

FLORINDA: But down there? Did you clean down there?

MARTA FELIZ: I washed my ears. I washed myself. I changed my underwear. I cleaned everywhere. I did everything.

FLORINDA: ¡Sinvergüenza!

MARTA FELIZ: I'm clean, tía.

FLORINDA: We are all dirty filthy creatures until we are washed in the blood of the lamb.

MARTA FELIZ: No!

FLORINDA: The one true God.

MARTA FELIZ: No!

FLORINDA: ¡Malcriada! ¡Necesitas un palazo!

MARTA FELIZ: You're not my mother! I don't owe you anything! (FLORINDA *reveals a large statue of the Virgin Mary. A church choir rises.*)

FLORINDA: She is your mother. She is a virgin. Her son died. And we must suffer. You hear me? Suffer! We are born to suffer! We live to suffer! It is our one true joy! (*Church choir bumps off.* FLORINDA *freezes as lights dim on her.*)

MARTA FELIZ: (*To audience.*) Poor Florinda. For her, crisis became a religion. When I think of her now, I always see her far away. And alone. (MARTA GRANDE *enters, fanning herself. It is a sultry, South Texas night.*)

MARTA GRANDE: ¡Ay, Marta Feliz!

MARTA FELIZ: When I think of my grandmother I'm always next to her. So close we can touch. (*Night sounds and a full moon rises.*)

MARTA GRANDE: ¡Qué calor!

MARTA FELIZ: (*To audience.*) I can see her skirt, her neck, her eyes, the cuts on her hands. I can recall the feel of her dress and the smell of her skin. She smells like chicken feathers, chicken feed and soap.

MARTA GRANDE: Mira la luna, Marta Feliz.

MARTA FELIZ: Every night she'd water her plants and then we'd sit on the porch and she would tell me stories.

.... SCENE EIGHT ....

El cuento de la luna / The Moon Story

MARTA GRANDE: Do you know the story of the moon, m'ija?
MARTA FELIZ: (*To audience.*) She'd wear a print dress which she
   made herself. The collar was always unfinished and the
   skirt was never hemmed. She'd wear cheap tennis shoes
   from the five-and-dime with no socks and she had green
   grass stains on her dress from gardening.
MARTA GRANDE: You see that circle around the moon, m'ija?
   It means rain. The bigger the circle, the more rain. The
   smaller the circle, the less rain.
MARTA FELIZ: The smell of comino was always on her fingers
   and in her hair. Cumin. Comino. For a while I forgot the
   Spanish name, but I never forgot the smell. And it was
   always hers.
MARTA GRANDE: Marta Feliz?
MARTA FELIZ: ¿'Amá?
MARTA GRANDE: Ven aquí. Do you know what the moon is,
   m'ija?
MARTA FELIZ: (MARTA FELIZ *transforms into a girl of ten.*) At
   school they told me the moon is a big cheese, 'Amá.
MARTA GRANDE: (*Unbelieving.*) ¿De veras? ¿Un queso? ¡Vál-
   game Dios!
MARTA FELIZ: Some people think the moon is the face of an
   unhappy man, the Man in the Moon.
MARTA GRANDE: ¿Así dicen los gringos?
MARTA FELIZ: Pos, sí. Some of the gringos think so.
MARTA GRANDE: Pos, la luna es otra cosa.
MARTA FELIZ: (MARTA FELIZ *transforms back into an adult.*)
   The moon, my grandmother told me, was really a window.
MARTA GRANDE: La ventana de Dios.
MARTA FELIZ: God's window. I remember the story perfectly.
   In Spanish and in English.
MARTA GRANDE and MARTA FELIZ: (*Simultaneously.*)

Y Dios abre la ventana.	And God opens the window.
Por parte del mes,	For part of the month,
la ventana esta cerrada.	the window is closed.
Pero por otra parte,	But for another part,
la ventana está bien	the window is wide
abierta.	open.

MARTA GRANDE: Y Dios siempre esta allí, viéndonos.

MARTA FELIZ: And God is always there, watching us.

MARTA GRANDE: When the moon is out, Marta Feliz, we're never alone.

MARTA FELIZ: One time I asked her about God, if she thought he really existed.

MARTA GRANDE: Pos, m'ija ...

MARTA FELIZ: Yes, 'Amá?

MARTA GRANDE: You see what you want to see. If you want God, you see God. If you want cheese, you see cheese. ¿Qué no? (*Lights fade on* MARTA GRANDE.)

MARTA FELIZ: (*To audience.*) Always practical. She was always so practical. And nothing about her was more practical than her chickens. (*A rosy dawn rises.*) Every morning, before dawn, we would feed them and collect the eggs laid overnight.

MARTA GRANDE: Pshst! Pshst! Pshst! Pshst! Pshst! (*Pause.*) Pshst! Pshst! Pshst! Pshst! Pshst! (*A rooster crows.*)

MARTA FELIZ: Some of our best times together were in the chicken yard. Maybe because, in the dark, I would tell her everything. (*Lights rise on* MARTA GRANDE *feeding imaginary chickens from a rusty, old coffee can full of feed.*)

MARTA GRANDE: Pshst! Pshst! Pshst! Pshst! Pshst! (*Chicken sounds rise.* MARTA FELIZ *transforms into a teenager.*)

.... SCENE NINE ....

Gallinas y la independencia / Chickens and Independence

MARTA FELIZ: 'Amá, I think I'm in love.

MARTA GRANDE: ¿De veras? Pshst! Pshst! Pshst! Pshst! Pshst!

MARTA FELIZ: Do you remember Michael McKay, the boy I loved from first to fourth grade?

MARTA GRANDE: No. Pshst! Pshst! Pshst! Pshst! Pshst!

MARTA FELIZ: Remember I told you he plays the church organ? Remember I told you he plays boogie woogies at night after the priests have gone to sleep?

MARTA GRANDE: No. Pshst! Pshst! Pshst! Pshst! Pshst!

MARTA FELIZ: Well, do you remember I told you he had decided to become a priest himself?

MARTA GRANDE: ((*Not pleased.*) ¿De veras? No. Pshst! Pshst! Pshst! Pshst! Pshst!

MARTA FELIZ: Well, now he has sideburns and he's decided not to become a priest. 'Amá, he's getting cuter everyday and by the time we graduate, he'll be irresistible!

MARTA GRANDE: ¿De veras? Pshst! Pshst! Pshst! Pshst! Pshst!

MARTA FELIZ: And graduation is only a year and a half away. There's only one problem.

MARTA GRANDE: Pshst! Pshst! Pshst! Pshst! Pshst!

MARTA FELIZ: He has asthma.

MARTA GRANDE: ¿Asmático? ¿Y gringo?

MARTA FELIZ: He's Irish, he can't help it.

MARTA GRANDE: Déjelo, m'ijita.

MARTA FELIZ: I can't drop him because of asthma.

MARTA GRANDE: Pshst! Pshst! Pshst! Pshst! Pshst!

MARTA FELIZ: And besides, I think I can get him to think of me now and to love me, and to marry me, and to take care of me.

MARTA GRANDE: ¿Y tu job?

MARTA FELIZ: 'Amá, when I'm married, I won't need a job.

MARTA GRANDE: ¿De veras? Pos, then, m'ijita, you better have some chickens.

MARTA FELIZ: 'Amá, Michael and I are not going to have chickens in our condominium.

MARTA GRANDE: (*Skeptical.*) ¿De veras?

MARTA FELIZ: Of course not. He's going to work in an office and give me money.

MARTA GRANDE: (*More skeptical.*) ¿De veras? Without a job, m'ija, a woman needs chickens. Pshst! Pshst! Pshst! Pshst! Pshst!

MARTA FELIZ: (*To audience.*) She always told me life was a battle. And for her, I guess it was. She was, in a way, like a general in the field. Kind of like a female Pancho Villa. With an army. An army of chickens.

MARTA GRANDE: Pshst! Pshst! Pshst! Pshst! Pshst!

MARTA FELIZ: Her entire theory of life, actually, revolved around chickens.

MARTA GRANDE: If you want to work with the men, m'ija, do it. If you want to stay home with your kids, do it. But whatever you do, you need chickens. Because with chickens, you always have something to sell. From hens you get eggs. From eggs you get chickens. Sell the eggs, and when the chickens get old, sell the pinche chickens.

MARTA FELIZ: Keep a rolling account, she used to say.

MARTA GRANDE: You buy. You sell. And never tell anyone how much money you have.

MARTA FELIZ: How American can you get?

MARTA GRANDE: Pshst! Pshst! Pshst! Pshst! Pshst!

MARTA FELIZ: One time, I asked her if my grandfather ever knew how much money she made.

MARTA GRANDE: Your 'Apá? ¡Pos, no! I learned a long time ago, m'ija, if your 'Apá doesn't know how much money I makc, I never have to tell him how much money I spend. (*Exits.*)

MARTA FELIZ: My grandmother, a ranch girl from Nuevo León, Mexico, independently discovered laissez-faire economics and state-of-the-art feminism all by herself. When I was older, I learned her other major theory of life. The "Fifty-Fifty" between the sexes. It was so important to her, I think it was her religion. (*Lights rise on* MARTA GRANDE *and* FLORINDA. *They are each sitting on a new matching couch and chair.*)

.... SCENE TEN ....

Los hombres y el dinero / Men and Money

MARTA GRANDE: You like my new couch and chair?

FLORINDA: No. You spent too much money.

MARTA GRANDE: Marta Feliz will like them.

MARTA FELIZ: (*Now a young woman in her early twenties.*) 'Amá, a new couch. And a matching chair. How'd you swing it?

FLORINDA: She blew your grandfather's insurance money. From that wreck he was in last year, ¿recuerdas?

MARTE GRANDE: Cinco mil dólares nos dieron.

MARTA FELIZ: You got five thousand for that truck?

MARTA GRANDE: It was a new truck, m'ija.

FLORINDA: Your grandfather blew out the transmission driving twenty miles an hour in first gear for the first three thousand miles, pero the insurance company never found out because he wrecked the whole truck before he wrecked the transmission.

MARTA GRANDE: He drives like a snail now. Pero it's okay because everybody can see him coming for a real long time.

MARTA FELIZ: So you spent the insurance money on a new living room?

MARTA GRANDE: Fifty-fifty, m'ija.

FLORINDA: Your 'Apá bought a new pickup ...

MARTA GRANDE: Que lo va a chingar ...

FLORINDA: ¡Ay, Marta! ¡No hables así!

MARTA GRANDE: Y tú, ¿qué sabes?

FLORINDA: Y tú, señora, ¿qué sabes?

MARTA GRANDE: He took his half and "blew it." And I took my half and "blew it."

MARTA FELIZ: Where did you two learn how to say "blew it"?

MARTA GRANDE and FLORINDA: (*Simultaneously.*) Pues— televisión.

FLORINDA: And you?

MARTA FELIZ: Me?

MARTA GRANDE: When?

MARTA FELIZ: What? (*Beat. To audience.*) Eventually, I did get married. But even with my grandmother as a perfect example of womanhood, I still managed to make a whole lot of mistakes. On the one hand, you could say I was lucky, because I was blessed with a lot of choices. But on the other hand, you could say I was unlucky, because I chose them all. And my first mistake was Rodney. (*Lights rise on the couch and chair.*)

.... SCENE ELEVEN ....

Familia, segunda parte / Family, Part Two

MARTA FELIZ: (*With an infant in her arms.*) ¿'Amá? ¿Tía? Rodney and I eloped.

MARTA GRANDE: Rodney? ¿Qué clase de nombre es Rodney?

MARTA FELIZ: It's just a regular name, 'Amá.

FLORINDA: RODNEY!

MARTA FELIZ: And this is Maury, our son. I know this is all very sudden ...

MARTA GRANDE: Maury?
FLORINDA: ¿Qué clase de nombre es Maury?
MARTA GRANDE: MAURY!
MARTA FELIZ: Irish? Jewish? American?
MARTA GRANDE: And how old is este Rodney?
MARTA FELIZ: Rod? He's twenty.
FLORINDA: Rod? ¿Qué clase de nombre es Rod?
MARTA GRANDE: Pos, m'ija, if Rodney is twenty, he has thirty
  years left. After that, you can forget it.
MARTA FELIZ: Forget what, 'Amá?
MARTA GRANDE: Everything. After fifty, m'ija, men aren't good
  for anything. (*Winking.*) ¿Sabes?
FLORINDA: (*Disgusted.*) ¡Dios mío! (*Exits.*)
MARTA FELIZ: (*To audience.*) She meant sex, of course. Accord-
  ing to her, I had thirty good years to log in with Rodney.
  But the marriage didn't last half that long.
MARTA GRANDE: ¡Ay, mi!
MARTA FELIZ: More crisis. But behind my grandmother's funny
  words that day was a deep pain as long as her marriage
  and as constant as the cancer that my grandfather brought
  back from the war. (*Lights rise on* JUAN.)
JUAN: The Germans practiced gas warfare, 'manito. In the
  trenches in France, 'manito. And I breathed it in. All
  the guys breathed it in.
MARTA GRANDE: Your 'Apá, Marta Feliz, got the cancer when
  you came to live with us. After fifty, m'ija, los pobres
  hombres aren't good for anything.
MARTA FELIZ: That's what she was really telling me. (*Beat.*)
  Soon after Maury was born, Rodney left. And my grandfather died.
MARTA GRANDE: Hijo de mi vida, se acabó.

.... SCENE TWELVE ....

El regalo de la viuda / The Widow's Gift

MARTA FELIZ: (*To audience.*) My grandmother wore a navy blue
  polka dot dress to the funeral.
MARTA GRANDE: I never liked black.
MARTA FELIZ: And afterwards we came home.
MARTA GRANDE: Marta Feliz?

MARTA FELIZ: ¿'Amá? (MARTA GRANDE *taking a small object out of her pocket.*) Para tí.
MARTA FELIZ: Your wedding ring, 'Amá?
MARTA GRANDE: Your 'Apá bought it for me in Méjico.
MARTA FELIZ: Pink gold. It's beautiful, 'Amá.
MARTA GRANDE: It's yours now, m'ija. I don't need it any more.
MARTA FELIZ: Are you sure?   .
MARTA GRANDE: ¡Pos, sí!
MARTA FELIZ: Gracias, 'Amá. Gracias. (*Beat. To audience.*) A week later, she sold my grandfather's pickup, rearranged the furniture and had all the walls painted a pale pink.
MARTA GRANDE: I always liked pink.
MARTA FELIZ: And she began all over again. A single woman of seventy-eight. I was single, too. So, Maury and I moved in.
FLORINDA: Hmph!
MARTA FELIZ: But when I tried to put Rodney's picture in the living room, my grandmother moved it.
MARTA GRANDE: I'm moving Rodney's picture, m'ija. I'm putting it in the hallway.
MARTA FELIZ: If you say so, 'Amá.
MARTA GRANDE: ¡Pos, sí! And if you get married again, m'ija, and the next marriage doesn't work out, I'm putting your next husband in the hallway, y pobre Rodney will be in the bathroom.
MARTA FELIZ: And if I get married a third time, 'Amá?
FLORINDA: Like your mother?
MARTA FELIZ and MARTA GRANDE: (*Simultaneously.*) Yes! ¡Igual!
MARTA GRANDE: Pues, after three marriages, mi'ja, I'll have to put el pobre Rodney in the backyard with my chickens. (*Pause.*) Unless you want him? Florinda?
FLORINDA: ¡Sinvergüenzas! Marriage is a holy sacrament, the work of God, pero divorce is perdition, the work of the devil. You are both mutilating the blessed sacrament of marriage and He will punish both of you for your sins. (*Waving the crucifix.*) ¿Lo veían? Do you see Him? How he suffered! Do you see Him?
MARTA FELIZ: (*To audience.*) We were happy.
MARTA GRANDE: Menos Florinda.
MARTA FELIZ: Until my grandmother got sick.
MARTA GRANDE: ¡Ay, Florinda! My stomach hurts.

MARTA FELIZ: And her illness was the beginning of the end. Because as my grandmother got weaker and weaker, day by day ...
MARTA GRANDE: ¡Dios mío! What did I eat?
MARTA FELIZ: Florinda got stronger. And stronger.

.... SCENE THIRTEEN ....

Dios y la enfermedad / God and Illness

MARTA GRANDE: (*Taking a bottle of Pepto Bismol from her pocket, opening it and drinking some of the medicine direct from the bottle.*) ¡Ay! Florinda, did I eat something bad? Did I sleep on the wrong side of the bed?
FLORINDA: You lost God. That's what you did.
MARTA GRANDE: ¡Pos, no, Florinda!
FLORINDA: ¡Pos, sí, Marta! You disgraced him with your bad words. Your maldiciones.
MARTA GRANDE: ¿Y por eso me chingo?
FLORINDA: ¡Válgame Dios!
MARTA GRANDE: I need to go to Mercy Hospital, Florinda.
FLORINDA: You have to go to the clinic now, Marta.
MARTA GRANDE: No, Florinda. I want to go to the hospital.
FLORINDA: The hospital is gone, Marta. Ahora they call it the health clinic.
MARTA GRANDE: Juan didn't die at the health clinic!
FLORINDA: ¡Se acabó!
MARTA GRANDE: Okay!
FLORINDA: ¿Sabes?
MARTA GRANDE: ¡Bueno!
FLORINDA: ¡Se acabó! ¡No hay más!
MARTA GRANDE: Okay, okay! I'll go to the pinche clinic.
FLORINDA: Bueno.
MARTA GRANDE: Pero, si me muero, Florinda ... (*Revealing a floral print dress made of light material.*) ... if I die, bury me in this dress. (*Pause.*) You like it?
FLORINDA: That is a dancing dress, Marta.
MARTA GRANDE: I made it after Juan died ... you like it? I like it.
FLORINDA: You haven't even hemmed it. And the top is too low. Te van a ver tus chi chis aplastadas. And where are the shoes?

MARTA GRANDE: Florinda, I don't need shoes.

FLORINDA: You have to have shoes when you die, Marta.

MARTA GRANDE: Florinda, the casket is half closed. ¿Tú sabes? All they see is your face and your chest. You don't need shoes when you die, Florinda.

FLORINDA: ¡Sinvergüenza!

MARTA GRANDE: You don't even need panties.

FLORINDA: ¡Desgraciada!

MARTA GRANDE: Nobody sees them except the pinche undertaker who dresses you. And I bet most of the time they steal the shoes and give them to their viejas.

FLORINDA: You are going to hell with no panties and no shoes?

MARTA GRANDE: Why not? That's how He made me!

FLORINDA: Y tú ¿qué sabes?

MARTA GRANDE: Y tú, ¿qué sabes?

FLORINDA: Y tú, señora, ¿qué sabes?

MARTA FELIZ: (*To audience.*) And so it went. But Florinda and my grandmother had one last thing to negotiate.

FLORINDA: Pos. God does not want you to die, Marta.

MARTA GRANDE: Pos, we all have to die, Florinda.

FLORINDA: ¡Claro!

MARTA GRANDE: ¡Pos, sí!

FLORINDA: Pos ... if the good Lord takes you, Marta ... if He takes you ... this house is mine. (*Pause.*) ¿Que no?

MARTA GRANDE: No, Florinda. I'm leaving it to Marta Feliz. I put it in my will.

FLORINDA: You made a will?

MARTA GRANDE: Pos, sí.

FLORINDA: American whore!

MARTA GRANDE: Ni modo. I made a will ... (*Gathering the floral dress.*) And now ... I'll go to the clinic. On the bus.

FLORINDA: Do you have the money?

MARTA GRANDE: For the bus? I always have money for the pinche bus. (*Pause.*) Bueno. Me voy. Que hagan lo que quieran. (*Exits.*)

MARTA FELIZ: When Maury and I came home that day, my grandmother was gone.

FLORINDA: The only thing I want, Marta Feliz, is this house. For me and my work with the church.

MARTA FELIZ: But, tía, I have a child.

FLORINDA: A bastard americano! He will never know who he is, just like you don't know who you are. Is he Jew? Irish? Mexican? Chicano?

MARTA FELIZ: Tía, I still need this house.
FLORINDA: Your 'Amá made me leave Méjico. I have had nothing here in Texas. Nothing but gringos, marijuanos, vendidos y maricones, that's all this country produces.
MARTA FELIZ: Tía, where is my 'Amá?
FLORINDA: You marry gringos and have children with no God.
MARTA FELIZ: Tía, I've only been married once. Where is my 'Amá?
FLORINDA: You carry sin. You give birth to sin. That's the only thing this pinche country is good for. Sin and confusion.
MARTA FELIZ: Tía Florinda!
FLORINDA: What about your race? What about your blood?
MARTA FELIZ: ¡Por favor! Where is my 'Amá?
FLORINDA: At the clinic. Dying. (*Lights rise on* MARTA GRANDE *barefoot and wearing her dancing dress.*)
MARTA FELIZ: (*To audience.*) On the way to the clinic I saw my 'Amá.
MARTA GRANDE: ¡M'ija! It's so good to see you! Come with me right now. I need you at the novena.
MARTA FELIZ: What novena? 'Amá, you don't go to church.
MARTA GRANDE: But this is my novena. The pinche minister wants to hurry up and stick me in the ground.
MARTA FELIZ: But, 'Amá, you're not dead.
MARTA GRANDE: Pos, sí, m'ija. I am. The pinche minister wants to run home and see the whores on "Dallas."
MARTA FELIZ: But, 'Amá, Maury needs you.
MARTA GRANDE: M'ija, I can't be raising any more kids. I'm dead.
MARTA FELIZ: No, you're not.
MARTA GRANDE: Pos, m'ija, don't contradict me.
MARTA FELIZ: But tía Florinda says you're at the clinic.
MARTA GRANDE: Before, yes, but now?
MARTA FELIZ: (*To audience.*) When I got to the clinic, she had just died. I slipped into her room when nobody was watching. She was lying on her side, her face turned away from the machines and the IV's. When I touched her, she was still warm. (*Cross fade to Anglo Texan doctor.*)
DOCTOR: (*Texan accent.*) I opened her up and closed her up again. I didn't like what I saw.
MARTA FELIZ: My mother is a nurse, doctor. If it was cancer ...
DOCTOR It was dirty in there. I didn't like what I saw.
MARTA FELIZ: But what is the diagnosis, doctor?
DOCTOR: I opened her up and closed her up again.

MARTA FELIZ: But doctor, that's not a diagnosis ...
DOCTOR: Don't you understand English, Mizzz. Gonzaleeez? I
   didn't like what I saw. Do you understand? I didn't like
   what I saw. (*"Marta Chica's Theme" rises.*)

.... SCENE FOURTEEN ....

El baile y la muerte / Dancing And Death

MARTA GRANDE: (*Cross fade to* MARTA GRANDE *in her floral
   dress and* JUAN *in his soldier's uniform, dancing.*) Marta
   Feliz! Your mother plays the piano like an angel.
JUAN: For you Marta, anything!
MARTA GRANDE: Juan said yes, he would marry me. Yes, he
   would dance with me. Yes, he would convert for me. He
   was so nice to the pinche Baptist minister in the river. I
   stood behind the minister and I whispered to Juan, "Say
   yes to him, pero después, take me dancing." We had six
   children. And you, Marta Feliz. But he never took me
   dancing. But now, m'ija, I can dance.

.... SCENE FIFTEEN ....

Transfiguración / Transfiguration

MARTA FELIZ: (*To audience.*) She had an obstruction in her lower
   intestine. It knotted up on her and then burst. Within
   hours, her kidneys failed and she started bloating. Her
   heart began to fibrillate and twice the doctors brought her
   back.
MARTA GRANDE: (*Dancing.*) ¿M'ija? Believe this! (*Cross fade
   to* DOCTOR *making notes in a medical report.*)
MARTA FELIZ: Looking at her, I remembered what the doctor had
   said. And more than ever I wanted to prove him wrong. I
   lifted the sheet, expecting to be horrified by fresh cuts and
   crude stitching from all her emergency heart and stomach
   operations. I expected to be revolted by the sight of an
   eighty-four year old with sagging tits, bloated from kidney
   failure. Maybe she was bruised. Maybe she was cut up.
   But what I saw was a small female body, legs tucked up
   neatly against her side, her breasts full, and her stomach
   smooth with no wrinkles at all. What surprised me most

were her beautiful thighs. (*Lights fade on* DOCTOR.) She
had transfigured all the doctor's disgust and fear. I was
vindicated but she, she was triumphant.
MARTA GRANDE: (*Stops dancing.*) ¿M'ija?
MARTA FELIZ: ¿'Amá?
MARTA GRANDE: Florinda is going to fight you for the house.
She's going to curse you with spells y voodoo y no sé qué.
Pobre Florinda. I don't know what happened to her. She
came to this country and went crazy. Maybe I should have
taken Flora, my other little sister, with me instead.
MARTA FELIZ: (*To audience.*) I laid the sheet over her. And
left. (*Lights rise on* FLORINDA *placing a large statue of
the Virgin Mary prominently in the living room.*) When
Maury was two, my mother died. She'd been married four
times and had had four children: me, Paulina, Juanita
and Joe. She did work hard all her life and out-lived all
of her husbands, even the younger ones. Then, widowed
for the last time, she bought a house. The same one she
had bought once before, twenty years earlier. And in that
house she died quietly from a disease that none of her
doctors could diagnose. Her life, to the end, filled with
mystery and crisis. My grandmother was buried in the
same plot as my grandfather. And the day after the funeral, Florinda went to see the lawyer. I tried to stay in
my grandmother's house but it didn't turn out to be easy.
And everything my grandmother had told me, as always,
came true. (*Lights fade to black.*)

ACT TWO

.... PROLOGUE ....

Four years later. Lights rise on MARTA FELIZ.

MARTA FELIZ: (*To audience.*) After my grandmother died, Maury
and I stayed in the house. And I did fight. Just like a Mexican. I began to see the house, small as it was, as my own
private Alamo. But it was becoming, I have to admit, a

peculiar kind of Alamo. (*Lights rise on living room. Children's toys are scattered here and there and religious objects abound—a statue of the Virgin Mary, a poster of the Pope waving from his gold Pope mobile, a high school-type Pope pennant and a large Pope button. The effect should be both touching and comical.*) And even though my grandmother had died, she didn't really go away. (MARTA GRANDE, *in her funeral dress, enters and sits by the piano.*) I saw her often and she kept telling me things. Even though it usually wasn't what I wanted to hear.

MARTA GRANDE: Things are not good, m'ija. Look at this pinche house. I don't even recognize it anymore. (FLORINDA *enters, surveying everything, clearly in her domain.*)

MARTA FELIZ: (*Continues.*) To be honest, my grandmother's visits, as I started calling them, seemed pretty normal. Compared to my Aunt Florinda anyway, who continued to spend most of her time looking for the one true God. One day, she posted a sign on our front door. (*A sign flies in.*)

ESTE HOGAR ES CATÓLICO—NO NECESITAMOS PROPAGANDA DE OTRAS RELIGIONES	THIS IS A CATHOLIC HOME—WE DO NOT NEED PROPAGANDA FROM OTHER RELIGIONS

MARTA FELIZ: (*Continues.*) It didn't keep anybody away. Jehovah Witnesses, Mormons, Baptists, Methodists, they all came knocking. Even Catholics knocked. Just to make sure. (*A loud knock is heard.*) And, one day, a priest came. (*Exits.* FATHER ERNESTO *enters.*)

FLORINDA: And so, Father Ernesto, I have been trying to turn this house into a home for the poor ...

.... SCENE ONE ....

Bendiciendo la casa / Blessing the House

FATHER ERNESTO: Blessed are the Poor.
FLORINDA: A home for those more unfortunate than us ...
FATHER ERNESTO: The Blessed Homeless.

FLORINDA: An honest house of God devoted to those forgotten by all of us.

FATHER ERNESTO: The Forgotten Blessed Ones.

FLORINDA: To those beneath us ...

FATHER ERNESTO: The Blessed Miserable.

FLORINDA: Who need refuge. In a home, with security.

FATHER ERNESTO: And guidance, Doña Florinda. Refuge, security and guidance.

FLORINDA: We think exactly alike, Father!

FATHER ERNESTO: Pos ...

FLORINDA: And in order to do these things, I have applied for grants.

FATHER ERNESTO: ¿De veras?

FLORINDA: City grants, county grants, neighborhood grants. I even applied for federal grants.

FATHER ERNESTO: Doña Florinda, such optimism!

FLORINDA: On the spiritual side, I have applied for a dispensation from our Bishop to lead a religious home.

FATHER ERNESTO: ¡Qué maravilloso!

MARTA GRANDE: Pos, that's what you think.

FLORINDA: And I also sent away for a framed blessing from the Pope. Even though it cost me a lot of money.

FATHER ERNESTO: Pos ...

FLORINDA: But I still don't have the rights to this pinche house, because the pinche lawyer ... (MARTA FELIZ *enters.*)

MARTA FELIZ: (*To offstage.*) Maury? You watch your little brother. J.J.? Listen boys, stay in the backyard or else you'll have to stay in the house with your tía Florinda. (*Pause.*) Of course, you can stay outside. Oh, tía, I thought you were at church.

FLORINDA: This is Father Ernesto. We are going to bless the house.

FATHER ERNESTO: Mucho gusto. (*A loud crash is heard.*)

MARTA FELIZ: (*Continues.*) Tory? What are you into now? Tory! (*Exits.*)

FLORINDA: My great niece. She has devoted her life recently to making children.

FATHER ERNESTO: She's very nice.

FLORINDA: No, she isn't. She goes out with men she doesn't know, then she marries them and has a baby with them, pero before they get to know each other, they decide they don't like each other.

FATHER ERNESTO: Maybe she is in need of guidance, Doña Florinda.

FLORINDA: Nothing can help her. She has dug her grave. And now she can sit in it.

FATHER ERNESTO: She can lie in it.

FLORINDA: What?

FATHER ERNESTO: The expression is "you dig your grave and you lie in it," Doña Florinda. (*Looking longingly in the direction of* MARTA FELIZ.) Lie in it.

MARTA GRANDE: Ay, 'manita ...

MARTA FELIZ: (*Enters, holding a squeaky toy.*) Squeaky toys. The only things that keep Tory quiet.

FATHER ERNESTO: ¿De veras?

FLORINDA: Father? We can start in the kitchen.

FATHER ERNESTO: Un momento, Doña Florinda. I want to talk with your niece, Mrs. ... ?

MARTA FELIZ: Miss.

FATHER ERNESTO: Miss? But you have so many children!

MARTA FELIZ: They're all legitimate, Father.

FATHER ERNESTO: But so many.

FLORINDA: (*Grabbing* FATHER ERNESTO.) Father?   The kitchen.

FATHER ERNESTO: But, Doña Florinda, your niece has had ...

FLORINDA: (*Pulling him out of the room.*) We will bless the refrigerator first ...

FATHER ERNESTO: Miss! Wait for me! (*They exit.*)

MARTA GRANDE: Marta Feliz?

MARTA FELIZ: ¿'Amá?

MARTA GRANDE: Before you came in, this fulano ... (FATHER ERNESTO *returns.*)

MARTA FELIZ: Father Ernesto!

FATHER ERNESTO: The refrigerator was too dirty.

MARTA FELIZ: Well, with the kids, you know.

FATHER ERNESTO: Yes, of course. (*Beat.*) Your aunt has told me everything about you.

MARTA GRANDE: Everything?

MARTA FELIZ: She has?

FATHER ERNESTO: You were in the Army. ¿Que no?

MARTA FELIZ: Me? No. That was my grandfather. I'm going to junior college.

FATHER ERNESTO: To become a nurse, yes?

MARTA FELIZ: Me? No. That was my mother. She was an R.N.

FATHER ERNESTO: How distinguished!

MARTA FELIZ: I'm just trying to finish my A.A. so I can go for
    a B.A.
FATHER ERNESTO: Pos, congratulations!
MARTA FELIZ: But it's not easy, you know. Not with three kids.
MARTA GRANDE: ¡Híjole! Even I didn't have them that fast.
MARTA FELIZ: ¡'Amá!
FATHER ERNESTO: And how is their father?
MARTA FELIZ: What?
FATHER ERNESTO: The father. Of your children? How is he?
MARTA FELIZ: Oh ... they're fine. They're all doing great. I
    think.
FATHER ERNESTO: They?
MARTA FELIZ: Rodney, Jorge and Mac.
FATHER ERNESTO: THREE fathers?
MARTA FELIZ: Well. Yes. Maury, J.J. and Tory each have their
    own father. I know that's a lot of children, Father ...
FATHER ERNESTO: It's a lot of fathers!
FLORINDA: (*Entering.*) Father?
FATHER ERNESTO: Doña Florinda?
FLORINDA: The refrigerator is ready.
FATHER ERNESTO: But, Doña Florinda, your niece, Miss ...
MARTA FELIZ: Marta Feliz.
FATHER ERNESTO: Marta Feliz. How joyous.
FLORINDA: (*Pulling him out of the room.*) Father?
FATHER ERNESTO: Marta Feliz, wait for me! (*They exit.*)
MARTA GRANDE: ¿M'ija?
MARTA FELIZ: What 'Amá?
MARTA GRANDE: Before you came, this fulano priest ...
FATHER ERNESTO: (*Returning.*) You have been married four
    times?
MARTA FELIZ: Me? No! That was my mother. I've only been
    married three times. Rodney, Jorge and Mac. Remem-
    ber?
FATHER ERNESTO: But isn't that a little ... playful?
MARTA FELIZ: Well, I wouldn't use that word exactly ...
FLORINDA: Father?
FATHER ERNESTO: For heaven's sake, Doña Florinda, the stove
    is too dirty!
FLORINDA: (*Petulant.*) Okay! ¡Bueno! (*Exits.*)
MARTA FELIZ: Father Ernesto, I don't know what my aunt told
    you, but I am a very responsible person.
MARTA GRANDE: You have checks with only your name on
    them.

MARTA FELIZ: Like my mother.
FATHER ERNESTO: Your mother? What about your mother?
MARTA FELIZ: My mother? Oh yes! My mother! I was just
    thinking that I have checks with my name on them. Just
    like my mother ... did.
FATHER ERNESTO: Pues, after three husbands, what is your
    name? I mean, your last name.
MARTA FELIZ: Well, now it's easy.
FATHER ERNESTO: On your checks, I mean.
MARTA FELIZ: Father, I thought about it for a long time ...
FATHER ERNESTO: And?
MARTA FELIZ: And ... I decided to use my favorite name.
FATHER ERNESTO: Which is?
MARTA FELIZ: The name I was born with. Miss Marta Feliz
    González.
FATHER ERNESTO: But, my child, it is the custom after marriage
    ...
MARTA FELIZ: But after EVERY marriage, Father?
FATHER ERNESTO: Well, if you only got married ONCE, like
    you're supposed to ...
MARTA FELIZ: But, Father, after my divorce from Jorge, my sec-
    ond husband, and the birth of J.J., Jorge Junior, my sec-
    ond son, I decided I was never going to change my name
    again. The way I look at it, Father, is you can always take
    the man ...
FATHER ERNESTO: ¡Dios mío!
MARTA FELIZ: But that doesn't mean you have to take his name.
    That's what REALLY complicates things.
FATHER ERNESTO: But, Marta Feliz, it is the custom ...
MARTA FELIZ: Father, just close your eyes and try to imagine.
FATHER ERNESTO: Pos ... for you ... (*Closes his eyes.*)
MARTA FELIZ: I've changed my name TWICE. On everything.
    Social Security, W-2 forms, school loans, employment ...
FATHER ERNESTO: What about the car insurance?
MARTA GRANDE: ¡Ay, the pinche car insurance!
MARTA FELIZ: ¡'Amá!
FATHER ERNESTO: What?
MARTA FELIZ: Yes. Yes. The car insurance. And the IRS, depart-
    ment stores, driver's license. And even my checkbook.
FATHER ERNESTO: (*Opening his eyes.*) That's a lot of work!
MARTA FELIZ: But it's even harder, Father, explaining it to peo-
    ple.
FATHER ERNESTO: Really?

MARTA FELIZ: Father, repeat after me.
FATHER ERNESTO: Bueno.
MARTA FELIZ: I am not González anymore. I am Fernández.
FATHER ERNESTO: I am not González anymore. I am Fernández.
MARTA FELIZ: That was Jorge's name. Again.
FATHER ERNESTO: I am not González anymore. I am Fernández.
MARTA FELIZ: How do you feel?
FATHER ERNESTO: Tired. Dizzy. And a little confused.
MARTA GRANDE: Priests. I never met a smart one.
MARTA FELIZ: Now, close your eyes again. And try to imagine.
FATHER ERNESTO: (*Closing his eyes.*) Bueno.
MARTA FELIZ: It's now one year later. Your marriage is over.
FATHER ERNESTO: Already?
MARTA FELIZ: Sometimes!
FATHER ERNESTO: Really!
MARTA FELIZ: And you're all alone with your kids. And now Father, try to imagine. Would you want to be identified with a man that you have to take to court to get child support payments?
FATHER ERNESTO: Pos, no.
MARTA FELIZ: And so you say to yourself, I won't be Fernández. Not anymore!
FATHER ERNESTO: No way.
MARTA FELIZ: So now, if you're not Fernández anymore, who are you?
FATHER ERNESTO: Pues, González.
MARTA GRANDE. ¡Claro!
FATHER ERNESTO: Of course.
MARTA FELIZ: You see? We agree, Father.
MARTA GRANDE: ¡Híjole!
MARTA FELIZ: After Jorge, I spent weeks changing my name. He just took his credit cards and left.
FATHER ERNESTO: But now, you are married now again, ¿que no?
MARTA FELIZ: Actually, I don't know.
FLORINDA: (*Entering.*) Father?
FATHER ERNESTO: In the name of God, Doña Florinda!
FLORINDA: (*Petulant.*) The stove is ready. (*Pulling him out of the room.*)
FATHER ERNESTO: (*To* MARTA FELIZ.) What do you mean, you don't know? Marta Feliz! Wait for me! (*They exit.*)

MARTA GRANDE: This fulano priest, Marta Feliz ... (*This time*
    FATHER ERNESTO *returns in a split second.*)
MARTA FELIZ: Father Ernesto!
MARTA GRANDE: Never gives up!
FATHER ERNESTO: I just want to know if you are married or
    not married.
MARTA FELIZ: Well, that's not easy to answer.
FATHER ERNESTO: Yes, it is!
MARTA FELIZ: No, it isn't!
FATHER ERNESTO: Where is your husband?
MARTA FELIZ: Which husband?
FATHER ERNESTO: The last one!
MARTA FELIZ: The last one that I married? Or the last one that
    I divorced?
FATHER ERNESTO: The last one!
MARTA FELIZ: The very last one?
FATHER ERNESTO: The last one! The last one that you last
    fornicated with! (*The phone rings.*) ¡Dios mío!

.... SCENE TWO ....

El fin del casamiento / The End of a Marriage

MARTA FELIZ: Hello.
FATHER ERNESTO: You are so confused!
MARTA FELIZ: Mac? How are you? (*To* FATHER ERNESTO.)
    It's my husband. The last one I fornicated with.
MARTA GRANDE: The pinche lawyer.
FATHER ERNESTO: Oh.
MARTA FELIZ: Interlocutory? You had a friend transfer title of
    the house to your name? And you're "doing something"
    with a new woman.
FATHER ERNESTO: ¡Dios mío!
MARTA FELIZ: That was a Hispanic priest, Mac.
FATHER ERNESTO: ¡Chicano, por favor!
MARTA FELIZ: No, we're still in the talking stage.
FATHER ERNESTO: ¡Dios mío! (*Into phone.*) ¿Qué clase de hom-
    bre eres?
MARTA FELIZ: You never have to pay for it?
FATHER ERNESTO: ¡Válgame Dios!
MARTA FELIZ: Well, most of us never sell it, you know. We
    just give it away, over and over and over again. Mac,

my lawyer will call you. (*Hangs up.*) My last husband. Always up to something.

MARTA GRANDE: M'ija, you can't afford a lawyer.

MARTA FELIZ: And I can't afford a lawyer!

FATHER ERNESTO: Pos ... very well, my child. Even though this last husband of yours es un poco "difficult," shall we say, I will pray that this marriage will work.

MARTA GRANDE: Not a smart one.

MARTA FELIZ: It's too late, Father. It's over.

FATHER ERNESTO: Well ... I guess you should know better than anyone.

MARTA FELIZ: Why should I know better than anyone?

FATHER ERNESTO: Pos ... based on all your extensive experience.

MARTA FELIZ: Father, that's the cruelest thing anyone has ever said to me.

FATHER ERNESTO: Ever?

MARTA FELIZ: Yes!

FATHER ERNESTO: Really?

FLORINDA: (*Entering.*) Father?

FATHER ERNESTO: ¡Válgame Dios, Doña Florinda!

FLORINDA: (*Petulant.*) The garaje is ready.

FATHER ERNESTO: You want to bless the garage too?

FLORINDA: Everything!

FATHER ERNESTO: Well ... actually that's good, Doña Florinda. That's very good. Marta, do you want to come?

MARTA FELIZ: Are you kidding? Up until now I didn't even know garages could sin, Father.

MARTA GRANDE: Me neither.

FATHER ERNESTO: ¡Híjole!

FLORINDA: (*Petulant.*) Father!

FATHER ERNESTO: I should never have got out of bed this morning.

FLORINDA: The garage, Father. ¿Por favor?

FATHER ERNESTO: (*Reluctantly following* FLORINDA.) Of course! Marta Feliz?

MARTA FELIZ: Yes, Father?

FATHER ERNESTO: I'll be back.

MARTA FELIZ: Take your time, Father. Take your time. (FA-

THER ERNESTO *and* FLORINDA *exit.*)

.... SCENE THREE ....

Independencia y gallinas, segunda parte / Chickens and Independence, part two.

MARTA GRANDE: Marta Feliz?

MARTA FELIZ: ¿'Amá?

MARTA GRANDE: Este Father Ernesto, I think he's falling in love with you, m'ija.

MARTA FELIZ: Come on, 'Amá!

MARTA GRANDE: Don't laugh, m'ija. It used to happen in Méjico all the time.

MARTA FELIZ: Really?

MARTA GRANDE: De veras. But don't worry. All priests get married. To Mother Church. Or the Virgin Mary. Or the Mother of God. To somebody.

MARTA FELIZ: So you're telling me he's taken, 'Amá?

MARTA GRANDE: Oh yes! Good and taken! Priests aren't good for much, m'ija. You just remember that.

MARTA FELIZ: All right, 'Amá. You know what? Ever since Mac, I don't believe in love anymore. You give them everything, 'Amá. You give it all away for free like a liberated woman, and they still get other ideas.

MARTA GRANDE: That's the way men are, m'ija.

MARTA FELIZ: And you know all that stuff you used to tell me about being independent, and having my own chickens? It doesn't work.

MARTA GRANDE: Pos, m'ija, the chickens have nothing to do with it.

MARTA FELIZ: The problem, 'Amá, is that the more independent you are, the more independent everybody expects you to be. It's not fair, 'Amá.

MARTA GRANDE: Pos, m'ija, if things were fair, nobody would ever have anything to talk about.

MARTA FELIZ: The problem, 'Amá, is that when you're independent, the men don't stick around.

MARTA GRANDE: I know, m'ija. Men come. And they go. And some women do the same thing. It happened during the Revolución. It's nothing new. But you know what I miss now, m'ija? More than anything? My chickens. (*Chicken sounds rise softly.*)

MARTA FELIZ: Pos, 'Amá, they're all gone. Tía Florinda wants to feed the poor, all right. But she wants to do it with grants. That's pretty silly when you think about it, isn't it, 'Amá? (*Chicken sounds fade.*)

MARTA GRANDE: Pos, mi'ja, if you ask me, my crazy sister is not the only crazy one in this house. Look at you. Three kids with no father. Problemas por todos lados. And no chickens. And now even a priest is in love with you. (*Chicken sounds rise faintly.*) I think I hear one.

MARTA FELIZ: 'Amá, you know we don't have any chickens ...

MARTA FELIZ: Just one. I hear one. Pshst! Pshst! Pshst!

MARTA FELIZ: ¿'Amá?

MARTA GRANDE: Nos vemos, m'ija. (*Exits.*)

MARTA FELIZ: (*To audience.*) My grandmother was right, of course. Things weren't so good. And with Father Ernesto around, they didn't promise to get any better.

.... SCENE FOUR ....

Reconciliación / Reconciliation

FATHER ERNESTO: Marta Feliz?

MARTA FELIZ: Yes, Father?

FATHER ERNESTO: I shouldn't have said those things to your last husband.

MARTA FELIZ: Mac? He can take it. But you know, Father, it does take two to tango.

FATHER ERNESTO: ¡Pos sí! And if it doesn't work out, pos, at least you've saved yourself a lot of time by not using his name. ¿Que no?

MARTA FELIZ: That's true, Father.

FATHER ERNESTO: Éste como se llama ... this last one. What is his name?

MARTA FELIZ: Mac.

FATHER ERNESTO: ¿Qué clase de nombre es Mac?

MARTA FELIZ: Irish? Scot? American? But don't worry, Father. Tory will use Mac's name. And Mac, of course, he uses his name all the time.

FATHER ERNESTO: ¡Pos vale! There you go!

MARTA FELIZ: You see? I'm not crazy. I'm not even wild.

FATHER ERNESTO: Still, THREE times, Marta Feliz.

MARTA FELIZ: But not four, Father. Not four.

FATHER ERNESTO: I guess you and your mother are just a little bit "experimental."

MARTA FELIZ: Maybe. But all my experiments have kind of failed, Father. Three kids under the age of six. That's not exactly a great record.

FATHER ERNESTO: Marta Feliz, call me Ernie.

MARTA FELIZ: Ernie? Like Father Ernie?

FATHER ERNESTO: No. Just Ernie.

MARTA FELIZ: But Father ...

FLORINDA'S VOICE: Padre nuestro que estás en el cielo, santificado sea tu nombre, venga a nosotros tu reino ...

MARTA FELIZ: My aunt.

FATHER ERNESTO: Praying.

FLORINDA'S VOICE: En la tierra como en el cielo, perdona nuestras ofensas, como nosotros perdonamos ...

FATHER ERNESTO: Marta Feliz ...

MARTA FELIZ: Father, can you find a job for my aunt in the parish?

FATHER ERNESTO: A job? I don't know, Marta Feliz. We are a poor parish.

MARTA FELIZ: Please, Father. You see it's very hard here ... (*Lights rise on* FLORINDA.)

.... SCENE FIVE ....

Avaricia / Avarice

FLORINDA: Puta. Your grandmother is laughing at you.

MARTA FELIZ: Please, tía.

FLORINDA: She took me from Méjico and brought me here. This is my house.

MARTA FELIZ: But tía, I have three kids now.

FLORINDA: Americanos.

MARTA FELIZ: And my 'Amá gave me this house.

FLORINDA: Yes. But the papers were never found.

MARTA FELIZ: Tía, I'm in debt up to my ears and I'm trying to stay in school, and I have no job security.

FLORINDA: I need this house! For my work with the poor.

MARTA FELIZ: But tía, I am the poor.

FLORINDA: You're supposed to take care of me! ¡Como familia! I have no one! I am alone. Abandoned. Have mercy on me! Have mercy on me!

MARTA FELIZ: Tía, please don't do this. (*A cross flies in.*)

FLORINDA: (*Watching cross intently.*) This is how God wants us to be. Bleeding, united with those who suffer ...

MARTA FELIZ: (*To* FATHER ERNESTO.) You see? She scares me.

FLORINDA: I am the chosen one. I will carry the cross for my Jesus. (*Embracing cross as it reaches her.*) For you, my Lord, I have suffered indignities. Like you, I was brought here. And like you, I bleed. On the cross. I am on the cross.

MARTA FELIZ: I talk to her, but she doesn't listen.

FLORINDA: Crucify me! Choose me! (*Secretly revealing a voodoo doll, with a marked resemblance to* MARTA FELIZ.) For you, my Lord, I have suffered indignities. For you, I suffer. With you, I suffer. Together, we suffer. And bleed. (*Black out on* FLORINDA.)

MARTA FELIZ: So you see, Father Ernesto, I need your help.

FATHER ERNESTO: She is devout.

MARTA FELIZ: Just a little job where she can feel like a saint. You know, humble but important?

FATHER ERNESTO: I understand, Marta Feliz. I'll speak to the proper authorities.

MARTA FELIZ: Father, I don't want the police ...

FATHER ERNESTO: The police? Of course, not! I'm talking about the church. We are much bigger than the police, Marta Feliz. (*Exits.*)

MARTA FELIZ: (*To audience.*) And, in this innocent way, I began fighting for my very soul. But, surprisingly, not with my aunt. (*Lights rise on* MARTA GRANDE.)

MARTA GRANDE: Marta Feliz, here comes the priest!

.... SCENE SIX ....

Guerrillero del alma / Soul Fighter

Lights rise on MARTA FELIZ *and* FATHER ERNESTO.

FATHER ERNESTO: Knowledge of self and belief in God, of course, are the only ways to salvation, Marta Feliz.

MARTA FELIZ: But Father, you do know that I wasn't raised a
    Catholic?
FATHER ERNESTO: The one thing your aunt forgot to mention.
MARTA FELIZ: My aunt is actually the first Catholic we've ever
    had in our family. You see my grandmother, who raised
    me, first she was a Methodist in Mexico, and then she
    came here, to Texas, as a Baptist. And then she went
    back and forth all her life ...
MARTA GRANDE: Not ALL my life!
MARTA FELIZ: But she was never, ever a Catholic.
FATHER ERNESTO: She never even tried it?
MARTA GRANDE: Are you kidding?
MARTA FELIZ: She always told me Catholics all over the world
    were underdeveloped, impoverished, disease-ridden, and
    undereducated. Second-class citizens, she called them ...
MARTA GRANDE: Asina.
MARTA FELIZ: In third-world conditions. Not a promising com-
    bination, she always used to say.
FATHER ERNESTO: Pos ...
MARTA FELIZ: So you see, Father, while I appreciate your sug-
    gestion, I could never be a REAL Catholic. So confessing
    to you is out of the question.
FATHER ERNESTO: But Marta Feliz, maybe there is a more mod-
    ern way to look at the confessional.
MARTA FELIZ: Like what, Father?
FATHER ERNESTO: The confessional, you see, more than any-
    thing else, sets us Catholics apart. Look upon it as a mys-
    tical exchange. Between yourself and God.
MARTA FELIZ: But Father, you told me that you would be there
    too. Pretending to be God.
FATHER ERNESTO: Marta Feliz! It is simply a doctrine of the
    church!
MARTA FELIZ: Okay! So, can I pretend too? Can I be God?
FATHER ERNESTO: No!
MARTA FELIZ: No?
FATHER ERNESTO: Not exactly. Marta Feliz, why don't you
    look upon the confessional as a process, as speaking to
    yourself. In speaking to God, you see, you could actually
    be speaking to yourself. Like therapy.
MARTA FELIZ: You mean like Freud or Jung?
FATHER ERNESTO: Yes. But with a religious twist.
MARTA FELIZ: Could that be an ecumenical twist?
FATHER ERNESTO: You mean like everybody?

MARTA FELIZ: A little from here, a little from there. But only
    Christian ecumenical, of course.
FATHER ERNESTO: Of course.
MARTA FELIZ: And only once a month.
FATHER ERNESTO: But, Marta Feliz, it is the custom to confess
    ...
MARTA FELIZ: But Father, with three kids under six, no husband,
    no social life and no money, I can't possibly have anything
    to confess every two weeks. Okay? (*Putting out her hand
    for a shake.*) Religious therapy. Once a month. Do we
    have a deal?
FATHER ERNESTO: (*Extending his hand slowly.*) Pos, Marta Fe-
    liz, I have never had a convert ...
MARTA FELIZ: Student.
FATHER ERNESTO: Student. Like you.
MARTA FELIZ: And the job? For my aunt?
FATHER ERNESTO: With the bishop. I have an appointment
    with the bishop.
MARTA FELIZ: Deal?
FATHER ERNESTO: (*Shaking hands.*) Pos, okay. Deal.
MARTA GRANDE: Híjole. I don't think this is a good idea.
    (*Black out. Light on* FLORINDA. *She is carrying a crudely
    made wooden cross. Four little dolls swing merrily from the
    horizontal bar, the replica of* MARTA FELIZ, *on one side,
    and three children, two blonde and one brunette, on the
    other side. The effect should be innocent and unsettling at
    the same time.*)

.... SCENE SEVEN ....

La familia de voodoo / Voodoo Family

FLORINDA: (*Swinging the cross like a toy.*)

    Blessed are those who suffer
    as it was in the beginning, now and forever.
    And blessed are those who cry.

    Blessed are those who hunger
    as it was in the beginning, now and forever.
    And blessed are those who thirst.

    First the mother and then the children.

First the tree and then the fruit.

Bless her with pain
and I will love you with all my heart and soul.
Bless her with torment
and my heart will flame for love of thee!
I am the Queen! I am the Bride!
I am the Virgin, untouched and sanctified!
Send them away and I will love you with all my heart,
with all my heart and soul.

> (*Black out. Lights rise on* MARTA FELIZ *on couch.* FA-
> THER ERNESTO *is kneeling in front of her. A large alu-
> minum bowl filled with water is next to him.* MARTA
> GRANDE *is nearby.*)

.... SCENE EIGHT ....

Amor sagrado / Sacred Love

FATHER ERNESTO: (*Washing* MARTA FELIZ'*s feet ceremoni-
ously.*) You are in my prayers now, always.
MARTA GRANDE: If this wasn't so ridiculous, m'ija, it would be
embarrassing.
MARTA FELIZ: Father, all I want you to do is find a job for my
aunt.
FATHER ERNESTO: But you need God's ministrations as well,
Marta Feliz. Right now you are being torn in many direc-
tions. Biculturalism. Bilingualism. Free love.
MARTA GRANDE: What does he know?
FATHER ERNESTO: Broken love affairs and fatherless children.
You have fallen far. And you are weak.
MARTA FELIZ: Father, I have a school scholarship. I have checks
with only my name on them. I have debts, three boys and
a lawyer on retainer.
MARTA GRANDE: ¡Híjole!
MARTA FELIZ: I can't be weak.
FATHER ERNESTO: But you ARE confused.
MARTA FELIZ: I don't think so.
FATHER ERNESTO: And broken.
MARTA FELIZ: Not lately.
FATHER ERNESTO: And needy.

MARTA FELIZ: I don't ... (*A realization.*) But you want me to
    be, don't you?
FATHER ERNESTO: Marta Feliz, Mother Church is waiting for
    you. We suffer daily ...
MARTA GRANDE: (*Ironic.*) ¡Ay, Dios mío!
MARTA FELIZ: You want me to be confused?
FATHER ERNESTO: Yes!
MARTA FELIZ: (*Taking her foot away.*) Men. You're all the same.
    No matter where you go to school.
FATHER ERNESTO: (*On his knees, trying to retreive her foot.*)
    Marta Feliz, though you have fallen far, this only means
    that your rise back to Mother Church will be that much
    higher and steeper.
MARTA FELIZ: You make it sound like rock climbing, Father.
FATHER ERNESTO: You're angry. Because I can't find a job for
    your aunt.
MARTA FELIZ: Father, stop wasting your time with the bishop.
FATHER ERNESTO: But the bishop knows many people, Marta
    Feliz.
MARTA FELIZ: Father Ernesto, have you ever thought of getting
    a real job? Where you improve people's lives, instead of
    maintaining the status quo?
MARTA GRANDE: ¡Ándale!
FATHER ERNESTO: But I can save you. This task I have chosen
    for myself. The most difficult in the whole parish.
MARTA GRANDE: I don't think she's THAT bad!
MARTA FELIZ: Father, I don't want you to save me! Just help
    me, Father, and then, I'll save myself. Oh, God!

.... SCENE NINE ....

La vida cotidiana / Daily Life

    Lights rise on FLORINDA *swinging her makeshift cross of
Marta Feliz and her children.*

FLORINDA:

    A little pain – and the stomach rolls.
    A little strain – and the legs stop.

MARTA FELIZ: My legs feel so heavy.
FLORINDA:

A little bump – and the eyes pop.
A little jump – and the feet stop.

MARTA FELIZ: Father Ernesto.
FATHER ERNESTO: What's wrong, Marta Feliz?
MARTA FELIZ: I don't know.
FLORINDA:

A little jab – and the lungs collapse.
A little stab – and the heart stops.

FATHER ERNESTO: Marta Feliz, without the love of God, you
    will get worse. I know these things.
FLORINDA: Pain in the morning. Pain at dinner.
FATHER ERNESTO: Here. Let me bathe your foot.
FLORINDA: Pain at night. For the lonely sinner.
MARTA FELIZ: (*Giving him her foot.*) Father, what is this? What's
    happening?
FATHER ERNESTO: (*Referring to her foot.*) You're hot, Marta
    Feliz. Burning.
FLORINDA: I am the Queen! I am the Bride. I am the Virgin
    untouched and sanctified. (*Black out. Spot rises on two
    chairs and* MARTA FELIZ.)
MARTA FELIZ: (*To audience.*) And so, sick and in a weakened
    state, I began my confessions. Maybe it was the accumu-
    lated sins of three marriages, maybe something else. But
    slowly, the house began to feel haunted, as if the walls
    themselves had plans. And even Father Ernesto couldn't
    stop the inevitable.

.... SCENE TEN ....

La confesión / The Confession

FATHER ERNESTO: (*Entering.*) You cannot resist her. Your aunt
    is giving you el mal ojo. And empacho.
MARTA FELIZ: Are you serious? Nobody gets those things.
FATHER ERNESTO: Folk medicine, Marta Feliz, as you well know,
    is practiced all over the world. Even here in Texas.
MARTA FELIZ: So?
FATHER ERNESTO: So folk medicine is designed to cure folk
    disease. You can't have a folk cure ...
MARTA FELIZ: Without a folk cause.
FATHER ERNESTO: ¿Que no?

MARTA FELIZ: Father, are you telling me my Aunt is hexing me?

FATHER ERNESTO: Your aunt Florinda gets her power from faith, my child. I have seen her in the dark. She has created a doll family of you and your sons. Recently she added the library at your old high school. (*Cross fade to* FLORINDA. *She is holding the cross with the voodoo family, only now there is a square, rundown stucco building hanging from it. She shakes the cross ever so lightly. The building collapses. She smiles.*)

MARTA FELIZ: Mrs. Norris!

FATHER ERNESTO: May she rest in peace.

MARTA FELIZ: She hired me. At the library. Father Ernesto, can my aunt really hurt me?

FATHER ERNESTO: You lost your scholarship. Let God enter you, Marta Feliz, and then, through me, turn your weakness to strength.

MARTA FELIZ: Oh, no. No, no, no, no. You are not gonna get me to start believing in this kind of stuff.

FATHER ERNESTO: It doesn't matter whether you believe, Marta Feliz. She believes. Faith is a very strong force. Where do you hurt?

MARTA FELIZ: Everywhere. Somewhere. Deep. Deep inside.

FATHER ERNESTO: (*Sincere.*) Soon, if you do not go to a curandero, you will get splotches on your face, your womb will tilt, blood will seep out of your ... breasts ... your teeth will fall out and you will turn dark and thick like a vegetable. An eggplant probably.

MARTA FELIZ: Where did you learn all this?

FATHER ERNESTO: In the seminary. Are you ready for your penance?

MARTA FELIZ: Okay. (*Black out.*)

. . . . SCENE ELEVEN . . . .

Las cosas extraordinarias occurren a la gente ordinaria / Extraordinary Things Happen to Ordinary People

Lights rise on FLORINDA.

FLORINDA: (*Catching a postal tube thrown from offstage.*) ¡Dios mío! (*Lights rise on* MARTA FELIZ *and* FATHER ERNESTO *in their chairs.* MARTA GRANDE *is nearby.*)

MARTA FELIZ: Yes, Father?

FATHER ERNESTO: Your aunt received her blessing from the
    Pope today.
FLORINDA: (*Reading from letter.*) "Continue God's work with
    the poor."
FATHER ERNESTO: He wants her to continue her work with the
    poor.
MARTA GRANDE: Good! If they're both lucky, they'll never run
    out of them.
FATHER ERNESTO: And you, Marta Feliz? Do you have any-
    thing to confess?
MARTA FELIZ: Well ... not much. I got a letter today. From
    Mac.
MARTA GRANDE ¿Qué quiere?
FATHER ERNESTO: He got married?
MARTA FELIZ: Again. Just like that!
MARTA GRANDE and FATHER ERNESTO: (*Simultaneously.*)
    ¡Vale! ¡Vale! (*Black out. A large sign drops from above.*)

HOSPICIO PARA LOS POBRES
HOSPICE FOR THE POOR

FLORINDA: (*Entering and standing underneath it.*) ¡Dios mío!
    (*Spot rises on* MARTA FELIZ *and* FATHER ERNESTO
    in their chairs. MARTA GRANDE *is nearby.*)
FATHER ERNESTO: Your aunt received permission from the
    bishop today. It's going to be announced next week in
    the "Parish News."
MARTA FELIZ: Well ... I guess she got to him before you did.
    So much for connections.
FATHER ERNESTO: I know God works in strange ways, Marta
    Feliz.
MARTA FELIZ: You're telling me!
FATHER ERNESTO: But God will help you. In other ways.
MARTA FELIZ: Well ... it better be soon.
FATHER ERNESTO: Are you ready for your penance?
MARTA FELIZ: Are you kidding? After this confession, Father,
    I think you should take my penance. And double yours.
    (*Black out. A sign, followed by a spot, flies in slowly.*)

ESTE HOGAR ES   THIS IS A CATHOLIC
CATÓLICO—NO   HOME—WE DO NOT
NECESITAMOS   NEED PROPAGANDA
PROPAGANDA DE   FROM OTHER
OTRAS RELIGIONES   RELIGIONS

FLORINDA: (*Enters and stands between all three signs.*) ¡Dios mío! I am blessed! (*Lights rise on MARTA FELIZ and FATHER ERNESTO at their chairs.* MARTA GRANDE *is nearby.*)

FATHER ERNESTO: Your aunt was awarded the house today, Marta Feliz.

MARTA FELIZ: Are you sure?

FATHER ERNESTO: It's going to be announced in the "Parish News" next week.

MARTA FELIZ: How could it happen, Father?

FATHER ERNESTO: The bishop, Marta Feliz, has a lot of power. ¿Tú sabes?

MARTA GRANDE Igual que la Revolución.

FATHER ERNESTO: The parish needs her, Marta Feliz. And the people love her. What could I do? Your aunt is respected. And loved.

MARTA GRANDE Get ready, m'ija. As the americanos say, "You ain't seen nothing yet." (*Black out. Dream lighting rises.*)

.... SCENE TWELVE ....

El sueño de los pobres / The Dream of the Poor

FLORINDA: Santa María, Nuestro Padre, el Espíritu Santo, the Virgin, y todos los Santos del universo. I am so happy to be here today. I see you suffering and my heart is filled with joy! I see you drowning in sin and doubt and God, our God is so far away but I, me, I am here, as it was in the beginning, now and forever, with love and refuge and lots of tortillas and spaghetti. (MARTA GRANDE, *wrapped humbly in the large shawl she was wearing earlier, approaches.*) Oh! People are coming!

MARTA GRANDE: (*As if receiving communion.*) Blessed saint, give me food. I suffer much.

FLORINDA: (*Pulling out a plate stacked high with tortillas.*) Here. Think of me with every bite.

MARTA GRANDE: (*With bowed head.*) Gracias.

FLORINDA: And remember me in your prayers. (MARTA FELIZ, *face downcast, enters.*) Another one!

MARTA FELIZ: (*As if receiving communion.*) Blessed señorita, I am a sinner, poisoned by sex, a big mouth, ambition and pride. A rebozo and beans are all I need.

FLORINDA: (*Pulling out a plate stacked high with pale-looking pink spaghetti.*) No beans today. But we have lots of spaghetti! (*Pulling out a dark-colored, large shawl.*) And here is a rebozo for you.

MARTA FELIZ: But this is black.

FLORINDA: I know. It's perfect! Remember me in your prayers. ¡Ándale! (*FATHER ERNESTO, in civilian clothes, enters.*)

FATHER ERNESTO: (*As if receiving communion.*) Oh, Virgin One, I lust for little nightingales surrounded by helplessness, poverty and shame.

FLORINDA: (*Pulling out a plate stacked high with tortillas.*) Try these. Handmade. Pray for me.

FATHER ERNESTO: (*With bowed head.*) Gracias, Doña Florinda.

FLORINDA: You know my name!

FATHER ERNESTO: Everybody knows your name. You are the rose of our parish. (*Rose petals fall softly over FLORINDA.*)

FLORINDA: Oh! They like me. (*Voices in Spanish all rise saying "Un poquito más, por favor."*)

MARTA FELIZ: Un poquito más, por favor.

FLORINDA: More?

MARTA GRANDE: Un poquito más, por favor.

FLORINDA: ¡Los Pobres! I hear you!

FATHER ERNESTO: Un poquito más, por favor.

FLORINDA: I see you! I love you! (*Voices in Spanish rise to a crescendo, as if all of the Spanish-speaking world were asking for help.*)

FLORINDA: People know me! I am loved! I am famous como Mother Teresa! So many to feed! So many to clothe! So many! This is good! So good! (*Spanish voices bump off, then black out. Lights rise on FATHER ERNESTO and MARTA FELIZ in living room. She is pale and disheveled.*)

.... SCENE THIRTEEN ....

Separación / Separation

FATHER ERNESTO: Marta Feliz, if you ask me, I think it's time for you to move.

MARTA FELIZ: What?

FATHER ERNESTO: For your health, Marta Feliz. God works in strange ways sometimes. But we must trust Him and follow his directions.

MARTA FELIZ: But Father, I'm scared.

FATHER ERNESTO: If you are scared, you should pray for strength.

MARTA FELIZ: This is the only home I've ever had. And now, since the kids, I don't know what it's like out there anymore. (*Lights on* MARTA GRANDE, *dressed as she was at the top of Act One, in her rebozo and carrying her morrales or hemp bags.*)

MARTA GRANDE: ¡Marta Feliz, mírame! I was scared, too. But I was young! I was alive! I knew something would happen to me! I ran, m'ija.

MARTA FELIZ: You ran?

FATHER ERNESTO: Marta Feliz?

MARTA FELIZ: My grandmother, I was just thinking ...

MARTA GRANDE: I ran, m'ija. Like the wind.

MARTA FELIZ: That fast?

FATHER ERNESTO: Marta Feliz?

MARTA GRANDE: Like the wind, m'ija. Like the wind.

MARTA FELIZ: You think I should leave, too?

FATHER ERNESTO: Marta Feliz?

MARTA GRANDE: But don't take this one with you.

MARTA FELIZ: Yes. I know. I know.

FATHER ERNESTO: Marta Feliz? Are you all right?

MARTA FELIZ: Father Ernesto? If I have to leave ... I think you should leave, too. ¿Que no?

FATHER ERNESTO: Pos ... I don't know ...

MARTA FELIZ: You need to get away from me. You know that. Don't you?

FATHER ERNESTO: Yes. I have made you the singular purpose of my vocation. You were my first assignment and I failed. I have fallen miserably, Marta Feliz, into the clutches of ego and desire.

MARTA FELIZ: Oh, come on! It wasn't that bad.

FATHER ERNESTO: Yes! I was the one consumed with worldly thoughts, not you, Marta Feliz. I wanted you to be my Mary Magdalene.

MARTA FELIZ: Well, it was kind of glamorous, sometimes. In a strange way.

FATHER ERNESTO: Please, don't make jokes.

MARTA FELIZ: You're right. We're not very good for each other,
    I think. You should definitely get away.
FATHER ERNESTO: Yes ... pero ... I don't know where to go
    either.
MARTA FELIZ: There are many places that need you, Father.
FATHER ERNESTO: You think so?
MARTA FELIZ: I know I've been a tough student ...
FATHER ERNESTO: But Marta Feliz, I'm scared, too. I pray all
    the time. All the time!
MARTA FELIZ: You should read books, Father.
FATHER ERNESTO: You think so?
MARTA FELIZ: Yes. Especially the bad ones.
MARTA GRANDE: Échele.
MARTA FELIZ: You know, my grandmother always said if people
    don't want you somewhere, it's because they have some-
    thing to hide. If you ask me, Father, you should pray a
    little less. And read a little more.
MARTA GRANDE Ándale.
FATHER ERNESTO: Pos ... maybe ...
MARTA FELIZ: Let's make a deal.
FATHER ERNESTO: Another one?
MARTA FELIZ: We'll leave together.
FATHER ERNESTO: (*Shocked.*) Oh no, Marta Feliz. I cannot
    leave the Church.
MARTA FELIZ: No! Not together together. At the same time, but
    in different directions.
FATHER ERNESTO: ¿Tú por un rumbo y yo por otro?
MARTA GRANDE: Asina.
MARTA FELIZ: Exactly.
FATHER ERNESTO: No, Marta Feliz. You know what? I am no
    longer worthy of the ministry. I have fallen from God's
    grace in this house. I know it. In my heart.
MARTA GRANDE: (*Putting down her hemp bags, concerned over*
    FATHER ERNESTO's *plight.*) Pobrecito. El Padre Ernie.
FATHER ERNESTO: I have fallen ... beyond redemption, beyond
    prayer ...
MARTA GRANDE: ¿M'ija? ¡Ayúdalo!
FATHER ERNESTO: And I'm certain that God Almighty will
    never forgive me.
MARTA GRANDE: Marta Feliz!
MARTA FELIZ: 'Amá. (*Gestures to her grandmother to be quiet.*)
MARTA GRANDE: What are you waiting for? Tell him the "Moon
    Story."

FATHER ERNESTO: From where He sits in his universe, I have become nothing but a speck of dust.

MARTA GRANDE: ¡Con gas! ¡Ándale!

FATHER ERNESTO: Especially in this house ...

MARTA FELIZ: Father? Did I ever tell you my grandmother's story about the moon?

FATHER ERNESTO: The moon? No.

MARTA FELIZ: Well, according to my grandmother, God has seen you everywhere, not just in this house.

MARTA GRANDE: Asina.

MARTA FELIZ: You see, the moon is a window ... (*A corrido of leave-taking rises. As* MARTA FELIZ *tells* FATHER ERNESTO *the "Moon Story," a moon rises slowly behind* MARTA GRANDE, *putting her in silhouette.*)

MARTA GRANDE: (*Stuffing her hemp bags once again.*) Bueno, Marta Feliz, tengo que juntar mis cosas ...

MARTA FELIZ: So you see, God is always watching us. And when the moon is out, we are never alone. It's just a kid's story, but I like it.

FATHER ERNESTO: Gracias, Marta Feliz.

MARTA FELIZ: You're welcome. (*Extending her hand for a shake.*) Well?

FATHER ERNESTO: I know. I should go. But I would like to do one last blessing before I leave.

MARTA FELIZ: Let her rip.

FATHER ERNESTO: (*Taking her hand, kneeling, and placing it on top of his own head.*) May Our Saviour and Redeemer bless us both. And may he give us the strength to live our lives with joy. Adiós, Marta Feliz.

MARTA FELIZ: Goodbye. (*Black out. Lights rise on* MARTA FELIZ. *To audience.*) From then on, the house seemed emptier without Father Ernesto. Even the presence of my grandmother couldn't fill it. But Father Ernesto didn't really go away. He called often and my aunt, through the "Parish News," knew what he was up to. (*Lights rise on* MARTA GRANDE.)

MARTA GRANDE: Ay, viene tu tía.

.... SCENE FOURTEEN ....

Padre por siglo veinte y uno / Twenty-First Century Priest

FLORINDA: (*Entering.*) Marta Feliz? Did you hear that Father
    Ernesto has left the parish?
MARTA FELIZ: Yes, tía.
FLORINDA: He asked to be moved to the largest barrio in the
    country. It's not here in Texas.
MARTA FELIZ: I know, tía.
FLORINDA: I got a letter from him today. He continues to pray
    for all of us. Even you, Marta Feliz.
MARTA GRANDE: Pos, it's the only thing he knows how to do,
    ¿que no?
FLORINDA: I heard from the bishop that they were thinking of
    promoting him.
MARTA FELIZ: Oh, yeah? Well, I never thought Father Ernesto
    was that smart.
FLORINDA: Y tú, ¿qué sabes?
MARTA FELIZ: Y tú, perdóname, ¿qué sabes?
MARTA GRANDE: Y tú, señora, ¿qué sabes? (*The phone rings.*)
FLORINDA: Probably some fulano for you.
MARTA FELIZ: Hello?
FATHER ERNESTO: (*Lights rise on* FATHER ERNESTO.) Marta
    Feliz? Don't tell your tía I'm calling.
MARTA FELIZ: Okay. (*Pause.*) How are you?
FLORINDA: Hmph!
FATHER ERNESTO: I like it in Los Angeles. The people are
    puro mexicano and the food is almost as good as in Texas.
    (*Pause.*) Have you gone back to school yet?
MARTA FELIZ: No. But I'd like to.
FLORINDA: ¡Pinches fulanos!
MARTA FELIZ: Are you doing all the things I told you?
FLORINDA: ¡Dios mío!
FATHER ERNESTO: Yes. I'm reading many different kinds of
    books. (*Pause.*) Even socialism.
MARTA FELIZ: You have to look at everything. With naked eyes.
FLORINDA: ¡Dios mío!
FATHER ERNESTO: ¡Pos, sí! And I'm walking out in the streets,
    Marta Feliz. Checking things out. And messing with the
    Raza.
MARTA FELIZ: Really?
FATHER ERNESTO: It's very exciting to be in the world, Marta
    Feliz. Now I know we are all brothers. Even those of us
    not in holy orders.
MARTA FELIZ: And just imagine, if we all took our clothes off
    ...

FLORINDA: ¡Sinvergüenza!

FATHER ERNESTO: We would all look the same, in the eyes of
God, ¿que no? And you?

MARTA FELIZ: Me?

FATHER ERNESTO: How are you? Really?

MARTA FELIZ: Here.

FATHER ERNESTO: Marta Feliz, come to Los Angeles.

MARTA FELIZ: No. It's too far away. (FLORINDA*'s eyes light
up.*)

FATHER ERNESTO: I'll help you find an apartment.

MARTA FELIZ: You will?

FATHER ERNESTO: And I'll feed you and your kids at the church
until you find a job. Marta Feliz, I want to help you. Not
save you.

MARTA FELIZ: Really?

FATHER ERNESTO: ¡De veras! (*Pause.*) I think of you often.

MARTA FELIZ: I think of you, too.

FLORINDA: Hmph!

FATHER ERNESTO: And I pray for you.

MARTA FELIZ: Well, thanks.

FATHER ERNESTO: Can I call you again?

MARTA FELIZ: Oh, yes! Please. Call again. Anytime.

FLORINDA: You don't have to beg them, Marta Feliz.

FATHER ERNESTO: Adiós, Marta Feliz. (*Lights fade on* FATHER
ERNESTO *as he hangs up the phone.*)

MARTA FELIZ: Bye. And thanks. (*Hangs up the phone.*)

FLORINDA: And who was that?

MARTA FELIZ: Ernie. (*Black out. Beat. Spotlight rises. After
a pause,* FATHER ERNESTO, *bible in hand, walks into
spotlight.*)

FATHER ERNESTO: My children, I am so happy to see so many
new faces in church this Sunday. I feel blessed to be your
new priest aquí en Los Angeles. Pero in my church, I want
smiles, bright colors, no crying, and no suffering. We deserve happiness, ¿que no? And prosperity. And full em-
ployment. And equality. And democracy. And a new and
better debt repayment policy. A more sensitive amnesty
program. A free trade agreement. And no ditches en este
lado, el otro lado y por todos lados! (*Pause.*) Pues, together, we will pray for these things, and I am sure that
God Almighty knows, in his mero corazón, that we deserve them. Pero, we should organize, too. Just in case.

¿Que no? (*Spotlight bumps off. Lights rise on* FLORINDA *and* MARTA FELIZ *and* MARTA GRANDE.)

.... SCENE FIFTEEN ....

Florinda ascendida / Florinda Ascended

FLORINDA: (*Putting lace doillies on everything, turning the house into a nineteenth century parody of itself.*) Everyone is giving me awards. The blacks, whites, chicanos, Elks, Moose, Rotarians ... Can you believe it, Marta Feliz, even the D.A.R.

MARTA FELIZ: The D.A.R?

FLORINDA: Pos, sí!

MARTA FELIZ: The Daughters of the American Revolution called you?

FLORINDA: Pues, why not? They are immigrants, igual que yo. And the Asians, Masons, Odd Fellows, NAACP, LULAC, MALDEF. Even the National Society of Latino Dentists has given me a plaque.

MARTA FELIZ: Well, tía, I think you should take care of your own familia first, and then take on the world.

FLORINDA: But I'm going to be on television next Thursday. The poor need me. I will, of course, be humble and thank them throughout for all this notoriety and fame.

MARTA GRANDE: (*To audience.*) At least she has the brains to thank the poor. Because without them somebody would have locked her up a long time ago, ¿que no?

FLORINDA: ¡Ay, pues! So much to do! (*Exits.*)

.... SCENE SIXTEEN ....

Revolución / Revolution

MARTA FELIZ: She got the house, 'Amá.

MARTA GRANDE: Igual como la Revolución.

MARTA FELIZ: The Revolution?

MARTA GRANDE: ¡Pos, sí! ¡Todo se fregó! ¡Sin tapa! ¡Se fue a la chingada!

MARTA FELIZ: 'Amá, for your information, a lot of people think the Revolution failed.

MARTA GRANDE: Pos, m'ijita, of course it failed! Why do you
    think I had to come to this pinche country in the first
    place?

MARTA FELIZ: But 'Amá ...

MARTA GRANDE: M'ija, listen to me. This house, and Méjico
    are gone for us. Don't become lazy, m'ija. Like all the
    other americanos. El Ernie is right. It is time for you to
    move. No kidding.

MARTA FELIZ: But I can't, 'Amá. Tía Florinda has made me
    sick. She's poisoned me with hatred and greed. I'm under
    a curse, and I'm going to ...

MARTA GRANDE: You're only pregnant, pendeja.

MARTA FELIZ: Pregnant? I'm only pregnant?

MARTA GRANDE: Pos, sí.

MARTA FELIZ: No hex? ¿No mal ojo? ¿No empacho?

MARTA GRANDE: Those things only happen to you when you
    think they can happen to you.

MARTA FELIZ: It's just a little crisis!

MARTA GRANDE: A girl. Pinche Ernie had it all wrong. (*Lights
    rise on* FLORINDA *now a girl of thirteen.*)

MARTA GRANDE: Mírala, when your aunt and me came over
    here during the Revolución, she was afraid of everything.
    She wouldn't even drink the pinche water. Now she's go-
    ing to be on television next Thursday. You know, your tía
    and me, we came from Méjico from that direction. What
    do you think?

MARTA FELIZ: I don't want to go to Mexico, 'Amá.

MARTA GRANDE: Really?

MARTA FELIZ: Really.

MARTA GRANDE: Are you sure?

MARTA FELIZ: Very sure.

MARTA GRANDE: Okay. The past is over. Only the future keeps
    repeating itself over and over again.

FLORINDA: ¡Ay, Marta!

MARTA GRANDE: Florinda? You want to go to the United States
    or what?

FLORINDA: Tengo miedo, Marta.

MARTA GRANDE: (*To* MARTA FELIZ.) Your tía was always a
    scared little thing. It wasn't easy, pobrecita, because in
    Méjico, Florinda and I had nothing. Our family lived on
    a ranch, but we didn't own it. The land was owned by
    the Church. And the patrones. When Porfirio Díaz began

to sell the land, the Church rebelled, of course. (*Bullet sounds rise.*)

FLORINDA: Marta? ¿Dónde estás? Marta?

MARTA GRANDE: So the patrones started shooting the politicians.

FLORINDA: (*Hitting the ground.*) ¡Dios mío!

MARTA GRANDE: And the politicians started shooting the students.

FLORINDA: ¡Ay, no! ¡Por favor!

MARTA GRANDE: And the workers, pobre malditos, they started shooting everybody.

FLORINDA: ¡Por favor! ¡Párense! ¡Ay, no! ¡No! ¡No!

MARTA GRANDE: (*Putting on her large shawl, or rebozo, and picking up her filled morrales, or hemp bags.*) And the poor people, like Florinda and me, we were in the middle. It is a curious thing, Marta Feliz. Pero Méjico, such a poor country, has never run out of ammunition. Imagínate ... (*Crowd sounds rise in Spanish.*) I was a girl of fifteen. The best thing my family could do for me was to marry me off to somebody. Anybody. Eso no, les dije. I will choose my own husband, and I will make my own life. (*Beat.*) Florinda? Levántate. Go get ready. We're going to Los Estados Unidos.

FLORINDA: Okay! ¡Bueno! Okay! (*Exits.*)

MARTA GRANDE: We had to become Baptists. So what? (*Crowd sounds rise in Spanish.*) And Texas was okay. But, all my life, Marta Feliz, you know what I missed most? Not hearing Spanish every day. (*Crowd sounds fade.*) No matter what anybody tells you, m'ija. Nobody wants to leave their country. Nobody. (*A moon begins to rise.*)

MARTA FELIZ: All you wanted to do was hear it. Just to make yourself feel better. 'Amá, if you had told me, I would have spoken more Spanish for you.

MARTA GRANDE: That's all over now, m'ija. Before this one is born, immigrate.

MARTA FELIZ: But where, 'Amá?

MARTA GRANDE: It's a big country. You decide, m'ija. But now, I have to go.

MARTA FELIZ: You're going? Where, 'Amá?

MARTA GRANDE: Where I've always been. Look up. Adiós,

m'ija. (*Exits.*)

.... SCENE SEVENTEEN ....

La despedida / Farewell

MARTA FELIZ: (*To audience.*) It was obvious. My tía Florinda
had turned into somebody I didn't know. And worse, into
somebody I didn't even like. And the house had changed,
too. The foundation was the same, but the rooms were
furnished with ghosts, dead memories, shadows and the
rotting remains of a dying Church. My grandmother was
right. Poverty is not a god and starvation has no virtue,
no matter what anybody says. I grabbed Maury, J.J. and
Tory. And ran. (*Lights rise on* FLORINDA.)
FLORINDA: (*Reading a note.*) "Dear Tía, I have immigrated to
Los Angeles. I'm scared, of course, but I'm young and
I feel alive. I think something will happen to me now.
Love, Marta Feliz." (*Exits.*)
MARTA FELIZ: Father Ernesto met me at the bus station. It didn't
bother him anymore that he couldn't save me, so I started
calling him Ernie. And Martita was born in L.A. I got my
B.A. Finally. Ernie came to my graduation. He was very
proud of me. (*Pause.*) And I got a job and then one day
the phone rang. My aunt Florinda had died. And then
the phone rang again. The neighbors told me the house
had gone up in flames. They said they saw fires inside,
and shadows on the wall, as if people were cooking. Of
course, they thought it was the wetbacks. (*Sounds of fire
rise.*) But I knew the shadows were my grandmother and
my aunt talking about Mexico ...
MARTA GRANDE: (*Offstage.*) El pinche Ernie owned it!
MARTA FELIZ: The Revolution ...
FLORINDA: (*Offstage.*) ¡Ay, Marta! ¡No hables así!
MARTA FELIZ: Television ...
FLORINDA: (*Offstage.*) I'm going to be on television next Thurs-
day.
MARTA FELIZ: And God.
MARTA GRANDE: (*Offstage.*) La luna, Marta Feliz, is a window
... (*Lights rise on the burnt-out shell of the house.*)
MARTA FELIZ: My grandmother, of course, is still with me. I
remember how she used to kid me about talking so much.

(*Lights rise on* MARTA GRANDE *in the moon.*)

MARTA GRANDE: Descansa, niña. Qué habladora eres.

MARTA FELIZ: Before she died, I never had the chance to tell her that I wasn't talking. I was dreaming. Just dreaming. (*Lights fade on* MARTA FELIZ, *then lights fade on* MARTA GRANDE *in the moon.*)

End of Play

A Dream of Canaries

Diana Sáenz

CHARACTERS

PAOLA BUNELOS: thirty-one years old, scientist, client of Nita's and also Nita's friend. Daughter of the former head of the Secret Service.

NITA DURME: nineteen years old, call-girl.

COLONEL SENSEZOZ: early forties, a military man in the Special Service, friend of Sra. Paca DeMas.

LALO FINOLINA: early twenties, soldier in the Special Service, bunkmate and best friend to Jesús.

JESÚS UTIMO: twenty-two years old, ex-gigolo to Sra. DeMas, soldier.

SERGEANT: thirty to fifty years of age.

CHAPA/DESAPARECIDO #3: call girl, involved in secret underground activities, Nita's friend.

SEÑORA DEMAS: forty, daughter of a General, in love with Jesús, a powerful and dangerous woman, closely linked with state matters.

OLD MAN PRISONER/DESAPARECIDO #1
YOUNG MAN PRISONER/DESAPARECIDO #2

Note: The cast should be from all races. A French, Spanish, Mideast, African, English accent for several characters would be excellent.

PLACE

From a country carved out of a jungle, the sets echo the silver screen a la Carmen Miranda. Costumes should be in neutral tones, white, black, beige, grey. The women should wear flowers when possible, dark red lipstick and nail polish. White flowers such as gardenias, orchids, lilies may decorate the sets. All this, juxtaposed with art-deco space-age gadgetry to give a sense of past, present and future, and thereby ease the viewer, distance him from the situation so he may absorb the immediacy of events.

ACT ONE

.... SCENE ONE: Cafe ....

A man sits at one table with a cup of coffee, reading a book.
NITA *and* PAOLA *are sitting together in a cafe.* COLONEL
SENSEZOZ, *whom they are discussing, is sitting downstage left.*

PAOLA: Is that less-than-toad, non-creature still staring at us?
NITA: Yes.
PAOLA: I know him.
NITA: From where?
PAOLA: A friend of my father's. Used to come around. Knowing
    what I know now, I think he was in love with my father.
NITA: He looks the type. (*Enter two soldiers wearing masks. They
    look at the* COLONEL, *who nods slightly. Soldiers cross
    to man reading the book and take him away.* PAOLA *and*
    NITA *watch.*
NITA: Don't start anything or I'll walk out right now.
PAOLA: Just like that.
NITA: I'm warning you, Paola. (COLONEL SENSEZOZ *crosses to-*
    *ward the two women. He is a man of multiple vanities and
    dubious sexual proclivities. He has the air of a gentleman,
    a British accent as authentic as the ex-prime minister's. In
    his dress, he is meticulous to a fault. His manner of speak-
    ing is as precise, as self-conscious as his rakishly tilted hat.
    However, he is not to be casually dismissed.*)
COLONEL: Excuse me for staring at you. Aren't you, Paola Bune-
    los, daughter of Ramón Bunelos?
PAOLA: Proof that you can make a silk purse from a sow's ear.
COLONEL: I beg your pardon?
NITA: (*Whispering.*) Paola!
PAOLA: Yes ... I am Paola and who are you?
COLONEL: Permit me to reintroduce myself. It's been at least
    ten years since I've seen you. Colonel Ignacio Sensezoz
    at your service. I knew your father. I am a great admirer
    of his. A great man, your father.

PAOLA: Oh yes, I do remember you. You seem to have done quite
   well. A Colonel now, is it?
COLONEL: Hard work, señorita, nothing but hard work. (*Takes
   a chair.*) Do you mind if I take a seat?
NITA: Please do, Colonel.
COLONEL: You had just been accepted to Yale, was it?
PAOLA: M.I.T.
COLONEL: Ah yes, M.I.T. Your father was so proud of you, as you
   must have been proud of him. Everyone admired him so.
PAOLA: Proud ... That man sitting there a moment ago, his coffee
   is still warm, did he admire my father? Probably not or
   he'd still be drinking latte, everything so civilized ...
NITA: (*Hissing to* PAOLA.) Would you shut up.
PAOLA: I wonder if my father kept as many secrets from us about
   his work as he did from you about his family. I keep his
   secret, Colonel, but I'll say one thing, my only regret about
   his suicide pact with those other two Neanderthals is that
   it wasn't my idea.
COLONEL: I am sorry you feel that way. (*Bows, clicks his heels
   and turns to leave.*)
PAOLA: Oh Colonel, no hard feelings. In fact, I insist upon a toast
   ... To the unresolved moments that last us a lifetime.
COLONEL: Good afternoon, señorita. (*He exits.*)
NITA: You're out of your mind! (*She exits.*)
PAOLA: Wait! Nita! You know you can't outrun me. (*Both women
   pass* SRA. DEMAS *as she enters.* SRA. DEMAS, *a handsome woman of forty, dressed in haute couture and fox furs
   has the habit of stroking the delicate fox paws which rest
   on her bosom. The only indication of her awry existence
   is perhaps too much jewelry, all unusual pieces. She is a
   mysterious agent, at least to those where her power and
   influence are felt: the military, the secret police, the Secret Service and the captains of industry. Her amorphous
   identity allows her to cross through the many facets of government and society. That this has made her the most
   powerful woman in the country would hardly impress her.
   But to say she is more powerful than most of the powerful
   men in the country would please her immensely. She is a
   woman who seldom reveals her weaknesses but, of course,
   like anyone else she is not without at least one.*)
DEMAS: Colonel, darling, I hope I'm not too late.
COLONEL: (*Rising to greet her.*) Not at all. What would you like?

DEMAS: A cigarette before anything. One of yours for a change. (*He gives her one and lights it.*) Thank you.

COLONEL: Did you notice those two young women that were leaving just as you got here?

DEMAS: Hardly. Why?

COLONEL: One of them was Paola Bunelos.

DEMAS: You mean Ramón's girl?

COLONEL: The very one.

DEMAS: Really? I wish I'd gotten a better look. Why, I haven't seen her for ages. She always was a bit on the quiet side. But then, who wouldn't be, living in the shadow of a great man like Ramón Bunelos. I don't recall that he ever had an unkind word to say about anyone. Single-handedly he turned our limping Special Services into a respectable machine. His devotion to my father ... Ah, a hero and a patriot. Ramón Bunelos' life and death were lessons and inspirations to me.

COLONEL: It's a pity his own daughter doesn't share your sentiments.

DEMAS: Can that possibly be true? (*They look deeply at each other and come to an unspoken decision.*) My. My, my, my. This country seems to be groaning under some insidious plague. And the border, any new developments?

COLONEL: I'm expecting a full report this afternoon. If it's what I fear, we shall need to double the troops there. Something we can hardly afford.

DEMAS: What we can't afford, Colonel, is to not double our efforts. Speaking of efforts, yesterday I met with the Minister of the Interior and the Archbishop.

COLONEL: Oh yes, how did that go? Bad entertainment, no doubt? (*Sighs audibly.*)

DEMAS: I ask you, Colonel, how did they ever rise to their present positions? An archbishop and a minister of the interior, I should think, would have loftier matters in mind than to ... well to squabble over who should lead a not particularly important ceremony. They waste my time— everyone's. I'm at a loss to explain such monumental stupidity. Do you think me cruel?

COLONEL: My dear extraordinary woman, how can you expect to explain the flaccid grey matter of half-wits. So, what finally happened?

DEMAS: I had them draw straws.

COLONEL: No, really?

DEMAS: I should've, believe me. I invited them to dine at the Ambassador, filled them with Boeuf ala Japonais and Gran Manier during which time I reminded them that a bishop ...

COLONEL: Archbishop! Please!

DEMAS: Lest we forget! And a statesman were put on this earth to work hand-in-hand. Then, because I am a woman, and women are taught to please, I asked the Archbishop to lead us in prayer and Martínez to lead us in singing the national anthem. That's all they're good for anyway.

COLONEL: Outrageous.

DEMAS: Don't I know it. I see no light at the end of the tunnel.

COLONEL: Paquita, this is not like you at all ...

DEMAS: Is our great cause lost? Was my father's dream nothing but that, and Ramón's martyrdom nothing more than a parting gesture? (*She is overcome by emotion.*) Forgive me!

COLONEL: This is only a moment ...

DEMAS: Forgive me my weakness.

COLONEL: No, no! A woman of quality, of blood, has sensitivities. We men can only bow our heads in respect. It always amazes me to think it is your brilliant strategy behind the scenes, like bolts of calcium into a curving spine. And because of that I forget—your delicate gender, that is—until I look into your charming grey eyes that hold the wisdom of Athena ...

DEMAS: The Goddess of War.

COLONEL: The wisdom of war, Francesca.

DEMAS: (*Modestly.*) Yes, I remember when my father first read that story. I ran to the mirror. Up until then, it seemed as though my eyes had always been hazel.

COLONEL: Mulattoes have hazel eyes.

DEMAS: Quite so. Then, suddenly, as if by will alone, my will, because I was so stricken by the myth of Athena, I had caused my eyes to change.

COLONEL: As grey as a winter lake. I am always humbled in your presence, as if Carlos DeMas passed on that magic to his daughter with his last breath, into her sparkling grey eyes of Athena.

DEMAS: You are always here when I need you most, dear friend. You lift my spirits. Life is so capricious. I wonder, sometimes when reason slips away and wishful thinking creeps in, what would've happened if you were not impotent.

COLONEL: Who told you that?
DEMAS: Why, it's general knowledge. It's not true?
COLONEL: Well, not always ...
DEMAS: Cheri, don't be ashamed. I'm unmarried, childless, dedicated to my beloved country. But a woman can hardly call herself one unless she has a platoon of children running after her. How else can she lay claim to her femininity?
COLONEL: Paquita ...
DEMAS: My point is, there's a bond between us. A commonality. My dear, dear Colonel Sensezoz. There are more unions than simply marriage made in Heaven. (*They both suck greedily from their cigarettes and blow a cloud of smoke as the lights fade.*)

.... SCENE TWO: Paola's Loft ....

The room is sparsely furnished, to suggest the home of a scientist. There is a computer, a microscope, telescope, a shelf of books, most notably a heavy red anatomy text, a container of pens and pencils, notebooks and, against the wall, a robot complete with microphone and microchip which is kept wrapped in a blue cloth in a box. From offstage, running footsteps can be heard. Enter NITA *and* PAOLA *gasping for breath.*

NITA: You tricked me!
PAOLA: What do you mean?
NITA: I never win.
PAOLA: I've let myself get out of condition.
NITA: Liar.
PAOLA: Look at me. I'm soaked!
NITA: You almost ran over that poor man with the cigar.
PAOLA: He stepped out from nowhere. That's the only reason you beat me. He made me break my stride.
NITA: I'm still mad at you. Very mad.
PAOLA: Next time, I won't let you win.
NITA: Aha! So you did trick me.
PAOLA: Tricked you, nothing. I have my pride, after all.
NITA: I mean, into coming here.
PAOLA: Even from here you smell like dried apricots.
NITA: Don't change the subject.
PAOLA: Nita, Nitaíta, you are the most serious person I know.
NITA: The Special Services are more serious.

PAOLA: Take off that dress before you ruin it.
NITA: I'm not sweating.
PAOLA: Perspiring. You will, now that you're inside. Outside it
was cool enough, but not in here.
PAOLA: (*Taking off her dress.*) How much was that dress?
NITA: Not much.
PAOLA: Liar.
NITA: It wasn't.
PAOLA: Take it off. It's too pretty to ruin. (NITA *consents to*
PAOLA, *taking her dress off. Both women are in their
slips.* PAOLA *kisses her on the neck.* NITA *allows her to.
While* PAOLA *hangs up their dresses,* NITA *begins playing
with the robot.*)
NITA: I wonder.
PAOLA: Good for you.
NITA: You're my strangest client, you know.
PAOLA: Flatterer.
NITA: I don't make a practice of sleeping with women. But when
you're not out-of-control, you can talk a snake out of its
skin.
PAOLA: Greed.
NITA: Ho! I charge you less than anyone. Why, it's practically a
give-away.
PAOLA: I'm not talking about money.
NITA: I don't get you, really. You're so pretty. Men act ridiculous
when you walk by in your little silk dresses smelling of
gardenias, and yet you hate them.
PAOLA: I don't hate men. They simply don't interest me.
NITA: Then why do you dress the way you do?
PAOLA: How should I dress, like a man? Why should I want to
ape an ape?
NITA: See, you do hate men.
PAOLA: Not men, Nitaíta, just their ideas.
NITA: Oh no! (*Holding a piece of the robot in her hand.*)
PAOLA: What happened?
NITA: It just came off. I hardly touched it—de veras ...
PAOLA: The cover plate again. Get me the tool box over there
in the corner. I need a soldering iron. It's always coming
off. (NITA *does so, then watches her work.*)
PAOLA: Hold this.
NITA: Like this?
PAOLA: There. You can let go now. (*She continues working on the
robot as* NITA *watches.*)

NITA: Paola?

PAOLA: What?

NITA: You say that we're born with only two emotions, love and fear.

PAOLA: Um-hum.

NITA: And that jealousy is a mixture of love and fear.

PAOLA: And?

NITA: Well, did your father love your mother and was he afraid she did not love him?

PAOLA: Yes, I suppose, but it's very twisted. Freud would've loved it.

NITA: And where does hate come from?

PAOLA: Fear.

NITA: Fear ... Are you afraid of the Special Services?

PAOLA: Absolutely not.

NITA: But you hate them. (*Pause as* PAOLA *ignores her.*) I mean, if you do hate them—and it sure seems that way to me ...

PAOLA: You're not letting me concentrate ...

NITA: But then, how can you hate them?

PAOLA: Why do you ask so many—oh, I don't know—I suppose I'm afraid for the world, Nitaíta.

NITA: One more question.

PAOLA: Is that a promise?

NITA: Why do you bother with me?

PAOLA: Nita?

NITA: I mean, there are plenty of women who do it for free ... even out of love.

PAOLA: Because I happen to like you very much ... and, I know at least when you're with me, you're staying out of trouble.

NITA: That's a joke. If anything ...

PAOLA: Quick. Get me those pliers by my bed. (NITA *does so.*) This one little bit here also keeps slipping out. I really must get solder.

NITA: How old are you?

PAOLA: Thirty-one.

NITA: Someday I'll be thirty-one.

PAOLA: Yes, and it'll serve you right. It'll seem like a snap of the fingers one of these days when you're happy and famous and very old.

NITA: And you'll be older. Let's tell him something.

PAOLA: Program him ... And I'm not so sure it's a he.

NITA: To me he is, even without the macho. Where's the book? (*Crosses to the bookshelf and finds a large red anatomy book.*) I put a marker at the page. See, even if it didn't work, just to give him some dignity—in the shower.

PAOLA: Water would ruin him. Shall we program something into him?

NITA: Okay. (*She opens the box and unwraps the blue cloth where the microchip is stored.*) It's so small. I would like to have my own robot.

PAOLA: You can have Xavier Valentine here, when I've got the bugs out of him.

NITA: Really? No, I couldn't. After all, he's your first man.

PAOLA: A girl should never settle for the first man who comes into her life.

NITA: No, I just couldn't.

PAOLA: I'll will him to you.

NITA: Don't be silly.

PAOLA: A paper, a piece of paper and a pen ... (*Writing.*) I, Paola Elena Bunelos de García, being of sound mind ...

NITA: Hah!

PAOLA: Bequeath my first mechanical man, Xavier Valentine, to Nita Durme, my dear friend. Oh yes, and also my red leather bound anatomy book, so that she may further her education in the safety of her own bed.

NITA: I would make him perfect. A gentlemen, generous, crazy about me. And I wouldn't settle for an idiot just because he was rich.

PAOLA: But what would you do when those hungry, hot and humid nights strike?

NITA: If he were smart enough to be rich, he'd know all he had to do was to start licking me all over.

PAOLA: A robot with a tongue. Hmmm. Some kind of latex by-product ... and a saliva solution would be as easy to simulate as any lubricant ...

NITA: I'm sure you'd figure something out. The rest, I'd teach him myself.

PAOLA: Program him ...

NITA: Program him with everything I know. See, he'd be exactly the way I wanted him.

PAOLA: Look what happened to Narcissus ...

NITA: What happened?

PAOLA: ... Dated this somber and august day of September ...

NITA: Don't sign it.

PAOLA: It's the only way to make it legal.

NITA: You signed it! (*She snatches it up and tears it to pieces.*) We
    have to burn it!

PAOLA: Nita!

NITA: It's bad luck! I can feel it in my bones!

PAOLA: How can you be so superstitious?

NITA: Where are some matches?

PAOLA: I don't know ... (NITA *is almost hysterical by now.*
    PAOLA *takes her in her arms and comforts her.*) You're
    being a goose, a chicken and a rabbit—an attack of un-
    scientific thinking. (NITA *is shaking.*) What's come over
    you?

NITA: I can't see you anymore.

PAOLA: Of course, you can.

NITA: No, I mean it. I warned you the last time. I shouldn't have
    even let you talk me into coming here again. You can't
    control your temper in public. One of these days some-
    thing is going to happen, and I don't want to be around
    when it does.

PAOLA: Let's program Xavier Valentine, shall we? And stop talk-
    ing like this.

NITA: I'm serious, Paola. (*Starts getting dressed.*)

PAOLA: Nita, I ... I can't blame you. I know, I'm an idiot. But
    they're such ...

NITA: See what I mean? It's as if you don't believe they're real.

PAOLA: I know how real they are.

NITA: But you don't care.

PAOLA: What if I promised never to ...

NITA: Forget it. It's like asking a baby not to cry.

PAOLA: It was stupid to talk about the great Ramón Bunelos the
    way I did to that ghoul. The Special Services take their
    work seriously. I don't know which one I hate more. But
    ... one last time, Nitaíta?

NITA: We have to burn that thing first.

PAOLA: I will, as soon as I get some matches.

NITA: You promise?

PAOLA: I promise. (NITA *stands transfixed. The two women gaze
    into each others' faces. Then slowly,* PAOLA *leans over
    to kiss* NITA *on the lips. Lights down. When lights rise
    again, it is morning. The bed is unmade.* PAOLA *enters
    in a robe with a cup of coffee in one hand and a book in
    the other. She sets the book and cup down. She finds a
    tape and turns on her tape deck. Vivaldi's "Four Seasons"*

*begins playing. Offstage the sound of a car pulling up is
heard. She crosses to the window to look out. A clatter
of heavy footsteps is heard, followed by a pounding on her
door. The door swings open. The* SERGEANT *and* TWO
ARMED SOLDIERS *enter.*)
SERGEANT: Paola Bunelos?
PAOLA: What do you want?
SERGEANT: You are under arrest.
PAOLA: On what charges?
SERGEANT: You and Colonel Sensezoz will have plenty of time
to discuss the details. (*He signals to the soldiers. Fade
out.*)

.... SCENE THREE: Nine p.m. - The Barracks ....

*Sparsely furnished with two bunks, each with a locker under
it. A bare wooden floor. A small window on the back wall.* LALO
FINOLINA *sits at his bunk shining his boots and reading from a
military text at the same time. He is in his early twenties. Enter*
JESÚS UTIMO, *the same age as* LALO *and fresh out of boot camp.
He is carrying a duffle bag and his rifle.*

JESÚS: Is this K-13?
LALO: What does it say on the side of the building?
JESÚS: Nothing.
LALO: What do you mean, nothing?
JESÚS: It's blackened out.
LALO: What? (*Getting up to look outside.* JESÚS *glances at*
LALO*'s book.*) Those jerks in K-7 better not have—
dammit! (*Enters.*) They did it again! (*Notices* JESÚS
is still carrying his gear.)
LALO: You can bunk down there.
JESÚS: Thanks. You got some kind of feud going or what?
LALO: Not me. Some of these guys think that's the way you keep
a gung ho attitude. I'll have to repaint it in the morning.
JESÚS: This happen often?
LALO: A couple times. They should get tired of it sooner or later.
JESÚS: You mean you just let them paint it over and you just fix
it?
LALO: Yeah, yeah. I'll get around to it. Right now I got more on
my mind than dumb-ass shit like that.
JESÚS: Utimo. Jesús Utimo.

LALO: Lalo Finolina.

JESÚS: Línea?

LALO: I-N-A. Its a fine line. The line that connects is the line that separates at the same time.

JESÚS: I get it. Pretty good ... Shouldn't let them get away with it.

LALO: Stoop to their level?

JESÚS: Lower. Paint the whole place pink.

LALO: Pink?

JESÚS: Yeah, the outside.

LALO: Pink. I like that.

JESÚS: I'll help you.

LALO: Yeah?

JESÚS: Sure.

LALO: I'll think about it.

JESÚS: (*Looking around.*) Lotta space for just two bunks.

LALO: Sure. Where were you transferred from?

JESÚS: Just got out of boot camp.

LALO: Come on.

JESÚS: Why?

LALO: I can usually tell when someone's walked the same streets I have and it don't figure you got a rich old man pulling strings for you.

JESÚS: More like up to his ass in piss and rotgut somewhere. My old man never had a job in his life.

LALO: Well, somebody up there's on your side. Don't you know about this place?

JESÚS: Know what?

LALO: You only get assigned here if you're on your way up.

JESÚS: Oh ... so you're on your way up?

LALO: Not that I got anyone up there either. I've had to work for every inch. It took me months of extra duty and book work to get this far.

JESÚS: Maybe they slipped up. I mean, maybe I'm the wrong guy.

LALO: Hey, whatever. Don't complain. The last guy I had in here was a pain-in-the-ass. A rich kid. I felt sorry for him. I think he descended from a jellyfish ... inbreeding. A mongoloid. Very thin skin, you could see all the veins on his forehead. Know what I mean?

JESÚS: Not your type.

LALO: You get some Nembutals in here. Suddenly, they're old enough to get it up and papito wants them to get serious.

Get serious. Hey, I ain't going to be babysitting you, am I?

JESÚS: What're you talking about.

LALO: I ain't kidding, some of these guys ... Well, what do I care as long as I know where I'm going. Work hard, do what you're told, you won't end up passed out in some alley. (*Pause.*) Pink. I like that. Hey, don't get me wrong, you're going to put out for this gig, but you get weekend passes, three furloughs a year and a few bucks more.

JESÚS: Yeah?

LALO: You'll notice the difference. I don't know what you've done to land here but take my advice and don't mess it up. (*Enter* SERGEANT.)

SERGEANT: Atten-hut! (*LALO and JESÚS come to attention. Enter* COLONEL SENSEZOZ.)

COLONEL: Get ready, men. You're going on a mission tonight. (*To* LALO.) You drive. Sergeant, see that this man gets a permit. Have you requisitioned a van before?

LALO: Yes, sir.

COLONEL: Good. Dismissed. (*The* SERGEANT *and* LALO *salute. The* COLONEL *returns the salute.* SERGEANT *and* LALO *exit.*)

COLONEL: So, you're the new man, eh?

JESÚS: Private Utimo, sir.

COLONEL: Mmm. At ease, Private. I am Colonel Sensezoz, your commanding officer. I run an A-One outfit here. I expect the best from my men and I get the best from them. I believe in communication. Communication is the best preventative. Any problems, you'll find my office is always open. The Sergeant will fill you in on your duties and other details, and you'll find First Class Private Finolina a first-class example of proper soldier conduct. For the first few months, you may find yourself in unfamiliar circumstances. I suggest you keep your eyes peeled and your mouth shut. Pick a role model, study him. I was given this sound advice. Now I'm passing it on to you. I was also advised to look before you leap. Words to live and die by. Any questions?

JESÚS: No, sir.

COLONEL: (*Inspects* JESÚS.) Not bad. You could put a bit more shine on those shoes, Private. No detail is too small.

JESÚS: Yes, sir.

COLONEL: You did very well on the exams. Where did you study?

JESÚS: Sir, I taught myself to read.

COLONEL: Well. Most of our draftees seem to have scraped their brains off the side of a fishing boat. You watch yourself, read the manual until you can recite it backwards. Another thing that separates the scum from the cream is to keep up your hygiene. Impeccable is the word. You know what that means?

JESÚS: Impeccable, sir? Perfect, without fault, sir.

COLONEL: Very good. Yes. There's plenty of room in the Army for people like you. You do well in this assignment and believe me, those that matter will hear about it. You get what I'm saying, Private?

JESÚS: Yes, sir.

COLONEL: Good. Ciao. (JESÚS *comes to attention again and salutes. The* COLONEL *returns the salute and saunters out. As soon as the* COLONEL's *steps fade out,* JESÚS *removes a dog-eared dictionary from his duffle bag.*)

JESÚS: Hygiene ... H-i ... (*Cannot find it.*) H-y ... g-e-g-i-e ... Hygiene ... The science of health ... system of principles for the preservation of health and prevention of disease. (*Enter* LALO.)

LALO: What the hell are you doing? Didn't you hear what the Colonel said? (LALO *grabs his rifle and exits. Offstage.*) Idiot fool. (JESÚS *scrambles for his gear. Fade out.*)

················· SCENE FOUR: Barracks ·················

Three hours later. Enter LALO *and* JESÚS. JESÚS *sits exhausted on his bunk. He lies down, his hands cupped behind his head, and stares at the ceiling.*

LALO: Tired? (*Proceeds to strip to his skivvies.*)

JESÚS: Um, nope. (*Pause.*)

LALO: It's a long drive.

JESÚS: Yeah. What was it?

LALO: Forty miles each way. I'm exhausted. These missions always take the hell out of me. (JESÚS *looks over at* LALO *who then turns to look at* JESÚS. JESÚS, *like a man caught staring, looks away.*) You mind if I turn off the light?

JESÚS: Go 'head. (LALO *does so. A blue light shines in from the moon.* LALO *returns to his bed.*)

LALO: You like women?

JESÚS: Women?

LALO: You know what they are, don't you?

JESÚS: Refresh my memory.

LALO: Short, freckles. Laugh over nothing, so what. Maybe she's got a friend. One whose mother never told her not to take money from strangers. I don't know about you, but I prefer the company of whores. Call-girls. You pay more, but it's worth it. Saturday. What're you doing Saturday?

JESÚS: Freckles, eh?

LALO: That one's mine.

JESÚS: Why not?

LALO: When we get back, we'll paint K-7 baby-butt pink. Sunday I won't mind waking up with a hangover. (*A cloud passes across the moon darkening the room. Enter* LOS DESAPARECIDOS, *three people with black hoods over their heads, barefooted with their hands tied behind their backs. They cross downstage, left to right and exit. Fade out.*)

.... SCENE FIVE: Hotel Room ....

LALO *and* JESÚS *are in a hotel room. They are dressed in civilian clothes.* LALO *is pacing the room.* JESÚS *is reading the newspaper. On the dresser is a brown paper bag containing a fifth of tequila, some limes and salt and some plastic glasses.*

JESÚS: Say, have you ever seen the Nativity scene in St. Adolpho's Church?

LALO: I heard about it. The sheep are as big as real sheep—and Joseph is six-feet tall.

JESÚS: Yeah, listen to this. "Late last night the life-sized plaster Baby Jesús was stolen from St. Adolpho's Church. This morning, Father Ramón received a ransom note. The note, composed from letters cut out from newspapers and magazines, said the Baby Jesús will be returned, unharmed, if the good Father leaves a case of German beer wrapped in a brown paper bag in one of the trash cans in Rico Plaza."

LALO: What's wrong with our beer?

JESÚS: Maybe the kidnappers were German.

LALO: More likely students. They like to think they know something. It's a damn stupid thing to do.

JESÚS: Kids, no doubt.

LALO: You think that matters?

JESÚS: I wouldn't exactly call it hygiene.

LALO: What?

JESÚS: Hygiene. I wouldn't call it that. Means the preservation
of one's health.

LALO: You got that. Holding the Baby Jesús for ransom is not
hygiene. What's keeping them?

JESÚS: It's early.

LALO: It's five to seven!

JESÚS: It's five to seven. Relax, read the funnies.

LALO: The best beer in the whole damn world they brew not seventy miles from here. Tecix. Seventy-six centavos a liter.
The best. I should've brought some. A shot of tequila and
a bottle of Tecix. You're shit-faced in no time. Your balls
get so swollen with semen, she never forgets the spanking
they gave her when you're on top of her. If you want a
family right away, you can fertilize both sides of her. Fra-
ternal twins. Hombre, I don't need to read the funnies.
A whore should at least be able to tell time.

JESÚS: A watched pot never boils. (*Knock at the door.*)

LALO: Bubble, bubble! (*Crosses to door and opens it. Enter*
CHAPA *and* NITA. CHAPA *is seventeen. She appears
sweet and amicable.* CHAPA *has been at her profession for
only a few months.* NITA*'s eyes are world-weary and spec-
ulative. The women are dressed in white summer dresses
with sandals. For a moment, they seem like proper young
ladies out for a stroll. They wear white flowers in their
hair.*) Well, what kept you two?

CHAPA: Are we late?

JESÚS: No, not at all. I'm Jesús.

CHAPA: I'm Chapa and this is my friend, Nita.

NITA: Jesús?

JESÚS: Yeah, I guess you already know Lalo.

LALO: You girls look great. (*On the side to* JESÚS.) Chapa is my
date. (*To the women.*) You girls want a drink?

NITA: Thanks.

CHAPA: Don't make mine too strong. (LALO *gets the tequila and
fills each cup. He cuts the lime into wedges with a pocket
knife.*)

CHAPA: So, you're in the Army, too?

JESÚS: Yeah.

CHAPA: My brother is in the Army.

JESÚS: Oh, yeah? Where is he stationed?

CHAPA: I don't know.

LALO: You don't know where your own brother is stationed?

CHAPA: He never writes. But then again, I'm always moving.

LALO: A deadbeat on your rent, eh?

CHAPA: (*Slightly offended but doesn't want to show it.*) It's not that.

NITA: There's a room in my building for rent. They won't bother you there.

LALO: What, the landlord wants a tip. Is he too fat?

NITA: (*To* JESÚS.) Is your friend always so charming?

JESÚS: He's a little highstrung tonight. (LALO *brings the cut limes and drinks to the coffee table.*)

CHAPA: Oh, thank you. (*She takes a sip and bites off the entire meat of the lime. She winces and shivers.*)

LALO: Drink some more. You can't feel that.

CHAPA: I'd better start slowly. Last time, oh brother.

LALO: Your turn. (*Hands* NITA *her cut. She drinks, bites and licks the salt. She watches* JESÚS *as she does this. Two men take their turns.*)

CHAPA: Oh, it doesn't take much for me to start feeling it. (LALO *drinks several swallows. Puts the whole lime slice in his mouth and gives them a "rind" smile. He then takes* CHAPA *by the waist and guides her into one of the bedrooms, singing unintelligible words behind the lime in his mouth.*) If I'm not out by ten o'clock, don't come looking for me. Get her to tell you one of her stories. (*The door closes behind them.*)

NITA: Maybe the best method after all is just doing it. (*They both pick up their cups and sip from them, eyeing each other.* PAOLA *enters, lingers a moment then exits.*) You remind me of someone I used to know.

JESÚS: But he's dead now.

NITA: Actually, yes. He choked to death on a glass eye. His glass eye. He was trying to shock this woman—a whore we called The Debutante. But she saw him drop it in. She switched their drinks when he wasn't looking.

JESÚS: (*Starts laughing.*) That's funny.

NITA: (*Starts laughing.*) I know. I know it's funny. We were such good friends.

JESÚS: (*Toasting her.*) Here's looking at you.

NITA: (*She chokes on the drink she was just about to swallow.*) If
   your right eye offendeth you ... JESÚS: Bottoms up!
NITA: So, what did you do before you were drafted?
JESÚS: I wasn't drafted.
NITA: Oh.
JESÚS: I was a gigolo.
NITA: (*Laughs.*) What?
JESÚS: A gigolo.
NITA: But why would you choose to go from being a lover to a
   ... a soldier. I mean, one is so extreme from the other. I
   mean ... oh, what do I mean ...
JESÚS: (*Putting her at ease.*) I've always hated the middle road.
NITA: Oh? So have I.
JESÚS: Boring.
NITA: I hate being bored.
JESÚS: And yet, you must often be bored.
NITA: You won't find me hanging around too long if he's a bore.
JESÚS: I suppose not. Yes. It's not that you're so beautiful—
   you're not bad-looking, not at all. There's something else
   I can see that lets you pick and choose.
NITA: You want to check my teeth?
JESÚS: Maybe later.
NITA: Hmph.
JESÚS: Another drink?
NITA: Sure. (*She accepts it with the attitude that she is doubling
   his dare.*)
JESÚS: So, what kind of stories do you tell?
NITA: Fairy tales.
JESÚS: You mean as in witches and princesses?
NITA: Yes, but they're not just any fairy tales. They're genuine
   fairy tales. They're as scary as real life.
JESÚS: We wouldn't want a phony fairy tale.
NITA: Exactly.
JESÚS: Tell me one of your fairy tales.
NITA: No.
JESÚS: Why not?
NITA: Because you're not the type to tell them to.
JESÚS: You know me that well already?
NITA: Enough to know you'll only want to argue and disagree with
   me.
JESÚS: And we wouldn't want that.
NITA: A fairy tale is what it is. I didn't make it up.

JESÚS: But you read them, and tell them to other people. Chapa for one, right? What about your other customers. Do you tell them these pretty lies?

NITA: They don't come to me to hear me tell them lies. They come to tell themselves lies. But you know all that, right?

JESÚS: The women I knew were always willing to listen to any pretty lies I was willing to tell them. But you, nothing? Never? Not one little white one? Not even an occasional make-believe groan of pleasure? Not one little thrust of plastic passion?

NITA: (*She looks at him a moment, then laughs.*) You see, no matter what I talk about, you're going to argue and disagree with me.

JESÚS: It makes me more interesting, doesn't it? (*She doesn't answer.*) I like you.

NITA: Why?

JESÚS: Because there's something going on up there.

NITA: How do you know it isn't just a calculator?

JESÚS: I think you like me, too.

NITA: Anyway, if I don't answer that, you'll answer it for me.

JESÚS: To please myself.

NITA: And that's the point.

JESÚS: Except you're not exactly building up my ego, but then again, you are pleasing me ... (*He looks at her, puzzled for a moment. His guard let down for that moment begins to unnerve her.*) But it would please me if you were pleased, too. I know, you must hear that all the time. But I mean it. Now I see that I've impressed you.

NITA: We could go in there and compare our skills.

JESÚS: I have an idea. Maybe we can make an arrangement.

NITA: What kind of arrangement?

JESÚS: How do you feel about once a week. This hotel. You get not an overly expensive bottle of champagne. How about one thousand pesos a month? Every Saturday starting at seven p.m. until two a.m. I have to be back at the base by three. Is it a deal?

NITA: You're so full of shit.

JESÚS: I'll pay you at the start of each evening 250 pesos a time. On the months where you get five Saturdays, we skip the last one. Vacation.

NITA: I'll believe it when I see it.

JESÚS: Hmm. Maybe I spoke too soon. Before anything ... the bed!

NITA: After this, you'll double the price. (*They exit through other bedroom door. Fade out.*)

.... SCENE SIX: Three a.m. - The Camp ....

LALO *enters with a gallon can of pink paint in one hand and a bottle of tequila in the other. He gestures for* JESÚS *who enters with two paint rollers in hand. They have just returned from the hotel. They are, of course, very drunk. Fade out*

.... SCENE SEVEN: Sunday Morning Eight a.m. ....

The sun streams down in harsh almost blinding light. JESÚS *and* LALO, *in impeccable uniform, nevertheless show signs of the previous night on their somewhat sickly faces. They are standing at attention, the pink barracks behind them. Other soldiers also stand beside them.* COLONEL SENSEZOZ *stands a few yards to the side while the* SERGEANT *delivers his speech.*

SERGEANT: I'm not interested in who did what, who started where and who did why. I am only informing you "men" that I am ending it now. Apparently you scum have failed to realize that you are the elite of this army and such activity as painting each other's barracks any color except regulation Grey #7 is conducive to neither the maintenance, the morale nor the operations of this camp. If I so much as find that anything even remotely similar to this type of activity occurs one more time, I will personally conduct an investigation if I have to beat it out of everyone of you. And when I find the parties involved, each and every one, including the so-called victim or victims, will never forget the consequences.

ALL THE RECRUITS. Yes, sir!

SERGEANT: I can't hear you!

RECRUITS: Yes, sir!

SERGEANT: Dismissed! (*The men fall out. Exit* SERGEANT.)

COLONEL: Finolina ...

LALO: Yes, sir?

COLONEL: At ease. Strictly between you and me, Private, I am setting this question to you because we consider you one of our most promising recruits. I realize you have set some admirable standards for yourself and, therefore, I know that you will give me a professional and objective assessment of Private Utimo.

LALO: My opinion of Private Utimo, without reservation, is that he is the finest soldier I have quartered with since I've been here, sir.

COLONEL: Dismissed, Private. (LALO *salutes. The* COLONEL *returns his salute. Fade out.*)

.... SCENE EIGHT: Cafe - Seven p.m. ....

JESÚS *and* LALO *are drinking beer at a cafe table, al fresco. Two empty chairs await the arrival of* NITA *and* CHAPA.

LALO: I'm telling you, it's no mistake that you landed in this outfit. Nothing happens by accident. Not you in this camp, anyway. Now, why does Lalo say that, you think.

JESÚS: Why has Private First Class Ferari Testosterone said what he just said.

LALO: Because you and I are different from most of the guys you see in there.

JESÚS: My papi never hobnobbed with their papies in the Yacht Club. They might have rubbed elbows since my papi was a waiter there for twenty-five years.

LALO: I thought you said your old man never worked a day in his life.

JESÚS: My real father didn't, but the guy who raised me worked 'til he dropped dead on their perfumed floor. He'd always tell me, "Don't be stupid and work your ass off the way I've done. If you can make a living at it, learn to lie, cheat, steal and deceive. They'll respect you all the more for it." He pissed right there. I saw it when I went to get him, a huge wet stain on their Persian carpet ... his coup de grace.

LALO: So you see, guys like us, they don't know exactly what to do with us. You gotta have brains and balls to have made it this far.

JESÚS: So, why are we scrubbing toilets?

LALO: Hey, that's what they call character building. But you can bet everything we do is noticed, reported and written down in triplicate. If we excel, they know it—and usually we do twice as good as any one of those dumb-

shits in K-7 but, on the other hand, every time we fuck
up, heads turn.
JESÚS: And ours roll.
LALO: Maybe. Except they need us and they know it. It's better
to have guys like us on their side. They need us to stay
alive.
JESÚS: (*Shrugging it off.*) Well ... they got us.
LALO: (*Enter* NITA *and* CHAPA.) Ho there—who are these beau-
ties? These flowers!
CHAPA: Are we late?
NITA: Hello.
JESÚS: How are you?
NITA: Fine. Lalo?
LALO: You're always late and you always ask. Buenos. (*They set
their jackets on the chairs.*)
CHAPA: Excuse us, we have to fix our faces.
LALO: I'll fix them for you—time is money. (*The women exit to the
ladies room.*) That little bitch—there's something about
her I can't get out of my system. She's got the whammy
on me, I swear it, from the first time I saw her, it stood at
attention.
JESÚS: You wouldn't know it by the way you talk to her.
LALO: Talk to her? How?
JESÚS: You know, you're ... well, an asshole.
LALO: Asshole? Fuck you! How else do you talk to a whore.
That's what they expect.
JESÚS: Maybe if you'd forget that, she might slip a little free stuff
to you on the side.
LALO: Hombre, a whore is a whore. Is that what Nita is doing?
JESÚS: Nah ... that's not the nature of her and me. It's different.
LALO: How different? You've been seeing her regularly.
JESÚS: Who told you that shit?
LALO: Chapa told me that shit. (*Lights dim on the men. Down-
stage left* NITA *and* CHAPA *sit facing downstage,* CHAPA
applying makeup and NITA *gazing at her image, suppos-
edly looking into the mirror. They are teasing and intimate
with each other.*)
NITA: I think Lalo is a little bit in love with you.
CHAPA: Are you crazy? He doesn't know if he should hate me
because I'm a whore or enjoy it because he's getting laid.
Who cares anyway. I have as much contempt for him as
he has for me. In love. You see the way he is—it's the
same in bed. An oaf all around. Period.

NITA: I still think he likes you.

CHAPA: Nita, you're too full of those fairy tales—ugly as they are—with Cinderella's sisters getting torn to pieces by wild bores and still ending happily everafter. What about Jesús?

NITA: Hah.

CHAPA: Hah, you better believe it. You cut them both and the same thing would ooze out. The same exact thing.

NITA: You're right, Lalo is crude and vulgar. I can't see how you stomach him. Jesús ...

CHAPA: Jesús is just a creamier version.

NITA: Maybe. Maybe not.

CHAPA: Ooze.

NITA: Oooooze.

CHAPA: You'd better believe it.

NITA: Just 'cause they pay for it, so what? The way of the world is ugly but it doesn't have to end badly.

CHAPA: Like your fairy tales. Can't you see? Paying for it ...

NITA: Where would you be without them?

CHAPA: I still spit on them. And paying for it, that's just one thing.

NITA: Name another.

CHAPA: They're soldiers. (*She looks at* NITA *who says nothing.*) I'd like to know just exactly ...

NITA: What?

CHAPA: Oh, never mind. Let's drop it. How does my hair look in the back?

NITA: It's flat.

CHAPA: Again? Fix it, Nita, you know how to do it right.

NITA: What do you do on Tuesdays?

CHAPA: (*A subtle wariness comes over her.*) Tuesdays? Nothing.

NITA: Who do you see?

CHAPA: Ouch—It's attached to my scalp, you know.

NITA: Sorry. Twice at the same time, I've seen you walking up Cordero and you're never at Rosie's on Tuesdays.

CHAPA: Well, if you have to know, I can only tell you he's a very discreet old man. Very distinguished.

NITA: Famous?

CHAPA: Very famous. Like Jack-the-Ripper. He made me swear on thirteen unblessed Bibles never to tell anyone his name.

NITA: Except me.

CHAPA: He said, especially don't say a word to Nita La Grita— Ow!

NITA: Sorry. Is he a politician?
CHAPA: He likes me to get undressed but to leave my shoes on.
    You've noticed my shoes?
NITA: He must be filthy rich.
CHAPA: As filthy as they get. Did you notice my shoes?
NITA: No.
CHAPA: Next time you see me, look at them. He sent me to a
    shoemaker and had them made-to-order. I also have to
    leave my stockings on. They're navy blue and come just
    over the knee.
NITA: Like a Catholic school girl: a virgin with a lot to confess.
    (*Lights begin to dim.*)
CHAPA: And wears mirror sunglasses.
NITA: That she traded for a few kisses.
CHAPA: And soon she'll stop confessing. (*Lights fade as they
    speak. Light rises on* LALO *and* JESÚS.)
LALO: What's keeping them?
JESÚS: They're talking about us.
LALO: How do you know?
JESÚS: What else would they talk about?
LALO: So, what are they saying?
JESÚS: They're comparing.
LALO: I wouldn't doubt it. (NITA *and* CHAPA *enter.*) It's about
    time. (*Taking* CHAPA's *sweater she left at the table and*
    CHAPA *by the hand.*) Come on.
CHAPA: Already? We just got here. Bye. Jesús ...
JESÚS: You need track shoes around Lalo.
CHAPA: (*To* NITA.) I'll see you at Rosie's.
JESÚS: (*They exit.* NITA *and* JESÚS *look at each other.* JESÚS
    feels compelled to explain.) She makes him nervous.
NITA: I know.
JESÚS: What can I get you?
NITA: A glass of wine would be fine.
JESÚS: Muchacho, un vaso. (*A* DESAPARECIDO, *wearing the
    ever-present black hood, enters with a wine glass on a tray
    and sets it on the table. Exits.*)
JESÚS: Would you like me if I were Lalo?
NITA: I wouldn't like you at all.
JESÚS: Would you still see me on Saturdays?
NITA: (*She hesitates.*) I would very much look forward to next
    Saturday.
JESÚS: Next Saturday?
NITA: It's the fifth Saturday of the month.

JESÚS: Oh yes, your day off. Aren't you looking forward to it?
NITA: It's what we agreed to, that's all.

.... SCENE NINE: Seven p.m. - Hotel Room ....

Two Saturdays later. Enter NITA. *She has a dozen white roses which she proceeds to arrange in a vase she also brought. Downstage right there is a dressing table so that when she looks into the mirror, she faces the audience. She picks up the phone.*

NITA: Room service. Please send up a bottle of champagne to room 609. Thank you. (*She hangs up the phone. There is an air of lightness about, almost as if she is meeting her sweetheart instead of a regular John. From her large bag, she pulls out a small radio and turns on the music. A salsa tune is playing. She crosses to the mirror and finds she is wearing too much make up. A knock at the door, then* JESÚS *enters. For a moment, he also has the air of expectancy about him. However, as soon as they see each other, they adjust to an attitude of studied nonchalance.*)
NITA: Hello.
JESÚS: Hi. It smells like roses.
NITA: Do you like them?
JESÚS: Mmm. Extravagant, don't you think?
NITA: Not if you know where to get them.
JESÚS: You look very nice. Beautiful.
NITA: It's a new dress. (*To their relief, there is a knock at the door.*) Room service, I think.
JESÚS: (*Answers the door. A* DESAPARECIDO *in a bellhop's jacket hands him champagne in an ice bucket.* JESÚS *gives him a tip and closes the door.*) So how was your Saturday off? Did you spend it profitably?
NITA: I dedicated the whole evening to myself.
JESÚS: You gave yourself a birthday party?
NITA: I just stayed at home and read.
JESÚS: Read what?
NITA: Well, did you know that if a gas line springs a leak in the desert, they mix the smell of putrid meat with the gas and wait for the vultures to come around.
JESÚS: Where did you read that, a believe-it-or-not comic book?
NITA: I have a subscription to this digest. It takes all the articles from science magazines, leaves out the words you don't

need and gets to the main point.

JESÚS: For people on the run.

NITA: For them, too.

JESÚS: So you read your science digest and slouched around eating chocolates.

NITA: I'm allergic to chocolate.

JESÚS: One less desire.

NITA: I can thank God for that.

JESÚS: Why don't you just thank pure dumb luck? A toast. To alcohol, the friend who will love you to death.

NITA: (*She drops three ice cubes into her champagne.*) One bone ... two bone ... three bone ... No one can ever know anyone.

JESÚS: Come here. (*She does so. He gives himself away in the gentleness of his touch. He kisses her. They begin to make love. Suddenly he stands up. He reaches into his pocket and pulls out the 250 pesos and hands it to her. He watches her put the money away.*)

JESÚS: What do you plan to do with all this money you're making?

NITA: I'm saving it.

JESÚS: That much I already knew.

NITA: When I have enough, I plan to go on a long vacation, maybe Barcelona. I'll have enough so that I can live like a lady and forget about sweaty hands and beer-breath.

JESÚS: For what purpose?

NITA: Isn't that enough?

JESÚS: You're saving all this money to go on a vacation?

NITA: What's wrong with that?

JESÚS: Not for you, you wouldn't waste your time and money on a silly vacation. I think you think you're going to cast a spell over some rich, handsome prince.

NITA: Do you expect to find me twenty years from now, pulling men into an alley? You think only you can get out?

JESÚS: You'll always think like a whore no matter where you go.

NITA: And you'll always think like a man no matter how up-to-the-minute you pretend to be. Besides, I'm not talking about becoming some idiot's mistress, I'm talking about marriage.

JESÚS: A prostitute only sells her body, a wife sells her soul.

NITA: What would you know about the soul? You spit on everything.

JESÚS: Now it's you who's wrong. You think dying is your ticket to happily everafter? The soul isn't some fog that escapes from the corpse—free at last! It's the animal in us since we were slime in a swamp. The missing link from ape to man, from man to whatever comes next. It's what keeps us going, what we don't know because we haven't discovered it. You ... you've never tried to understand it further than a caveman staring at the fire. But never mind all that because the fact of the matter is, your plan will never work.

NITA: And why not?

JESÚS: As soon as you drop a chunk of ice into your champagne ...

NITA: For your information, I saw the President's daughter do it ... (*He looks at her in amused disbelief.*) On the television.

JESÚS: They'll see you coming from the far end of the poop deck.

NITA: I know how to dress.

JESÚS: You think a couple of expensive dresses will make a lady out of you?

NITA: I know I'm no rich, fancy ass bitch ...

JESÚS: It's everything about you, Nita, the way you stick out your hip ...

NITA: I've already thought of that, Mr. Know-It-All. I'm taking classes where they teach you everything. The problem with you is you just shoot off your mouth before knowing all the details, those unimportant details like charm school, where you can learn how to say thank you, or how to raise one eyebrow and, since you mentioned it, how to tilt your ass at the right angle so even experts like you can't ...

JESÚS: Nita, Nitaíta, face it. This sounds cruel only because I want you to face the truth.

NITA: Truth? What truth? That you can't imagine anyone changing their life except the great Jesús?

JESÚS: That you're nothing but una rascuachi.

NITA: Rascuachi!

JESÚS: To the bone, to the core ...

NITA: Rascuachi!

JESÚS: From the way you breathe in, to your worn-down heels ...

NITA: Look at my heels. Are they worn down? Are they worn down?

JESÚS: You're going to find yourself out-classed by the rest of the gold diggers swarming after a very limited market. Not to mention the ones with money who are looking for a suitable match. You'll be competing with women who think the pavement is a carpet between the doorman and a limousine.

NITA: (*Gathering her things to leave.*) Your thinking is as free as twenty pesos an hour. I've known profesores, writers, scientists and ... you know what? They were smart enough to know when I had something to say about something, and to give it some consideration. They respected me, because they respected themselves. But with you, there's something inside you, something ugly and alive and it fills you up with contempt so that you think you're safe. But one of these days, what's inside will eat you up and become your outside so that everyone will see it, not just me.

JESÚS: You can't leave ...

NITA: Fuck you, I can't leave.

JESÚS: (*Gently.*) One thousand pesos, one thousand homeruns, Nita, chipita. One thousand. (*She prays for the day she'll no longer know men like this one. She pauses. Gritting her teeth, she turns away from the door. He watches as she circles around the room.*)

NITA: Hurry up then. I want to get this over with.

JESÚS: Four hours left to go, chipitita. You can start with the paint on your face. But first ... I want you to say, thank you. The way they've taught you in charm school.

NITA: Sometimes you forget that you're only a trick. (*She takes out the lotion she was about to use to remove her makeup before he came in and proceeds to clean her face. Fade out.*)

················ SCENE TEN: Nita's Room ················

PAOLA*'s robot sits serenely in one corner alongside a microphone and some of her books, in particular* PAOLA*'s red anatomy reference text.* NITA *enters, back from her ordeal with* JESÚS.

NITA: Jealous, that's what he is. Jealous of what? That I can do as well as he's done? What's he done that's so great? Jealousy, love and fear. He loves only himself and fears only that I might do better than him. Jealousy is a man with no cojones. Cojones ... (*Takes the anatomy book and begins looking through it.*) Hmmm. He thinks he knows everything ... Ah, pencil, pencil and a little paper. (*Finds pencil and paper and returns to the open book, carefully printing t-e-s-t-i-c-l-e-s.*) Testicles. And ... eyes, eyes ... Hmmm. Pupil, tearducts ... retina ... the layer of cells sensitive to light ... optic nerve fibers ... carried to the brain. Retina. (*Writing, R-e-t-i-n-a. Picks up the microphone, blows into it, and speaks into it, referring to her notes on the specific words.*) Lesson Number 37. Men have a weakness in their retina that causes them to mistake the demon of jealousy for testicles. Your eyesight will be perfect. (*Fade out.*)

················ SCENE ELEVEN: Barracks ················

JESÚS *is lying in his bunk, reading the manual. Enter* LALO.

JESÚS: ... Capture upon shot be will soldier offending Any .inexcusable and cowardly is enemy the of face the in Desertion.
LALO: Section 1.4, Paragraph 24. Backwards.
JESÚS: Very good. I thought you had a date with Chapa?
LALO: The bitch stood me up.
JESÚS: Stood you up?
LALO: Stood me up, stood me up—what are we, parrots?
JESÚS: Well, it's not like her. I thought she was in love with you.
LALO: What does a whore know about love.
JESÚS: So, why didn't you find another one—what the hell?
LALO: I got into a card game waiting for her to show up.
JESÚS: So now you're broke.
LALO: So what, it's only dirty money.
JESÚS: Dirty? Why do you say that?
LALO: (*Agitated.*) No reason. Money is dirty—haven't you ever noticed how your hands get when you handle it all day long?
JESÚS: Since when do you handle money all day long?
LALO: Aw, never mind. It's best if you don't talk to me for a while.
JESÚS: Well, it might cheer you up to know that the Baby Jesús has finally been recovered.
LALO: So what.
JESÚS: Careful, blasphemy is very unattractive. (*Picking up the newspaper. He reads.*) "The Baby Jesús was discovered

in Rico Plaza by a Doña Juanita Carmona who has been feeding the pigeons for over twenty-five years in the same spot at the same time. She noticed a flesh-colored something, which turned out to be the heel of the Baby Jesús, sticking out of a brown paper bag in one of the trash baskets."

LALO: She knew something was afoot.

JESÚS: "The kidnappers had taped over the eyes and mouth of the plaster Baby Jesús, otherwise the little idol was unharmed. Father Ramón plans to install an electronic eye and alarm system to prevent further vandalism."

LALO: Science in the service of God.

JESÚS: I think it shouldn't be just any alarm but one that sets off special effects of thunder and lightning.

LALO: I repent! I repent!

JESÚS: Here, I beg you, take my money ...

LALO: All of it ...

JESÚS: Do you suppose it was a plot cooked up by the priest and the pigeon lady?

LALO: The celibate Father Ramón and the virgin Doña Juanita!

JESÚS AND LALO: (*Simultaneously.*)   Oh-ho-ho!   (*Enter* SERGEANT.*)

SERGEANT: Attention!   The van is being prepared for another mission.   Be ready to move out in ten minutes. (SERGEANT *exits.* JESÚS *and* LALO *stare after the* SERGEANT. LALO *makes the first move and* JESÚS *follows. Neither one can look the other in the face. Fade out.*)

.... SCENE TWELVE: Hotel Room ....

NITA *and* JESÚS *are in bed. She seems preoccupied.* LOS DESAPARECIDOS *all sit at farthest part of the stage.*

JESÚS: What's the matter?

NITA: I don't know ... I guess I'm worried ... about Chapa.

JESÚS: Chapa? What about her?

NITA: Well, she hasn't been home for several days now. She hasn't been to Rosie's since Wednesday, but since she never goes on Tuesdays, I don't know if she's been gone since Tuesday or Wednesday. But then I wasn't there on Monday ...

JESÚS: What're are you talking about?

NITA: Well, it's just that people disappear.

JESÚS: Disappear? How do you know?

NITA: How do I know? Everybody knows. People disappear. We live in that kind of world. That old man, maybe he did something to her.

JESÚS: What old man?

NITA: Some kook she went to every Tuesday.

JESÚS: (*Somewhat relieved.*) Oh, some degenerate. I thought you meant something else.

NITA: She's not political.

JESÚS: What do you know about politics?

NITA: The unmade bed. A girl I knew, but Chapa never talks about anything more political than ... (*She hesitates, remembering her last conversation with* CHAPA.)

JESÚS: Than what?

NITA: Than the wisdom of fairy tales. But this one, her name was Paola, she was a scientist. She'd say anything to anybody. I warned her. Finally, I even had to stop being her friend. Then I heard that she hadn't been seen for weeks. I went to her place ... The bed in Chapa's room was like an echo. They're all degenerates! (LOS DESAPARECIDOS *speak so that #1 and #3 overlap as #2 is speaking.*)

DESAPARECIDO #2: You are that sickness. Tell her everything. She can help you.

DESAPARECIDO #1: Dígale.

DESAPARECIDO #3: Tell her everything.

DESAPARECIDO #1: Cúrame.

JESÚS: What would you do if I said I was one of those men?

NITA: What?

JESÚS: Nitaíta.

NITA: What men are you talking about?

JESÚS: Nitaíta, remember we have a deal.

NITA: What men.

JESÚS: You would at least owe me this. Owe me the rest of the night. (*He pulls her to him, kissing, biting her ear.*) Nitaíta, Nitaíta, I live for you. I am alive because of you. I have all my money invested in you. All I ask from you is a cheap bottle of champagne and your soft, wet kitty-cat.

NITA: I think you've lost your mind.

JESÚS: Mind—yes! And now I've just spilled my guts to you. (*Affectionately.*) And on top of that, I live for a whore. (*Pushing him away. He has a way of ruining the moment.*

*The next line comes not from actual suspicion but from an
intent to injure.*)

NITA: So what're you, some kind of executioner?

JESÚS: Not so loud!

NITA: Then it's true?

JESÚS: No, it's not true, but you don't have to shout it to the
world.

NITA: Then why did you say it?

JESÚS: I don't know, it was a bad joke.

NITA: More than a bad joke—a cruel one.

JESÚS: A cruel joke. Nitaíta, I'm sorry.

NITA: Why are you calling me that all of a sudden?

JESÚS: That's how I always hear your name.

NITA: I shouldn't have agreed to this ...

JESÚS: But you did.

NITA: I can always back out.

JESÚS: You still owe me the night and by the time I'm finished
        fucking you, you'll be addicted to Felicidad here. Have I
        ever told you about Felicidad?

NITA: It's your favorite story.

JESÚS: I might have missed something.

NITA: I doubt it.

JESÚS: The wisdom of Felicidad tells us all women are lesbians at
        heart. Put a dress on him and she relaxes. It's like playing
        with herself. She smiles. She laughs. She tickles herself.
        She knows exactly what to do.

NITA: Yes, and like I've already told you, even in my heart I'm
        not a lesbian. I know that for a fact.

JESÚS: For a fact, eh? You never told me it was factual knowledge.
        Hm, well then, call him, Señor Felicidad.

NITA: Even if it were true, it's only because men make us that way.

JESÚS: And the women who'd sleep with you and me? Who made
        them so charitable? It's not up-to-the-minute thinking,
        Nita. It's so easy to blame men for everything. We're
        scapegoats. Oh well, we save you the trouble of searching
        out the truth.

NITA: So, without poking through your rubbish and reading your
        mail, I'll be right ninety-eight percent of the time.

JESÚS: You don't mind being two percent blind?

NITA: I can live with it.

JESÚS: As I was saying, women are lesbians because they come
        from slime.

NITA: Oh ho!

JESÚS: If you were to take a woman and a bit of slime and put samples of each under the microscope, you would find they are of the same ingredients. It started way before we even had eyes.

NITA: Oh, that's a new one. What I want to know is where do you get these ideas?

JESÚS: I've been making love to women since I was nine.

NITA: Before they had eyes, I'm sure.

JESÚS: Eight and a half.

NITA: So where do men come from?

JESÚS: Slime, innocent slime. That's why we are the way we are.

NITA: Not so innocent slime.

JESÚS: (*Sadly.*) Maybe you're right. Slime without innocence ... It leaves a bad taste in your mouth. Something like the metallic smell of blood ...

NITA: You're full of ugly thoughts, tonight more than usual, and I don't like you calling me Nitaíta. I think I should go.

JESÚS: (*Holding her down.*) You've already said that.

NITA: You can have your money back.

JESÚS: I've glued you to the bed. You can't move. (*He kisses her.*) Where is your make-believe tonight, Nitaíta?

NITA: Safe. I have it in a safe place. (*He begins kissing her until she responds. Fade out.*)

.... SCENE THIRTEEN: Jesús' Nightmare ....

JESÚS *is asleep in his bunk. The most noticeable aspect of this scene is the presence of color. The actors wear an incongruity of colors to give a sense of a demented Mardi gras, of torment and disharmony. The music speeds up and slows down before giving way to other sounds. The sound of a party is faint at first. The crystalline sound of ice in mixed drinks, the splash of a diver as he hits the water with shrieks of gaiety. In the antiquated accent of an old talkie, as if speaking through a megaphone, a voice is heard, "get on your mark, get set ... " The thunderous sound of a starter gun makes* JESÚS *sit up in his dream. Enter* SRA. DEMAS *in riding gear and* LALO *wearing regulation boxer shorts and socks, a colorful bandanna around his neck.* JESÚS *is the invisible entity circling the player in his own dream.*

DEMAS: Jesús?

LALO: What?

DEMAS: Tan sucio ... You're the only man I know who refuses to walk around naked. You never open your eyes when we make love.

LALO: You never close them.

DEMAS: What would make you lose the shame of Adam?

LALO: The revenge of Ophelia. (DEMAS' *laughter melds eerily with the clash of the party. LALO crosses to her, blending into her arms.*)

DEMAS: Such a clever boy. Such a clever, clever boy. Have you always been so clever?

LALO: My father died in your house.

DEMAS: He ruined an heirloom.

LALO: A fond farewell.

DEMAS: It's so difficult to find good help these days. What about you?

LALO: When I piss I always hit my mark.

DEMAS: Clever boy. (*Her words are muffled as they kiss in a particularly disgusting parody of passion. A melodious doorbell rings. The chimes ring slow and fast as if the technician is also in conflict with his mixer.*) Answer the door. (*With the back of their hands, they simultaneously wipe the saliva of their kiss from their lips.*)

LALO: Answer the door. (LALO *staggers to his feet and veers toward an imaginary door where a* DESAPARECIDO *stands holding an oversized telegram.*)

DEMAS: What is it, darling?

LALO: A matter of life and death, I presume.

DEMAS: But not ours. Come to me, Jesús. (*She opens her arms.* LALO *opens his likewise, dropping the telegram and falling into her arms as they begin the struggle of lovemaking. Suddenly from the upstage side of the bed,* CHAPA *sits up. She is wearing a colorful though ragged dress. Her hair is in plaits. She is a girl of twelve.*)

CHAPA: Jesús! Jesús!

LALO: What?

CHAPA: Hurry!

LALO: Hurry?

CHAPA: There's no time. Time is running out. We've got to catch up. Hurry!

LALO: (*Suddenly sober.*) I can't be seen like this.

CHAPA: Here. (*She hands him a black hood with a red streak across it. He puts it on. They exit.* DEMAS *stands up and follows them as far as centerstage, then stops. As they exit,*

LOS DESAPARECIDOS *pass them. Salsa music begins playing a bit too slow.* LOS DESAPARECIDOS *encircle* DEMAS. *One gets on all fours like a seat for her while the others begin removing her clothing. She remains motionless, staring after* LALO *and* CHAPA. JESÚS *crosses to retrieve the fallen telegram.*)

DEMAS: A matter of life and death. (JESÚS *returns to his bunk and with his back to the others begins to open the telegram.* LOS DESAPARECIDOS *leave* DEMAS *as she turns to watch them. They surround* JESÚS, *pushing him to lie supine on the bed and begin pulling at his T-shirt in an effort to undress him. He resists them, turning their efforts into a struggle.*)

JESÚS: No! Get away from me—auhhh!

LALO: Jesús! Jesús! Wake up!

JESÚS: What?

LALO: You must been having some dream. (LALO *returns to his bunk.* SRA. DEMAS *backs out as* JESÚS *watches her.*)

JESÚS: It was a bad sign.

LALO: Must've been a good one.

JESÚS: You were in it. And someone I once knew. You were lovers.

LALO: If she was good-looking, it's too bad it wasn't my dream.

JESÚS: (*Pause.*) Lalo.

LALO: Yeah?

JESÚS: Where do you think they come from?

LALO: Who?

JESÚS: Those guys.

LALO: What guys?

JESÚS: You know what guys.

LALO: Who knows.

JESÚS: I know.

LALO: Then why are you asking me?

JESÚS: Some of them are from ...

LALO: Just shut up and get some shut-eye.

JESÚS: The same place ...

LALO: Don't you get it? So like I said, shut up. (*Silence.* LALO *at last feels forced to speak.*) It's all very practical. You ever thought of that? You can't see them, they can't see us. They're gagged, too. Can you tell? In a shooting range, too. All you ever hear in a shooting range are shots.

JESÚS: Sometimes I imagine abuelitas, little grey-haired abuelitas in their rebozos, sewing on pedal machines, black hoods for twenty-five centavos a piece. They stop for lunch, take out their minute amounts of black beans and cold tortillas and eat slowly, chewing with their two good teeth. Then they go back to sewing black hoods.

LALO: You sure like to torture yourself.

JESÚS: And who makes these gags? Who makes the cloth? Who dyes it? And I start thinking about the sandalmakers ...

LALO: Sandalmakers?

JESÚS: One of them wore sandals. One of the guys we shot last time. Somebody made those sandals. And the sandalmaker never thought, I am making these sandals for a dead man. And when the dead man put them on in the morning, he didn't think, this is the last time I'll be putting on my sandals.

LALO: Don't be an idiot. They know what they're doing, more than you or me. Don't start driving yourself crazy.

JESÚS: And I see scores of people, hoodmakers, sandalmakers, hat weavers, gag dyers, standing around a shooting range, staring, like dumb animals at their work, soaking up the fresh blood. You and me next to them. Nobody says a word.

LALO: Canaries.

JESÚS: What?

LALO: My aunt had a yellow canary and the cat ate it and it didn't make a peep, not a sound. That's what they are. Consider that you already know more than you should about them. Are you hearing me, Jesús?

JESÚS: It's already too late. Three the first time. Two tonight. (LOS DESAPARECIDOS *dance in the periphery of their view, making them both jumpy.*) Five canaries. How many for you?

LALO: I haven't counted them.

JESÚS: Yeah, I guess it's better to not know.

LALO: You're damn right, hombre. It's either the dirt under your boots or the dirt in your mouth. It's a fine line, one that I don't care to challenge. I didn't ask for this duty, but I'm here now and I'm not about to make a stink. ¿Qué te pasa, hombre? Go back to sleep and think about Nita ... when she's lying in bed, looking at you through sleepy eyes. If you don't mind, I'll think about her, too. Since that other one stood me up, I'm going to think about not thinking about her. (*He turns his back to* JESÚS. *The music begins.* LOS DESAPARECIDOS *dance across the stage in their tumbling, weightless kind of dance. Fade out.*)

. SCENE FOURTEEN: The Office of Colonel Sensezoz .

COLONEL SENSEZOZ *is gazing at his reflection on the glass of the President's portrait.* SRA. DEMAS *is sitting behind* COLONEL SENSEZOZ' *desk.*

DEMAS: Well?

COLONEL: I was thinking, Paca.

DEMAS: You were admiring your reflection.

COLONEL: I was doing both. (*Switches on his intercom.*) Lieutenant, have Private Utimo report to my office. (*Switches off the intercom.*)

DEMAS: Why do you hesitate?

COLONEL: He'll be here soon enough.

DEMAS: You're pleased, I can tell that much.

COLONEL: I must admit, I had my doubts at first.

DEMAS: Go on. (JESÚS *enters stage right, passing under the* COLONEL's *window. He recognizes* SRA. DEMAS' *voice immediately and stops to listen.*)

COLONEL: However, one thing puzzles me. He claims to have enlisted.

DEMAS: Is that so? Why would he say such a thing?

COLONEL: I thought you could shed some light on it.

DEMAS: You don't think he knows I was the one who got him drafted, do you?

COLONEL: Anything's possible.

DEMAS: But very unlikely. Pride.

COLONEL: Pride. That makes sense. Whatever reason, I don't think you'll be disappointed.

DEMAS: I would hate to be disappointed. (*Suddenly she remembers the importance of her own existence and is overcome by rage and indignation.*) You can't imagine, so much incompetence these days. Now, that Colonel Peña ...

COLONEL: He's turned in his resignation, you know.

DEMAS: My father would've had him court-marshalled and shot.

COLONEL: They felt it would've been bad for morale ...

DEMAS: Losing a whole district to those ... people, isn't that bad for morale? This world has lost its mind. Sometimes I think you and I are the only ones who understand the situation along the border is critical.

COLONEL: As long as the Capitol is overrun by an embarrassment of senile Santa Clauses writing each other's meal tickets, we will continue to ...

INTERCOM: Private Utimo is here, sir. (*The* COLONEL *and* SRA. DEMAS *realize the preposterousness of their respective positions. She hurries to the chair in front of his desk and the* COLONEL *sits in the chair she has just vacated.*)

COLONEL: Have him come in. (*A moment later* JESÚS *enters.* DEMAS' *back is to him.*)

COLONEL: Private Utimo, prepare to chauffeur Sra. DeMas ...

DEMAS: Jesús!

JESÚS: (*Also feigning surprise.*) Hello.

COLONEL: You know each other?

DEMAS: Of course, Jesús is the son of the gardener who worked on my father's estate for years.

COLONEL: The gardener's son? What a small world it is.

DEMAS: Well, I must be going, Colonel. It's been a lovely visit. The Colonel has been a friend of the family for many years. Do take care, Colonel, and see if you can find some time in your busy schedule to look up an old friend.

COLONEL: Of course, my dear. Private Utimo, see to it that you're back at the base by twenty-two hundred. We may be needing you this evening.

JESÚS: Yes, sir. (*They exit. Fade out.*)

.... SCENE FIFTEEN: The Home of Sra. DeMas ....

The room is adorned with Mexican artifacts, chairs, a coffee table. A vase of flowers, a bar downstage right. The mirror is to be over the bar, so anyone looking into it is facing downstage. Various liquors, mixes, elegant glasses. In a corner, almost unnoticeable, a DESAPARECIDO *sits. He is wearing a sombrero and is sitting like a sleeping Mexican statue, his head resting on his knees.* JESÚS *is looking into the mirror.* DEMAS *watches him.*

DEMAS: Julian redecorated it. Remember Julian?

JESÚS: You mean the one in see-through socks?

DEMAS: How true. It amuses me, I must admit. I had to buy a new wardrobe just to sit in this room. What is it? You seem different.

JESÚS: Something about this mirror . . .

DEMAS: The man I bought it from told me that if you look into it long enough, it'll trap your soul.

JESÚS: Without a soul we'd never jump from a cliff wearing canvas wings. (*He turns away from the mirror.*) Would you believe, I had a dream about you last night?

DEMAS: I hope it was a good one.

JESÚS: You were half undressed.

DEMAS: Was I?

JESÚS: Do you mind if I have another?

DEMAS: (*Mimicking his politeness.*) Oh, please do, Jesús.

JESÚS: How lucky you are, you're exactly where you want to be.

DEMAS: If that were true, I'd have nothing to strive for.

JESÚS: To the champion of rhetoric. (*He drinks.*)

DEMAS: You are different.

JESÚS: Thank you. After all, it's been what, six months?

DEMAS: Six months next week.

JESÚS: But who's counting? I've changed my life since the last time I saw you. I've grown up. Don't laugh. I mean, when you're small, you notice that behind the sofa is a brighter color, a butter knife is like a finger, a steak knife is like a mouth. The way your mother kisses you before she goes dancing. Then whack, a whole new world, right between the eyes and you begin to notice those secondary details . . .

DEMAS: Such as?

JESÚS: Such as, your bad taste in jewelry. How easily "the gardener's son" rolled off your tongue. And also . . . that it was you who got me drafted. Pulling strings.

DEMAS: I didn't mean to . . .

JESÚS: Paquita. You are not the kind of woman who does something without weighing all the possibilities. So let's be honest from now on. Okay? There was something wrong with my life—even I knew that. Maybe that's why I wasn't upset about the notice. See, I left the country to give myself room to think and . . . in case I wanted to skip out. If I came back, it would be because I wanted to. (*The* DESAPARECIDO *stands. He has the curiosity of one who has never seen luxurious surroundings. He stands at the periphery of the stage.*)

JESÚS: So there I was, having this Tahitian-fantasy of a drink when who do I run into but good, old Carlos.

DEMAS: Carlos who?

JESÚS: You wouldn't know him. An old acquaintance. At one time we were almost inseparable. He taught me a few tricks. Well-preserved ... except for these two lines at the mouth. Deep lines, as if he'd been deeply disappointed.

DEMAS: Disappointed, yes.

JESÚS: All that time ... nothing had really happened. Do you know what I mean?

DEMAS: I'm not sure.

JESÚS: He had become the aging, desperate, lonely version of the women he had used. He wanted to know—not that he ever said a word—if he'd changed much. His looks. Very important. But of course it was clear, it was all slipping away from him. And that's what had been bothering me for some time before the draft notice. The difference between Carlos and me was that it didn't show. (*Pause.*) I heard you and the Colonel. Outside, from the window. (*He makes himself another drink.*) Do you want another?

DEMAS: Not yet.

JESÚS: No matter if I lived to be eighty, romancing invalid women, if I died humping, prick on duty, the successful gigolo, I would still be sick of myself. And always, in the back of my head, I kept hearing, this isn't me. I don't belong here. So opportunity knocked and I said why not?

DESAPARECIDO: Right up your alley. (*The* DESAPARECIDO *blows on* JESÚS' *neck.*)

JESÚS: I don't know if I should thank you for having enough concern for me to try and turn me into a man, or walk out of here because you played me for a fool.

DEMAS: I just—I don't know why. I couldn't suggest it ... I didn't think ...

JESÚS: To land in officer's training camp, like a cat on all fours ... Everyone there is there because they know someone. It's the way of the world. Right?

DEMAS: A world you've just been born into, one of leadership and power ...

JESÚS: To a new life.

DEMAS: To a whole new life. Come, darling. (JESÚS *picks up the bottle and crosses to her, knowing he is still under observation. He falls into her arms in an ecstasy of self-loathing.*

Fade out.)

.... SCENE SIXTEEN: Nita's Apartment ....

Lively South American music plays from the radio. NITA *enters with a plate of fruit. She sets it next to the robot. She is cleaning the robot with a small brush and solution. She is wearing old slippers and an ancient robe. She wears glasses. Loud knock at the door.*

NITA: Who is it?

JESÚS: Nita?

NITA: (*Opens the door.*) Jesús! How did you find me?

JESÚS: I've been all over trying to track you down—are you alone?

NITA: Yes. What's the matter?

JESÚS: You've been saving the money I've been giving you?

NITA: Now wait a minute ...

JESÚS: Listen to me. Your vacation, it's time. Listen—listen, you take the money and buy a round trip ticket to Calibari. I can't explain right now. The round trip ticket is to confuse them.

NITA: Who?

JESÚS: They might even know about us and they can't know you're leaving the country ...

NITA: But why?

JESÚS: Let me finish, dammit. It's Thursday. Saturday, if I don't send you a box of candy by two o'clock, you go. You understand me? Pack vacation clothes. Nothing else. I'll meet you. There's a cafe on the main boulevard ...

NITA: Which?

JESÚS: There's only one main boulevard—just ask. Miguelitos, you got that?

NITA: Miguelitos ...

JESÚS: Tonight, I don't know when, except very soon—I got the deep, in-here gut feeling. Nita, meet me, will you?

NITA: Jesús, what's happened?

JESÚS: I know what you're going to think, but I can't argue now, damn you. Don't you see, you'd shoot my argument to shit ... one minute, one moment. (*He crosses to the table with water pitcher and basin and unzips his trousers.*)

NITA: What are you doing? (*Washing himself.*)

JESÚS: What does it look like I'm doing?

NITA: Why?

JESÚS: Los desaparecidos. There's nowhere to hide from them.
I know where they go, what happens to them. Me—I'm
what happens to them—but I didn't know, Nita, I swear, it
was that shark. What a fool I was to think for the spilling
of a few lousy sperm ... You can't beat them at their own
game. Remember that, Nita. And to think I laughed at
you while all this time she had me sized up.

NITA: You never wash up after we finish fucking.

JESÚS: Because when we fuck—when we make love—when I'm
laying there, the smell of you, of us on my skin in the
sheets, it's the only time I feel like an honest man ...

NITA: But then who were you with?

JESÚS: *La puta Muerte*, what does it matter? You can tell when
they're from the city, the gutter, like you and me, or the
country, the mud, dried mud on the cuffs of their pants.

NITA: Who?

JESÚS: ¡Los desaparecidos! The hoods don't matter, their eyes are
still open. Or gagging them? They still grunt when they
fall, gasp when they're shot, like a fish screams when you
hit it, you hear it in the palm of your hand. I don't know
what I know. I mean, I'm not sure about what I know,
but that I need you with me. They should eat shit! God,
am I one of them? Nah, just their dog. Ex-dog, got that?
Nita, say it's not too late ... I can't believe ... I mean,
yes! There comes a time when it's too late, but this is not
one of those times. Nita, forgive me. Nita, Nitaíta, you
be my god, you be my god and bless me! (*He kisses her
and staggers out. He re-enters.*)

JESÚS: Is that a robot?

NITA: Oh, yes.

JESÚS: Oh. (*Exits.*)

NITA: Paola gave it to me before she ... (NITA *unwraps the microchip and carefully slips it into the robot.*) The poorest
are sometimes the richest. Do you understand that? How
could you, with your microchip and your ... your metal
plate. No blood. It leaves you and you die. It warms you,
it gets hot and you must ... Do something, something
crazy when it gets that hot. Maybe it was a microchip
that thought of making the gas smell like putrid meat. A
mean trick, if you ask me. If I could make you perfect,
what would that mean for me? You perfect and me all
alone. You need pain to make you change. And you don't

understand pain or dreams. Paola would say ... Paola ...
You would only be scientific. Paola was always scientific
... and she's gone. I know. I know, I know, I know. But
I don't know. It's my heart. My heart knows something
I don't know up here ... Or is it the other way around?
It could be. Maybe the heart is the scientist, the way it
beats, like a motor. And the brain is stupidity. It could be.
As long as you aren't sure, anything could be. Even Jesús.
Even Jesús has learned something. Maybe even me. (*A
DESAPARECIDO enters and stands behind* NITA.) You
don't have a heart. You don't have a brain. Oh no, the
microchip doesn't count because it doesn't need blood or
know about an empty stomach. Empty stomachs make for
many ... mistakes. Wanting to keep it full. How would
you know? I've been wrong to think that I, of all peo-
ple, could make a perfect man. Even God didn't do that.
Me, so unperfect. I ran from Paola. I could've made her
understand. But I was only looking out for myself. (*The
DESAPARECIDO removes the black hood. It is* PAOLA.)
I should've stolen you away like Xavier Valentine here.
PAOLA: I would've laughed at you.
NITA: Not scientific at all.
PAOLA: Only ninety-five percent is science.
NITA: Even when you're dead, you're funny.
PAOLA: The rest is blood. And empty stomachs. And empty
hearts.
NITA: Demanding to be filled.
PAOLA: Sated.
NITA: What happened to you? Where did you go?
PAOLA: I was taken by the evil wishes of others, by the non-
creatures from hell. I was sacrificed for you.
NITA: For me? No. Don't say that. Why for me—a whore! And
you, a ... a ...
PAOLA: The beginning.
NITA: Beginning? Beginning of what?
PAOLA: I can't tell you everything.
NITA: I should've loved you. I should've loved you more. I
should've ... I should've said something more than these
stupid tears ... (PAOLA *picks up the microphone and
blows into it.*)
PAOLA: Lesson Number 38: A man begins to understand women
when he learns to weep for those outside of him ... (*She*

hands the mike to NITA *and slowly exits leaving the hood behind.*)

NITA: And a woman ... begins to understand men when she learns to speak for those outside of her. Until then, we are all cavemen staring at the fire. (*Fade out.*)

.... SCENE SEVENTEEN: The Firing Range ....

LALO *and* JESÚS *enter, carrying their rifles.*

JESÚS: Lalo, let's get the hell out of here.

LALO: Soon, soon.

JESÚS: I mean now. We can't go on killing these people every few weeks.

LALO: What? Have you lost your mind? We have our orders.

JESÚS: They said, jódete to some order. Now it's up to us to do the same.

LALO: We're soldiers and we follow orders.

JESÚS: I know a safe route to the border. We could get there by dawn ...

LALO: Don't you see, they're just testing us. It's not what we're going to be doing a year from now.

JESÚS: Right. Next year we'll be signing the order to kill or worse.

LALO: We've been through this before and now is not the time for second thoughts. We disobey orders and they'll hunt us down and stick our head on a pole as examples of bad hygiene. I have no intention of risking my life for a few filthy prisoners. So, what'll it be? (JESÚS *realizes* LALO *will not only not be moved, but will prevent him at all costs.*)

JESÚS: Y—you're right. It's very bad hygiene. But you see what I mean, it can turn you against your own best friend.

LALO: I ...

JESÚS: No. There's no need to explain. You're absolutely right. There's nothing we can do about it except ruin our lives.

LALO: Worse.

JESÚS: Worse. It must've been just as hard for you in the beginning.

LALO: It's still hard. All we can do is wait it out. The better we do, the sooner they give it to someone else. Okay?

JESÚS: Yeah. This is just between you and me, right?

LALO: Compañeros.

JESÚS: I'll get them. (LALO *watches him exit. Offstage, van doors open. Three prisoners enter,* JESÚS *behind them.* LALO *and* JESÚS *line them up and take aim. In the last moment,* JESÚS *swings his aim at* LALO *and in a burst of fire,* JESÚS *shoots* LALO. LALO *falls and lies dying.* JESÚS *kneels beside him.*) Why ... why wouldn't you come with me? You hated them as much as I did.

LALO: The Major asked me about you. I told him you were a great guy. (LALO *dies. His eyes staring at* JESÚS. JESÚS *closes them. He crosses to the prisoners and unties their hands. As their hands are freed they remove the black hoods and gags.* CHAPA *is one of them.* CHAPA *and* JESÚS *stare at one another.*)

OLD MAN: You know him?

JESÚS: (*To the* YOUNGER MAN.) Take his uniform and put it on. Cover his head with this.

OLD MAN: ¡Apúrense! (CHAPA *takes her hood and slips it over* LALO's *head. Salsa music begins. Lights fade to black.*)

End of Play